SEAGULL ESSAYS

Series Editor: ALBERTO TOSCANO

A trial, an attempt, a test. But also a weighing up, an assaying of unknown quantities and imponderable qualities. The essay has been called 'the strictest form attainable in an area where one cannot work precisely' (Robert Musil) and the essayist depicted as one who composes in the very act of experimenting, who attacks their object from multiple angles and 'puts into words what the object allows one to see under the conditions created in the course of writing' (György Lukács).

An art of transitions, thresholds, mediation and impurity, the essay evades the posture of the objective expert just as it refrains from the subjective cult of creativity. Exacting without a pretence to exactness, its subject matter, Adorno once suggested, 'is always conflict brought to a standstill'.

Seagull Essays is a wager that, in times pervaded by formulaic writing and automated script, the essay is a living form, open to further trials and tests, insubordinate to rigid demarcations between the arts, the sciences and the humanities.

SEAGULL
BOOKS
•
CELEBRATING
40 YEARS

BENJAMIN NOYS

The Matter of Language

Abstraction and Poetry

LONDON NEW YORK CALCUTTA

Seagull Books, 2023

© Benjamin Noys, 2023

First published in volume form by Seagull Books, 2023

ISBN 978 1 80309 074 0

British Library Cataloguing-in-Publication Data

A catalogue record for this book is available from the British Library

Typeset by Seagull Books, Calcutta, India

Printed and bound by WordsWorth India, New Delhi, India

CONTENTS

ACKNOWLEDGEMENTS

I would like to thank Alberto Toscano for inviting me to write for this series, for his friendship and for his support. I would also like to thank Daniel Katz, Sean Bonney, Joshua Clover, Simon Hadjani, Anthony Iles, Federico Luisetti, Gregor Moder, Alenka Zupančič, Samo Tomšič, Mark Francis Johnson, Sophie Carapetian, Paul Buck, Verity Spott, Dean Detloff, Ben Gook and Marina Vishmidt. Harrison Fluss has been a valuable philosophical friend. My family has, as always, supported and sustained me. Finally, I would like to thank Fiona Price, who made this possible.

In material terms, the first chapter, '1844: Direct Language', draws on Benjamin Noys (2016), the second chapter, '1901: Freudful Mistakes' on Noys (2018), and the eighth chapter, 'Hex Position' on Noys (2017). I would like to thank the editors and publishers for their permission to reuse this material and their support for the original publications. Also, various parts of this book have been presented in London, Ljubljana, Zagreb, Canterbury, Stockholm, Malta, Atlanta, Cambridge, St Gallen, and Warwick. I would like to thank the organizers for the invitations and the audiences for their participation in these events.

The War of Language

If the twentieth century was the age 'when language invaded the universal problematic' (Derrida 1978: 280), then the twenty-first has seen the repulsion of this invasion. The recent turns to the digital, the material, the statistical, to realism and to the nonhuman or the inhuman have all tried to stem and reverse the invasion of language in different ways. Instead of the twentieth-century pre-occupation with the limits of language within language, today language itself appears as limited; we are called to breakout of the 'prison-house of language' (Jameson 1972) and inhabit the material *great outdoors*' (Meillassoux 2008: 7). As the wave of language has receded what remains is the flotsam and jetsam of matter to be recovered—resistant to being inscribed in language, as well as to any relation with the human. In contradiction to these claims, I want to tarry with language in its relation to the material and materiality, as well as in its relations to the conceptual and to the problems of abstraction. If language remains somehow unsatisfying today in its lack of materiality and in its function as a mere medi-ator of reality, then I want to suggest that we live with and work through this dissatisfaction. Rainer Maria Rilke, in his 1923 collection *Duino Elegies*, wrote, 'we are not dependably at home / in an interpreted world' (2021: 5). If language, as an interpretative exercise, seems to distance and alienate us from the world, it also, at the same time, allows us to start to overcome forms of alienation and abstraction. For Rilke, humans are not only homeless but also find their homeland in language, in the 'sayable' (71). We must not abandon language, as a form of abstraction and mediation, but relearn to live with it.

1

The claim made about language in the twentieth century was also a claim about its materiality, about matter itself. What the British neomodernist poet J. H. Prynne called 'the acrid wavering of language' (2016: 19) was celebrated as a materiality secreted within language—as the possibility of a new understanding of materiality as radical alterity. This would be the signature gesture of those forms of thought that became known as poststructuralism. Language would now be the path to a matter that resisted any stable inscription. I would not want to deny the experience of 'the acrid wavering of language', which is vital to the poetic. As Jacques Derrida put it, this is language perceived as 'sweet nourishment or as excrement, the trace as seed or mortal germ, wealth or weapon, detritus and/or penis' (1978: 231). This 'acrid wavering' is the moment of language—the resource for speech and its frustration—in which we find the word eluding us on the tip of our tongue and experience language as a painful struggle for expression.

This 'acrid wavering of language' was, however, treated by many twentieth-century writers and thinkers as the fundamental or transcendental form of language. Language experienced as material, as a taste, would figure matter resisting expression in language. We shift focus from the search for matter in language to a transcendental claim that language itself leads to a new form of matter that is fundamentally indeterminate. Language and matter fuse together, but remain unknowable. This was, as Hegel recounts (1977a: 98), the gesture made by Friedrich Heinrich Jacobi, who used the indeterminateness of language and representation to suggest a space beyond reason. In the twentieth century such gestures would produce peculiar forms of materialism in which language would become a matter that resisted all determination. These gestures would also lead to a political vision of language as a means to a materiality that would offer a perpetual source of subversion and resistance. The trail of language would, we were told, lead to a subversive materialism that could no longer be contained within the traditional limits of matter or language.

While aiming for radical subversion, such a stress on the materiality of language as radical alterity served a theological agenda—a leap of faith into a mystical fusion with what cannot be said. Jacobi treated language as indeterminate to deliberately open a space for faith in a *beyond*, but this articulation of radical alterity presented itself as secular—bringing the theological down into matter. By leaving such radical alterity beyond comprehension, however, the result was a materiality that remained indeterminate. This left space for a god or gods, in this indeterminate alterity, and left us with the mystical gesture of accessing this beyond by a fusion with the indeterminate. This tendency to ascribe a theological or mystical potential to language and matter is part of the reason why more recent materialisms are dissatisfied with poststructuralism and the stress on language. They feel that poststructuralist materiality and alterity remain too immaterial and potentially religious. The difficulty is that if the new materialisms reverse the terms, by putting matter before language, they do not escape the theological and mystical.

From those perspectives which push language to the limit, associated with poststructuralism, we approach the unsayable and the mystical point when language exhausts itself. This is evident in Wittgenstein's famously enigmatic assertion at the end of the *Tractatus*: 'Whereof one cannot speak, thereof one must be silent' (2001: 89, under #7). Drawing the limits of language is not simply an act of modesty, but creates a new domain of the unsayable. Of course, the new materialisms claim to answer this by saying what lies outside language is matter. It is matter that has priority, and a concern with language and what can be said is surpassed by an active experimentation with matter. The emphasis on matter is important and necessary, but in detaching matter from language they risk rendering matter as unsayable. In this case, matter is the site of a *beyond*, a site of mystical fusion, which remains another site of faith. My suggestion is that we see a strange convergence between the emphasis on language as leading to radical alterity and the more recent proclamations of matter as primary and Other to language. What we are offered in both cases is the possibility of mystical fusion, but what we lack in both is the ability to think through the relations between language and matter.

This transition from language, as site of the unsayable and indeterminate, to matter, from what we might call the ideology of language to the ideology of matter, can be found in the work of Martin Heidegger. Certainly, Heidegger is seen as one of the dominant thinkers of language, especially poetic language, as the primary means of disclosing the world to us. It is difficult not to agree with Fredric Jameson that the 'unctuous and contemplative solemnity of the Heideggerian meditation' (1994: 89) partially resembles the spontaneous ideology of much commentary on modernism. Heidegger's jargon of authenticity, acidly analysed by Adorno (1973), is the jargon of Being on the way to language and on the way away from language. Language is the fundamental event that also discloses the concrete world around us. In Heidegger, it is not just a matter of the celebration of language, but also a stress on how language reveals historicity and matter. This stress on the power of language resonates with the attempts by modernist poetics to reconnect language and matter in a new meaningful relation. For Heidegger language discloses the fourfold of earth, sky, gods, and mortals, revealing that they exist in a *primal* oneness' (1971: 149). Lukács observed that Heidegger's ' "authentic historicity" is not distinguishable from ahistoricity' (1963: 21). While claiming to uncover a primal moment of language connected to the world and the unfolding of history itself, Heidegger's vision remained a myth of origins that left history indeterminate and subject to a dubious Greco-German nostalgia.

Today, the prophets of the new materialisms argue that we have left behind Heidegger's toxic nostalgia for origins for a new world of hybrid matter. In contrast to Heidegger's traversal of language and search for 'primal oneness', we are witnesses to the turn towards science and other forms of materiality to celebrate the diversity of matter. The passage from Heidegger's meditations on language as a means to materiality to contemporary meditations on hybrid matter by thinkers like Bruno Latour (2004) and Graham Harman (2005) is, however, a short one. The qualities Heidegger assigned to language—the means of veiling and unveiling matter and Being—are now simply attributed to matter itself. It is matter which veils and unveils itself, without the need for language, or only with the need for a chastened language that can recognize its own inferiority. In Heidegger, what persisted was a sense of the relation of language to matter, even if this was presented in a highly mystified form of 'primal oneness' and mythic origin. Now, however, in the new materialisms all forms of relation are absorbed into matter, which presents itself as self-disclosing. Matter is preserved as beyond or prior to language, but only by making matter abstract and exempt from relations. Far from surpassing the Heideggerian or poststructuralist ideology of language, we find in these new materialisms a displacement or inversion that leaves matter as a mystical form absorbing all forms of relation—a new ideology of matter.

To begin to displace this structure I want to work through two different gestures that push at the limits of language and matter. The first aims to push language to the point at which it collapses into matter—a gesture that runs parallel to the poststructuralist subversion of language. The second aims to recover matter as what is mute, indeterminate and resistant to language, a tendency that resembles the contemporary new materialisms. These extreme gestures will help reveal the contours of the structure I have sketched above. They are both examples of the war on language. The first gesture declares war on language by pushing language to its limit in a guerrilla war waged on language from within itself. It aims to exhaust language and prise open its materiality as it falls silent. Such a guerrilla war is characteristic of twentieth-century avant-garde movements, modernism and the theoretical forms known as poststructuralism. The second gesture is the war on language from the outside, a war of attrition waged from the resources of matter.

This erodes the power and privilege of language, by invoking a materiality that exists before and after it. This gesture of turning against language in the name of the primacy of matter has become strident in the new materialisms of the twenty-first century.

For my example of the guerrilla war on language from within I use the American writer William Burroughs. In Burroughs' fiction, especially in his most experimental works, we find a violent resistance to language, which is seen as the mechanism of domination and control. His fiction aims to return us from the mystifications of language to a sense of reality. Yet, in trying to destroy language and uncover a reality beyond it, this reality takes on a mystical form, irreducible to any mode of expression. Burroughs, an American Artaud, mimics the latter's violent war on language that sees it as excrement. Antonin Artaud wanted to purify us from this excremental language, but in Burroughs we are left to welcome the fusion of language with excrement and materiality. The victory over linguistic control is bought through a deliberately fragmented and incoherent fusion of language and excremental matter.

In contrast, for the second gesture of the war on language waged from outside language on the side of matter, I turn to the art historian T. J. Clark. Clark argues that painting proposes a vision of intolerable materiality. Contrary to interpretations that conceive of paintings as compositions of linguistic signs, Clark proposes a more radical form of materiality that escapes determination. Such a materiality, for Clark, is registered at the edge of the frame of paintings and at the historical margins. Here matter is posed against materialism, especially historical materialism. If historical materialism looks at how matter is integrated and transformed by historical forces, Clark looks for an intolerable materiality beyond language and history. Clark expresses the desire to recover this matter, to attest to this strange materiality that persists despite the attempts to give it a linguistic form. The mute work of painting involves the attrition of language and the revelation of matter as what remains at the edge of the frame.

The symmetry of Burroughs and Clark lies in the fact that their wars on language end in silence: the silence of a language reduced to muteness in Burroughs, and an unspeakable silence of a matter in Clark. This reiterates Wittgenstein's gesture, in which silence is the edge or limit that opens the mystical and the ethical as the unsaid. It is such a limit I wish to cross by tracing the relation of language to materiality and conceptual thinking. We must not remain silent, but speak or write of the determinate forms of abstraction and language. It is this activity that makes possible a transition from the abstract to the concrete. Instead of a war on language, as we see here, we must transition to the war *of* language, a civil war, which opens the relation of language to matter and the concept. This can be done by interrogating the gestures of Burroughs and Clark. By reading them against the grain we will see how they reveal the complex war of language at work within their claims to transcend language.

Plan D

Burroughs conceived of the word as a virus, as a violent intrusion or invasion: 'The word may once have been a healthy neural cell. It is now a parasitic organism that invades and damages the central nervous system' (1999: 208). Here language, the material of Burroughs' practice as a writer, is rendered toxic and infectious. But how can one mount a resistance to this viral infection by language? It is this problem that preoccupies Burroughs. The violence of the word has to be met with another violence, such as the cut-up—the excision and recombination of words—and the fold-in—combining two texts by folding vertically. The result, similar to Antonin Artaud, is an escha-scatology, an apocalyptic writing that renders the end of language as the surpassing of the body and the excremental (Derrida 1978: 182–83).

This apocalyptic moment of the appearance of the invasion of the word virus, as well as its end, is presented in Burroughs' 1964 fold-in novel *Nova Express*:

What scared you all into time? Into body? Into shit? I will tell you; *'the word.'* Alien word *'the.'* *'The'* word of Alien enemy imprisons *'thee'* in Time. In Body. In Shit. Prisoner, come out. The great skies are open. I Hassan-i Sabbah *rub out the word forever.* If you I cancel all your words forever. And the words of Hassan-i Sabbah as also cancel. (1968: 10)

The word constitutes a fall into time, the body and excrement. Hassan-i Sabbah was the leader of the Order of Assassins, known in the West as the Old Man of the Mountains, who reputedly declared on his deathbed 'nothing is true, everything is permitted' (Murphy 1997: 116–30). Here he promises to *'rub out the word forever'*, thus overturning our fall into language and the body. Burroughs may also be fusing Hassan-i Sabbah with his successor, Hassan II, who in 1164 announced that the chains of the law were broken at the mountain fortress of Alamut (123–30). The word (and law), that which imprisons the human, will be abrogated, annulled.

Nova Express is a science-fiction novel that explores a guerrilla war on language as a cosmic war; a war to cancel language by the use of language. This war is fought between Nova Criminals— embodiments of the language virus who are draining our world of time and will eventually 'nova it' out of existence—and the Nova Police. The Nova Criminals include Sammy the Butcher, Mr Bradly and Mr Martin, and the Subliminal Kid. It is Burroughs' authorial surrogate Inspector J. Lee who primarily represents the Nova Police. Other players in this cosmic war include The Insect People of Minraud, the Virus Power of the Vegetable People, Venusians and Uranian street gangs. In this war, the Nova Criminals are aligned with language, morphine, addiction and control, while the Nova Police are aligned with silence, apomorphine (a morphine addiction 'cure') and liberation. The schema is binary and apocalyptic, with 'Total Resistance' to be achieved by erasing the word with apomorphine (Burroughs 1968: 62), as 'a powerful variation of this drug could deactivate all verbal units and blanket the earth in silence, disconnecting the entire heat syndrome' (38). The moment of the apocalypse is the moment of silence and the guerrilla war on language aims to annul language to reveal this silence.

Hegel once pointed out, 'to want to think without words as [Franz] Mesmer once attempted is, [. . .] , a manifestly irrational procedure which, as Mesmer himself admitted, almost drove him insane' (1990: §462). Madness, as Foucault also suggested, might be the absence of work, a sort of absence of language (1989: 287). It is also important to note, however, that in madness, as R. D. Laing argued, language becomes a confused 'word salad' (2010: 196). Burroughs' desire to transcend language and achieve silence falls into this space between the madness of silence and the madness of linguistic disturbance. Burroughs is well aware of this paradox of trying to transcend language through language. This is why double agents and traitors populate his universe, which foreshadows the writer who betrays silence to fight the word with the word: 'The purpose of my writing is to expose and arrest Nova Criminals.' (Burroughs 1968: 12) Burroughs turns fink and lawman in calling for war against all the 'boards'—the corporate domination of the earth. While aiming to erase language to escape the body and control, Burroughs knows that such an erasure can only be waged from within language.

If language, the Enlightenment and reason are the enemy—imposers of total control—Burroughs is also well aware that they are also the only possibility of resistance. Nothing could be more resonant of the Enlightenment than Burroughs' 'Plan D', which 'called for Total Exposure. Wise up all the marks everywhere. Show them the rigged wheel of Life-Time-Fortune. Storm The Reality Studio. And retake the universe' (55). Total exposure is an almost parodic version of the desire for transparency and clarity associated with the Enlightenment. Burroughs' aim to 'Wise up all the marks' is also a classical vision of the educational role of the Enlightenment intellectual. To be educated, to be 'wised up', is then to evade the snares of control.

While these aims are, for Burroughs, posed against a reason that has become irrational, we can still see the retention of a peculiar dialectic of Enlightenment. Burroughs makes us of the tools of reason to dismantle the controlling rationality he regards as dominating the world. This is evident in the fact that Burroughs' war with language is an internal war, in which we 'Shift linguals' and 'Cut word lines' (57) to bring language to a halt. The tools of reason and language are used against reason and language, in a fashion that remains unstable. Burroughs is poised between the desire to reveal the forms of control and the desire to enter into a space beyond reason and language.

This is not to underestimate the reactionary aspects of Burroughs' libertarian visions of revolution. The opposition to control is so general as to make possible any number of alignments: from freedom to do as one wants within the form of the market to the more radical forms of guerrilla war and liberation that Burroughs adopts in *The Wild Boys* (1971). Burroughs' satire is, like nearly all satire, politically problematic in its own attachments and blank ironies. Instead, the importance of Burroughs lies in the complexities and impasses of his war on language, which turn it into an internal war. In this way, matter is not simply gestured towards as a utopian outside, especially in the sexualized bodies of adolescents, but also appears as an inside, in which those bodies exist in relation to language.

We can sense this relation and struggle in the ways in which the abstractions of Burroughs' own text start to foreshadow the determinations of capitalist society. The 'Time–Money–Junk' equation of the Nova Criminals would be Burroughs' realization of Marx's 'general formula of capital': M–C–M', in which *money* transforms into *commodity* into *money as surplus value* (1990: 257). In Burroughs' equation, time—the point of origin of the extraction of surplus value—is rendered into money and then into junk—drugs, not simply surplus value but value as addiction. Burroughs' revised formula suggests a material addiction of capital at work within the abstractions of time and money.

This might seem an unlikely projection of Marx into Burroughs' text. After all, Burroughs' cartoonish pulp figures of science-fiction war hardly seem to grasp the subtleties of the capitalist value form. They appear more indebted to his pulp namesake Edgar Rice Burroughs, best known for the John Carter of Mars stories. The Subliminal Kid, the Insect People of Minraud, the Vegetable People might be laughable bad lore or at best good parodies of bad science fiction. And yet, the very cartoonish virulence of Burroughs captures something of the war of language that engages bodies and images, and tries to disrupt how they are chained together to forms of abstract value. The parallel can be made with Balzac: Lukács notes that Balzac's 'stylising' might seem 'romantic and grotesque', but 'is faintly reminiscent of the corruption of Marx's "economic character masks" ' (1983: 6). In a similar fashion, the excess of Burroughs' pulp characterizations renders the corruption of our own pulp character under late capitalism.

If we live in societies in which 'individuals are now ruled by *abstractions*' (Marx 1973: 164), then we also live in societies in which individuals become abstractions. Slavoj Žižek suggests that 'in certain specific social conditions (of commodity exchange and a global market economy), "abstraction" becomes a direct feature of actual social life, the way concrete individuals behave and relate to their fate and to their social surroundings' (2000: 105). We can go further and say we take on the character of abstract types, we become the bearers of these abstractions, and so we become abstract. Burroughs' science fiction pulp tells us something of abstractions turned pulp(y). The personifications forced on us by the form of value, companion to the reification of things, are not themselves necessarily clever or sophisticated. The much-vaunted sophistication of capital and value is, at the same time, a base materialism grafted onto bodies and turning us and the world into cartoon figures, while denying the possibilities of liberation that haunt cartoon worlds (Leslie 2002). Capitalism might be a bad cartoon, as much as an intricate and infinitely complex network. This deflation is also necessary to avoid the return of solemn Heideggerian tones to the contemplation of language. Poetically dwelling with gods and mortals, earth and sky, is nothing compared to living with The Mayan God of Pain and The Intolerable Kid, the Grey Room and The Reality Film. In Burroughs we confront the cartoon world of capitalist value as science-fiction comedy and horror.

Intolerable Materialism

On the other hand, matter can appear as the promise of an exit from 'the acrid wavering of language', from the pain of speech and writing. Unlike the anguished war from within language, the turn to matter proposes a liberation from the torture of the word. This liberation is, however, ambiguous. T. J. Clark, writing in *The Sight of Death* on Poussin's 'Landscape with a Man killed by a Snake' (1648), remarks:

> It would not anyway be bearable, for human subjects, to have the world offer itself every second as a fully material thing, a constant proximity, a presence, a place of mere events, all of them physically impinging on us—part of us, touching us, winding themselves into our very subjectivity. Materialism, in this sense, is a great and intolerable vision. (Clark 2006: 237)

Here materialism appears as negative—a vision of the collapse of mediation and of representation, in which distance vanishes. Escaping the pain of language only leads to the claustrophobia of an intrusive matter. If anything, this vision resembles the putrefactive materialism of the sixteenth-century peasant Menocchio, detailed by Carlo Ginzburg (1980). This is the vision of the world in continuous generation, rotting and regenerating. In this materialism, matter is at one with us and we realize our continuity with matter. It forms, in a strange way, an inverted vision of 'the acrid wavering of language'. If language started to appear too invasive and intimate, as a virus, then materiality too can start to appear as an intolerable intrusion into our world.

Clark, in his practice as an art historian, is a proponent of materialism in a form that turns to matter in its 'muteness and ungrammaticality' (2018: 136). There is a very strange symmetry with Burroughs. If Burroughs turned to silence as the opposite of language, Clark turns to matter as the moment of silence. This is evident in Clark's *Heaven on Earth* (2018), which explores painterly visions of the-life-to-come in works by Giotto, Bruegel, Poussin and Veronese. While Clark was known for his work in the social history of art and his use of historical materialism here things are different. Now we have a transition from a materialism that is attentive to the social to its antithesis—a materialism that turns matter against (historical or dialectical) materialism. The book certainly reaffirms Clark's controversial suggestion that the left must take the politics of tragedy as its guide and give up ambitions to shape the future, but what interests me more is the enabling discourse around materiality (2012). If we are to give up making heaven on earth, as Clark puts it, we must endorse an 'earth-bound' painting of 'humble or unregenerate materials' (2018: 8).

This is most evident in Clark's discussion of Bruegel's *The Land of Cockaigne* (1567), which for Clark is a material form, however equivocal, of the peasant utopia of realized material satisfaction. It is a project of peasant materialism that bears an odd resemblance to that of John Berger's arguments about the necessity of considering peasant experience (1992), and also to the 'absolute immanence' of the peasant utopia of Andrei Platonov's novel *Chevengur* explored by Frederic Jameson (1994: 73–128). For Clark this peasant materialism is both antidote and answer to those who claim to realize transcendence by achieving heaven on earth, whether that claim is explicitly religious or secular. The down-to-earth is the anti-utopian utopia, in which materiality is resistant to all attempts to impose plan or organization. Familiar tropes of anti-utopianism and anti-Communism are reworked in a new register of resistant materiality aligned with those perennial victims of history, the peasantry, seen as bearing the brunt of all projects of modernization, regardless of their political colouring.

It is remarkable that, in his reading of Bruegel, Clark is so quickly dismissive of any reading of the paintings as expressions of 'derision and sanctimony' (2018: 120). While Clark recognizes the potential in reading Bruegel's vision of the peasantry as one that is pessimistic, condescending and calculating, he wants to resist this way of seeing. What is surprising here is that Clark does not say more about the class politics of this gaze, especially as he had already done so convincingly with the twentieth-century British painter L. S. Lowry (Clark 2013). If Lowry's position as rent collector could, according to Clark, imply a gaze that was both sympathetic and condescending to the working class, even cruel at times, then Bruegel's own vision might also be subject to a critical reading that could admit its pessimism while not eliminating sympathy. In fact, what both painters share, in Clark's analysis, is an attentive gaze on people with disabilities and the ill, which wavers between disgust and sympathy. In Clark's proclamation of the down-to-earth, what we lose is a sense of who is proclaiming this position and from where: is it the painter or Clark? Are we really going down to earth or merely seeing the earthly from a distance?

What is also remarkable is that historical mediation only appears in the text as the violence of war and, more specifically, religious war. It is transcendence, imposed by force, which is the phobic object of Clark's book. The reference here is to the campaigns of Islamic State to achieve a global caliphate in the years before the book's publication. The violent attempt to bring heaven to earth by some religious believers is what concerns Clark, although the implication is to cast doubt upon any leftist projects that aim at realizing a material heaven on earth. This phobia is marked by the turn to 'painting's muteness' against language and any speech that would violently impose itself on matter (Clark 2018: 11). In opposition to religious war, there exists the silence of matter as the registration of exclusion and suffering. The silence of matter becomes a silencing of language and of social mediation, which can only intrude in a violent form. In the end we are left to contemplate this moment of silence.

Clark is relentlessly critical, often to the point of seeming exasperation, with contemporary art history, especially with its linguistic approach to painting. While Clark wants to escape language for materiality, he obviously attempts this escape in language itself and has considerable skill as a stylist. Therefore, language remains a problem and a necessity, which is resolved by Clark's endorsement of Paul de Man's 'challenge to more familiar (and comforting) versions of materialism' (2018: 275n40). De Man's materialism is one of language rendered as senselessly material in its own material inscription (1996: 90). At this point, the radical force of inscription escapes the control of philosophy. This is 'the prosaic materiality of the letter', which escapes aesthetic judgement, symbolic mastery and pathos. This is even what brings de Man into alignment with Burroughs vision of language as a virus, since de Man sees language as an 'inhuman faculty' (Jameson 2019: 27). We can see the convergence of de Man's subversion of language from within, the guerrilla war on language, with Clark's war on language from without, his war of attrition. In both cases we find matter remains as a form of indeterminate radical alterity, resistant to sense and meaning.

Clark is far from de Man's cool tone of materiality or Burroughs' experimental excess. Instead, he finds pathos in the foundering of language over the material and a materiality not indebted to language. The material stands for all that is excluded, from peasants to all the other victims of modernity (Clark 1999). Matter appears at the edge of the frame, as what is registered at the limit. Clark also tries to occupy this external and sidelong position (2018: 164). We can speculatively locate the sense of being on the outside or to the side in Clark's own political history. This was marked by his brief membership of the English chapter of the Situationist International, from which he was expelled in 1967. From Guy Debord's work (1995), Clark took the concept of the spectacle as an abstraction that determines forms of value in modernity (Clark, et al. 2005). The spectacle captures the movements of life in staged forms and encourages us to participate in these limited forms of display. This is a much broader conception than that of media, at the same time, it is narrower than representation, in that it gauges a particular mode of power and separation that capitalism has exacerbated and perfected.

While Clark pioneered the social approach to art history, clandestinely operating through such a conceptualization of abstraction, his more recent work totalizes the spectacle form, which can then only be resisted through matter. Instead of the recognition of materiality as shaped by natural and historical forces, we now have matter as marginal, at the edge of the frame, a surplus escaping capture by representation, especially in the form of language. Matter pokes through at the edge of the abstract. Matter is left as the remnant of power and so as the site of resistance. Here the war on language only leaves behind a residue of matter and the spectator standing to the side or looking to the edge of the frame. And yet, of course, Clark is producing a relation, a particular configuration of language and matter, of text and image, even if that relation threatens to become static or mystical.

In the case of Clark, vision is revealed as a mechanism of abstraction and subsumption in a further radicalization of Debord's notion of the spectacle. This is a parallel totalization to Burroughs' understanding of control, and one equally vulnerable to the problem of leaving only the remnants of matter as the moment of resistance. What is more valuable in Clark's work, and occluded in the totalization of the spectacle, is the analysis of matter, class, value and relation to the work of art. This is more evident in his work on Lowry than in the essays that make up *Heaven on Earth*, which has inverted the religious transcendence it violently rejects. We are called to exchange the aim of transcendence, of making heaven on earth, but only by a negative transcendence, a strange making of the earth earthier. The turn to immanence, which is not foreign to the religious impulse to find god everywhere, is not the solution or inversion of the religious that Clark claims. Also, while standing to

16

the side and on the outside is claimed as a position of modesty, it is also a position of surreptitious power. To be at the edge, to be outside, is not only to be excluded but also to have a position where one is unaffected. Clark's vision is more solemn and weighty than Burroughs' cartoon abstractions, but it also articulates the persistence of class vision within the undifferentiated vision of spectacle or control. Even Clark's attempt to stand at the edge or outside does not escape questions of class and power that complicate the opposition between the spectacle and matter. It demonstrates a moment of struggle in that moment of standing aside from commitment and action. This is certainly equivocal, but again it indicates that the war *on* language is not simply opposed to the war *of* language. The war on language is a poorly waged war, a misunderstanding, a fractured variant of the war of language.

Implacable Stickiness

The conclusion would appear to be simple. Burroughs and Clark, in very different ways, mistake a war on abstraction for a war on language. Their concepts of abstraction, control and the spectacle are overinflated, and thus it is easy to slide from abstraction to language itself, or from abstraction to the world. The solution would also be comparatively simple. We would need to separate out language from the forms of capitalist abstraction. This would be a Mallarméan task of purifying the words of the tribe, which have become contaminated by abstraction. I want to suggest things are not so simple. The war here is dual, on both abstraction and on language, and in both cases, it needs modification.

Yet Burroughs and Clark are not simply wrong. Their anguish speaks to the penetration of abstraction into language, as do their moments of comedy (more prevalent in Burroughs, but not absent in Clark). While language has often been associated with the force of abstraction and been seen as the enemy of concrete particularities, the increasing subsumption of language by capitalism has given rise to a capitalist language of 'implacable stickiness'

(Barthes 1975: 29). Capitalist value is an arrangement of language and matter in the service of the abstraction of value, but presented as something that cannot be separated. In this situation, calls for the purification of language or plain speech can often sound a reactionary note, but we must also resist the notion that an increasing difficulty or complexity of language will defy capitalist value. In fact, what is challenging about the language of the commodity is that it appears both simple and complex, cartoonish and serious, binding us in relations between language and matter that leave us blind to those relations.

The first point to make is that we are not conducting a war on abstraction as such. Abstraction is necessary to thought and, if anything, language is what makes this most evident. Hegel, while an implacable foe of abstraction, grasped the necessity of the force of abstraction against puerile empiricisms. The very 'units' of empirical stuff are themselves abstractions. We cannot exit this for some pure experience of materiality or for some unadulterated experience of language as the primal connection of sign and referent. A war on abstraction, then, already has to be nuanced into a war on real abstractions that structure forms of value and power, most notably, as Marx indicated, 'abstract labour' (1973: 103–5). Abstract labour, the notion of a general category of labour, is not merely an idea, nor is it just the result of capitalist value rendering all labour comparable through the measure of value. Abstract labour is also something materially produced by all those processes of discipline and punishment that result in organized labour, as well as by all those social and technological forms that embody, regulate and make available forms of labour to all. The technological subsumption of labour—for example artistic labour in the form of music or art software—constitutes that labour as abstract.

This is an abbreviated account of *real abstraction* (Sohn-Rethel 1978). Both words of this expression must be understood closely— 'real' indicates that these abstractions are embodied and given physical form, while 'abstraction' indicates how these abstractions organize and subsume the differences between things into the homogeneous category of value. Abstract labour takes all the different experiences of labour and homogenizes them into one calculable and exploitable form—work. Value, as is well known, renders all commodities—and potentially, everything—fungible, equivalent, at the level of the general equivalent: money. At the same time, however, capitalism generates stratifications and striations through this form of value, a multiplication of differences and identities that fragment any unity that might be achieved through the homogenization of all activities into the form of value. Our world is not only one of simplification, where all activities, rendered as forms of labour, only matter in so far as they generate value, evident in the notion of monetization. It is also a world of complications, in which we witness a proliferation of roles, commodities and lifestyles, each embodying or containing different forms of value, which all serve the process of value generation.

A similar effect takes place in the transformation of language into capitalist language. This is a process by which language becomes commodified, which makes it serve the production of value and become an object of exchange. This can be seen in the process of simplification, in which language is reduced to a slogan, buzzword, or meme. Here language operates in this most rapid and condensed form to generate value through facilitating capitalist exchange or even becoming the object of exchange. This is familiar and a familiar cause for complaint. We can add, however, that language can also become capitalist language by becoming more complex. Here language is not rendered equivalent but differentiated, through new linguistic forms, but also through modes of expression, accent, and levels of verbal mastery. The complexity of language renders capitalist reality opaque, and also access to these different levels of complexity serves to differentiate class position. Both the simplification and differentiation of language serve capitalist ideology, by rendering language as easy to exchange and by creating new hierarchies and exclusions within that process of exchange. It is easy to focus on the first, simplification, as negative, itself a class-bound vision, focusing as it does on the working class or other minority positions as bearers of these simplifications. We must also be aware of how complexity and linguistic variety and density can serve an ideological vision of hierarchy and domination. In both cases, however, we are concerned with the resources for resistance and the possibilities of language beyond the service of value. This is particularly the case when the very possibility of resistant language starts to seem archaic or a mere matter of historical interest, rather than a dissident tradition.

This absorption of language by capitalism helps lead to the desire to abandon language as something irredeemably tainted. The implacable stickiness of capitalist language we confront, in which abstraction has penetrated into language and in which language becomes a form of value, does not mean we should abandon language as irredeemably tainted, replacing it for the supposed purity and innocence of matter. Instead, we have to work through the critical possibilities of language as a force of abstraction that will allow us to tease out the forms of real abstraction without succumbing to silence. To return to Rilke, the *Duino Elegies* concern not only the human capacities of language that mediate between angels and creatures, a power of naming things, but also 'how money breeds more of itself' and 'the private parts of money' (2021: 79). Here Rilke, as poet, uses poetic language to try and state how money and value operate under capitalism. Poetic language is not only compromised by capitalism, but can also offer us ways to speak and understand how language is drawn into capitalism.

Poetry is important here, as the means to both grasp the limits of language and to think about the relations between language and materiality. Both Burroughs and Clark resort to poetry, or to the poetic functions of language, to speak to materiality. Burroughs is a novelist and does not make resort to poetry in any direct fashion. Yet, he makes constant material interventions into language, breaking up the text, fracturing prose by deploying new modes of enjambment. Agamben defines poetry as enjambment, the breaking of the line of text, as the disjunction of sound and sense (1999a: 109). The cut-up and fold-in of Burroughs produces a similar kind of disruption, as does the fact that much of this prose began in spoken routines, brief performances of the various personas Burroughs inhabits. T. J. Clark also makes recourse to poetry, notably religious poets like T. S. Eliot and George Herbert, to explore the limits of language in its relation to materiality. Here religion is explicitly identified with an embrace of immanence and the material as against a religious fanaticism that would try to change matter or the world. These gestures, while problematic, suggest how the turn to poetry emerges as crucial mode of the war on language, as well as how it can be used to complicate this war into the war *of* language. This is why we will pursue poetry as a form that is engaged with thinking about the disruption of language, of the disjunction of sound and sense, but also the possibility of new relations between sound and sense, language and matter. Laura Riding remarked that poetry is a craft of 'verbal rituals that court sensuosity' (1970: 12), and it is this relation between language and matter that concerns us here.

This book is written with symmetrical attention to thinkers or philosophers who engage with language and matter and to poets who do the same. They all carve a passage through a rather brief moment of time, as Guy Debord might have put it, and that passage involves the transition through language. In terms of thinkers, I return to Marx, Freud and Saussure—progenitors of theoretical movements we have not yet exhausted. The ways in which they tarry with language and matter continue to raise the problem of the relations between language and matter, especially as they bear on abstraction. I also return to Donna Haraway, in a more critical vein, as a thinker demonstrating the desire to surpass language for matter, while at the same time as someone who still maintains difficulty of language. In terms of poetry, my selection is idiosyncratic and personal, but aims to speak to how poetry explores both the great and intolerable materialist vision and implacable stickiness of capitalist language. These poets include David Jones, Diane di Prima, William Blake, Leslie Kaplan and a number of contemporaries. For me, these are all poets concerned with the pursuit and disruption of abstraction and are poets not only of difficulty but also of the simplicity of direct language.

I have presented these thinkers and poets through a series of dated chapters. Each chapter is intended as a largely self-contained essay on the thinker or poet, but also as a link in a chain that develops the relations between language and matter. The dating of particular chapters will recall, obviously, the 'plateaus' of Gilles Deleuze and Félix Guattari's 1980 work *A Thousand Plateaus*, which are chronologically marked and can be read in any order. In contrast, my chapters are rather moments of punctuation, intended to be read in the order they are presented. They take the flow of historical language and interrupt it with particular moments of historical and conceptual understanding, in which the relations of language and matter are rendered visible. The aim is to progressively illuminate the possibility of these relations. Bourgeois ideology often claims that freedom is found in monadic subjectivity and in escaping our relations with others (Caudwell 2009: *xxi*). Instead, I argue, our freedom is found in our relations with nature, history and with others. It is the experience of collective life, which is already prefigured in the collective experience of language. This recognition of our relation to reality is, I hope, where we can begin to think of better ways of living together and to fashion new relations of freedom.

CHAPTER ONE

1844

Direct Language

In a famous act of ventriloquism in *Capital* (1867), Marx has a coat—a commodity—inform us 'that its sublime objectivity as a value differs from its stiff and starchy existence as a body' (1990: 144).[1] The commodity addresses us to make us aware of value, of its irreducibility to the material and how it enables the exchange of seemingly incommensurable objects. The language of the commodity also informs us of how labour creates that value through the process of being rendered into abstract labour. All of this is not only spoken by the commodity through the gift of language; the structure of language as a system of signs suggests how this gift is associated with the fluency of the commodity. Language is a system of different but equivalent signs, and the realm of the commodity and its language is one that translates all differences into different comparable values. In particular, Jacques Derrida (1994), in *Specters of Marx*, and Werner Hamacher (2008), in response, have drawn out the possibilities and impasses of Marx's comparison of the structure of the commodity form to language.[2] The structure of language, according to Hamacher (170), renders the 'arithmetical propositions of relation', but language as an original promise also

---

1 Peter Stallybrass (1998) has offered a powerful account of the personal resonance of the coat for Marx as a material object both owned and regularly pawned for money.

2 Fred Moten's (2003: 12) discussion of the slave as living commodity and the 'irreducible materiality' of 'the commodity's scream' is a vital supplement to this discussion of commodity language.

exceeds this dimension of exchange. In this way, language promises a route out of commodity language. This is not, however, Marx's route, which instead rests on the promise of what Marx calls 'direct language' (1975: 276). The promise of language for Marx is the possibility of the use of language to express directly the true relations of humans as well as the distorted relations of capitalism.

My reading of Marx and language will also be a reading of Marx and Derrida. This will not involve an interpretation of commodity language in *Capital* and Derrida's commentary on that discussion in *Specters of Marx*. Instead, I want to read the early Marx and the early Derrida together: the Marx of the *1844 Manuscripts* and the Derrida of *Writing and Difference*, specifically the essay '*La parole soufflée*' on Antonin Artaud (Derrida 1978: 169–95). I am returning to the problem of Marx and language as a problem of alienation. Today alienation is commonly regarded as a problem that belongs to the past. While Althusser remains largely out of fashion, his criticism of the early, humanist Marx's model of alienation continues to resonate (1969). A parallel criticism of the early Marx was made by Derrida, especially in his 1968 verdict of anthropologism (1982: 117). Of course, today such dismissals of alienation and language are often made in the name of the new materialisms that claim to transcend the problems of the human into nonhuman matter. Marx's concern with humanism, species-being, essence and alienation is treated as passé in a posthuman world. Even amongst the scattered bands of historical or dialectical materialists, the current taste is more for *Capital* than for the early Marx. In the context of crisis and the dominance of capitalist abstractions, the discussion of alienation seems to have little to offer us. I want to resist this consensus. For Marx, the problem of alienation persists into his discussions in the *Grundrisse* and in *Capital* (Ollman 1976: *xv*), and there are signs of its recovery in the present day. Alienation, thought through language, is vital to grasping the abstractions, the sublime objectivity of value, which dominate us today.

This return to alienation also constitutes a return to labour, to add another unpopular word. Labour is often seen as a problem of capitalism, and the focus of the early Marx on labour is critiqued as an anthropological and historical mistake for regarding it as a central ontological and transhistorical category (Postone 1993). While I am sympathetic to the criticisms of the celebration of labour as an anticapitalist category, the desire to be rid of labour does not resolve the problems it poses. Jacques Rancière reminded 1970s radicals who proclaimed the abolition of work that the struggles of workers often began from the assertion that 'those who will not work will not eat' and the demand that idlers work 'is the banner of every working-class revolt' (2012: 111). Work remained a crucial dividing line between the working class and the bourgeoisie. Certainly, the experience of alienation that persists into the present is one of being bound to labour: either we are among the many who must labour to live, or among the few who live off the labour of others. We are bound to labour. It is our future, from cradle to grave. It is required of us, it is something we are linked to and cannot escape. This is true when, as Marx writes, for the worker 'work itself becomes an object which he can only obtain through an enormous effort and with spasmodic interruptions' (1975: 324). The instability of labour, what is today often called its precarity, does not allow us simply to escape labour. To declare labour theoretically bankrupt is to fail to address this problem and the fate of labour or work in the future, including after a future revolution. It is to fail to grasp the persistence and the possible over-turning of alienation.

This is why, at a theoretical level, I want to return to the early Marx and the early Derrida to grasp the persistent problems of language, alienation and labour. In this exchange between Marx and Derrida, language is conceptualized as a form of alienation as well as a possibility of escape from alienation. Language must not only speak alienation, for Marx, but offer an alternative direct language that can speak our liberation from alienation. Such a possibility might seem strange or phantasmatic to us, used as we are to supposing the permanence of alienation. It might also seem strange because direct language is invoked here in an overtly theoretical text, which is not seemingly speaking in direct language. The language of Marx, of course, is a complex and theoretical language, but one that aims at directness. In fact, Marx suggests, this direct language is occluded by the language of commodities and 'the estranged language of objective values appears as the justified, self-confident and self-acknowledged dignity of man incarnate' (1975: 276–77). In this situation the pursuit of direct language might seem strangely indirect or offensive.

Archi-alienation

> 'So bind me if you want.'
>
> Antonin Artaud,
> *To Have Done with the Judgement of God*

The turn to the early Derrida to consider the early Marx is not merely wilful. It is in Derrida's essay on Antonin Artaud that we find one of the few instances, before *Specters of Marx*, when Derrida mentions Marx.[3] This happens in a long footnote, which argues that the reconstruction of Artaud's thought reveals a very close, not to say identical, syntax and vocabulary with the early Marx. Derrida points out that Marx explored the inversion by which the value-producing labour of the worker leads, proportionately and inexorably, to the depreciation of the value of the worker. This inversion, in which an increase in value leads to depreciation of the body, is also found in Artaud. For Derrida, what is shared between Marx and Artaud is not only the problem of labour, but also a metaphysics

---

3 Derrida's most extensive discussion of Marx prior to *Specters of Marx* (1994) can be found in *Positions* (1987a: 37–114). Derrida also makes brief mentions of Marx in *Archeology of the Frivolous* (1987b: 214) and in *Margins of Philosophy* (1982: 216). The seminar on Marx and Marxism, from 1976, has now been published as *Theory & Practice* (2019).

of the proper and of alienation (1978: 325n20). This is a metaphysical desire for presence expressed as a desire for some original moment of the proper, and a sense of the loss of that moment though a fundamental experience of alienation that separates us from presence. In particular, according to Derrida, Marx and Artaud are unified by a common desire for the proper and resistance to alienation, one which touches on the essential dimensions of philosophy. Beyond the fascination with Artaud as a figure, especially a figure of madness (Foucault 1989: 287), we can find in the encounter between Artaud and Marx a revelation of alienation as the experience of labour.

These questions of the proper and alienation are played out in a shared language. What is the language of Artaud? Derrida explores Artaud's texts as divided: on the one hand, there is a desire to establish a work that is pure and fully present, lacking the marks of difference that are associated with language: 'the dream of a life without difference' (1978: 180). This is the Artaud who wants to re-establish the original purity of a life not sullied by the sign or writing; it is the Artaud who has a 'horror of all derivation' (Bersani 1976: 262). His is the purest of returns to presence. On the other hand, Artaud insists on the existence of an original theft or alienation of every form of writing—of every voice. This supposes the ruination of any form of property or propriety, the impossibility of a moment of presence 'prior to all dissolution' (Derrida 1978: 183). The original theft, prior to any purity or unity, is what Derrida would later call the 'ex-appropriation' of language, as language 'alienates' but 'lacks nothing that precedes or follows it' (1998a: 25). This is an alienation without any original loss and is the 'property of language' as 'inalienable alienation'.

In a later text on Artaud, Derrida, in a moment of ventriloquism, writes: 'I have been robbed, not of this or that, but myself robbed of myself, in the very stuff of myself' (1998b: 93). In the same text, Derrida summarizes this operation of theft as a sexual operation carried out by fiends, succubi and vampires, 'who come to suck your very substance, to subjugate you to steal what is most truly yours' (63). Creatures that drain vital fluids, especially sperm, preoccupy Artaud. Artaud certainly could treat this vampirism metaphorically, yet he also gives it a corporeal sense. It is not difficult to hear the echo in Artaud of Marx's comment that 'Capital is dead labour, which vampire-like, lives only by sucking living labour' (1990: 220). While Marx is making use of a gothic metaphor, we could, reading such passages along with Artaud, insist on the bodily violence and violation at work in them. The metaphor draws materiality into language and into the violence by which labour is rendered abstract.

Artaud's extreme sensitivity to loss and theft places him at the limit of the problem of alienation. Alienation is no longer simply the loss of something, but a loss that robs us of 'nothing', a loss of loss. In this sense, it is Artaud who is the true frontier figure of Western metaphysics, as a metaphysics of presence, not Heidegger, as Derrida claims (1989a). Artaud pushes the dream of presence to its limit and shatters it by forcing the dream into an expression that cannot contain it. This limit position can be graphically understood through Artaud's 'scato-logy', as Derrida puts it (1978: 182). A writing and a logic of excrement and inscription is what dominates Artaud's thinking. We can trace this from Artaud's claim in his letter to Pierre Loeb of 23 April 1947 that the human body is an 'alembic of shit' and a 'cask of fecal distillation' (1988: 516), to his declaration that 'All writing is to Pigshit' (1965: 38–39), and finally to his radio play, *To Have Done with the Judgement of God* (1947), which announces that Being is shit, God is shit, and that faecality is everywhere (1988: 559–61). This soiling threatens to encompass all values and forms, but at the same time Artaud, again, wants to resist this archi-alienation and recover an unsoiled being. Artaud does not simply celebrate the excessive or the abject. Instead, for Artaud, this ontological faecality must be cleansed from the body to reveal the true body. Absolute alienation is, for Artaud, a reversal towards a restoration of the purity of the body. In contrast to the figures of the vampire and the succubus, stand the 'daughters of the heart', those beings of angelic purity, young women, to whom Artaud turned as saviours (René 2014).

The body is also the site and subject of a dual articulation, a locus of alienation and recovery. Artaud writes, 'Man is sick because he is badly constructed', and 'there is nothing more useless than an organ' (1988: 570, 571). This disarticulation can be undone and a new body constructed in place of the old. It is possible to recover a body without differences, a real body that is 'without organs', without automatic reactions, and so a body of 'true freedom' (571). Our usual lives are dominated by automatic reactions, a machine-like existence in which our existing organs determine our behaviour. Freedom, for Artaud, is achieved by living without these organs, and so without the automatic reactions and habits that structure our existence. In this way we achieve the freedom of the body without organs. Artaud demonstrates a vitalism that poses life against deadening habit, represented by the automatic reactions of the bodily organs. It is this body without organs that Gilles Deleuze and Félix Guattari will explore in detail (1983: 9–16; 1988: 149–68). Loss, loss of the organs, is not simply ruin, but also a ruination that reveals this true body, beyond the forces and forms of habit and convention. Alienation is written on the body or into the body in the form of organs that dictate reactions. In the case of Artaud, the removal of alienation requires the removal of these organs and the construction of a cleansed and angelic body.

The extremity of Artaud's dream of a life without difference places him beyond Marx—an observation Derrida does not discuss. For Artaud (quoted in Esslin 1976: 109), Marx and Marxism remain bound to European barbarity: 'Have come to Mexico / to flee the Barbarity of Europe / last example of European Barbarity: Marxism'. The flight to Mexico in 1936 was, in part, a flight from Marxism, as 'the revolution invented by Marx is a caricature of Life' (Artaud 1988: 357). When the Surrealists had shown signs of embracing Marxism, in the mid-1920s, Artaud had violently denounced this as a 'revolution of eunuchs' (Shafer 2016: 77; see also 69). If Marxism only offers a 'fragmentary life', although one that corresponds with 'a real movement of history' (Artaud 1988: 357), real revolution must go beyond the material. Marx remains transfixed by what he opposes, tied to capital, tied to the facts: 'But he too remained fixated on a fact: the capitalist fact, the bourgeois fact, the congestion of the machine, the asphyxia of the economy of the age caused by the monstrous abuse of the use of the machine' (358). Against this Marx, which for Artaud is the materialist Marx, Artaud suggests 'the youth' demand a 'total metaphysics' that 'will reconcile them with the life of today' (358). Such a metaphysics circulated among many dissident Surrealists, notably with the group around the journal *The Great Game* (Duncan 2015).

Artaud's criticisms of the materialist Marx remain strikingly anticipatory of many of the later criticisms of Marx, especially as summed up by Baudrillard's (1975) suggestion that Marx was only 'the mirror of production'. For Artaud, Marx remains too attached to capitalism because he remains too attached to labour.[4] As a result, Marx's revolution was a mere change in who was in charge of the machine, not a fundamental rupture with the culture and consciousness that structured capitalist society. Hence Artaud's call for spiritual revolution. While Artaud's criticism has faded, the criticism of Marx as too attached to labour has found its most well-known and most magisterial formulation in Heidegger, especially his 'Letter on "Humanism" ' (1998[1946]: 259). As well as being echoed by Hannah Arendt (1959), it can also be felt in Michel Foucault's (1970: 262) claim that Marxism swims 'like a fish in water' in nineteenth-century conceptions of labour, especially those of David Ricardo. It underpins Derrida's understanding of Marxism as only offering a restricted economy (1978: 251–77), compared to the potentials of Georges Bataille's general economy. While these

---

4 For this accusation that the early Marx remains too attached to labour see Louis Althusser (2009: 42n18), and for the parallel charge against the later Marx of *Capital*, see Antonia Birnbaum (2011: 24).

references might be largely displaced today, the same point is often redeployed by the new materialisms. Marx is condemned, as he was by Artaud, for being bound to the concept and reality of capital and labour and unable to transcend this fatal pairing.

The scene of reading Marx with Artaud and Artaud with Marx, which Derrida implies, suggests, I think, that the bind to labour cannot be so easily undone. Artaud's flight to Mexico, like his later flight to Ireland, are attempts to physically escape the alienation of labour and the alienation of existence or Being itself. These flights would end in failure and madness. Artaud's own invocation of the purity of life echoes in contemporary vitalist theories, which also try to evade the binding of labour by evoking the capacities and potentialities of the living body beyond any determination. Instead of this flight, and the subsequent Icarian crash back into binding, my suggestion is that we now need to read Marx not only with but also against Artaud. In fact, reading Artaud with Derrida and Marx suggests the intractability of the binding to language and labour, and the concomitant experience of alienation, as one that must be more carefully worked through. This is not simply to embrace the pessimistic suggestion that we cannot escape capitalist labour, which is simply the inversion of the dream of purity. Perhaps, the solution lies instead in the traversal and interrogation of the binding to labour and language implied by Artaud's scatology. It is in working through the binding of labour and language that we might find a way out of alienation.

Bound to Labour

It is not difficult to see a parallel between Derrida's reading of Artaud and Derrida's later reading of Marx in *Specters of Marx*. To summarize that reading briefly and brutally, Marx is seen as intuiting and enacting the structure of spectrality, of hauntology, which dislocates metaphysics, by hinting towards the primacy or better irreducibility of spectrality. Marx's discussions of ideology and the commodity insist on the spectral dimension of value and a general spectrality in which we exist. At the same time, Marx will also always desire to exorcize this spectrality, to establish or re-establish presence, a transparency, an ontology or metaphysics of presence that can bring an end to the *'madly spectral'* dance of ghosts (Derrida 1994: 57). Marx will insist on a use value, on species-being, on a rupture with the spectral forces and forms of capital. For Derrida, this desire to establish presence is particularly true of the early Marx. Derrida (2002: 147–198), in the wake of Althusser, assimilates the early Marx to a humanism of 'total man' (a phrase belonging to Henri Lefebvre (1968)) 'for whom the ghost must be nothing' (Derrida 1994: 30). The dream of total man and humanism seems to remain the chief ingredients of a seemingly irresistible reading and subsequent dismissal of the early Marx.[5] The parallel with Derrida's reading of Artaud is that Artaud also inhabits this double movement: an insistence on a radical experience of alienation and loss that shakes the metaphysics of presence, but also the will to re-establish presence and purity in a more secure fashion. The difference is that Derrida is more sympathetic to Artaud's more extreme pursuit of presence through radical loss than he is to Marx's more materialist reading of this movement.

We can, however, offer another interpretation. If the language of the early Marx, read through a Derridean lens, bears a precise resemblance to Artaud, and if Artaud is split between presence and its ruin, recovery and theft, then we can reread Marx as someone who also probes this fracture. While Derrida's reading of Artaud remains more generous, and more troubled, there is no obvious reason why we should not extend that generosity to Marx. It may be that contrary to Artaud's dismissals Marx offers something that allows a stabilization of Artaud's excess. Whereas Artaud transforms the tension of life and labour into a world-historical drama of life trying to detach itself from labour, a hyperbolic or exorbitant speculation on life without difference which reveals and ruins this

---

5 This reading of Marx and the purity of property, in relation to Stirner, is prefigured by a long footnote in Derrida's essay 'White Mythology' (1982: 216–17).

dream that lies within metaphysics, I want to suggest that Marx's attention to the binding of life and labour insists on the fact that the bind cannot simply be cut. Marx, on this reading, leaves us within a stricture, within the bind of the economic, but this paves the way for another interpretation, another possibility.

I want to begin with labour before proceeding to language. Contrary to the image of alienation as a deviation from unity, and disalienation as a return to unity, we will see that Marx complicates this experience without giving up on critique. Marx begins the discussion of 'estranged (or alienated) labour' by interrogating the central assumption of political economy—that we start from private property. If we begin from the assumption of private property as primordial then the result is a disconnection between all the elements that constitute political economy—especially labour, capital and landed property—which appear separately. This fragmentation is licensed by the positing of 'some imaginary primordial condition', as Marx puts it (1975: 323); in the language of Derrida the 'dream [. . .] of full presence, the reassuring foundation' (1978: 292). In the case of political economy, this 'imaginary primordial condition' is later specified by Marx in the *Grundrisse* as the fantasy of the *Robinsonades*: those visions of a human detached from all bonds and a self-sufficient creator of value found in the figure of Robinson Crusoe by political economists (1973: 83). This fantasy that does not reflect the reality of human origins, but rather the atomized conditions of contemporary capitalist society that treats all humans as isolated and independent units of value. Instead of this imaginary beginning, Marx suggests that we must begin from the worker's position as a commodity, for whom their labour and its products 'stand opposed to it as *something alien*' (1975: 324). The paradox, a socially produced paradox, is of a beginning in division, in alienation, a divided beginning, which while still referring to a unity is, as we will see, more complex than an invocation of prior presence.

Marx argues that for the worker the separation from their own product and subjection to the form of civil society results in a loss of reality. What's more: 'So much does the realization of labour appear as loss of reality that the worker loses his reality to the point of dying of starvation' (324). Labour is not just a social category, but a material experience and one that fails to provide a living for the labourer. To labour in capitalist society is to risk starvation as a matter of course. The result of this loss of reality is that the worker's exertion increases his alienation; this is an insight that Derrida explicitly linked to Artaud. In this situation life is displaced: 'the life which he has bestowed on the object confronts [the worker] as hostile and alien' (324). The process of alienation is for Marx, as it is for Artaud, a corporeal process, in which the worker 'from being a man becomes an abstract activity and a stomach' (285). Artaud's 'body without organs' is realized by capitalist labour as a 'body of work with only one organ'. The body lives out the alienated splitting of production and self-reproduction, of work and eating, of the experience of alienation as antagonism. If some might be tempted to say today this issue has been resolved, for some in the world, by the availability of cheap food (Patel and Moore 2018), then the return of food banks and the poor nutritional quality of that cheap food, suggests that the alienation of the stomach has simply been raised or modified to a different form.

This process of alienation begins with nature, with 'the *sensuous external world*' (Marx 1975: 235), which is the first object of appropriation. Again, a displacement operates in which the identity of being a worker, which is secondary, comes to overlay the condition of being a '*physical subject*', and determines our very existence as human beings (325). This is reminiscent of the Freudian logic of 'deferred action', in which a later sexual trauma comes to reactivate the original sexual trauma, which only exists through that later event (Laplanche and Pontalis 1988: 111–14). In this case, the traumatic imposition of the identity of the worker and its deprivation of reality come to reactivate the struggle for survival that underlies our physical being. The original dependence on nature for survival is overwritten and overdetermined by the secondary dependence on capital, which now becomes the primary condition of access to subsistence and natural substance.[6] Capital becomes nature or, better, a second nature that overlays natural existence (Lukàcs 1971: 64). The discourse of political economy conceals this trauma by suggesting that we are born without dependence and so always make a 'free' choice for exchange and alienation. It disavows both natural bonds and the remaining, fragmentary and weak, bonds of capitalist society, but especially the despotic imposition of labour as binding.

There is no choice to labour, no choice over the binding dependence on production to sustain life, which is also the separation from the means of subsistence that Marx will analyse under the form of 'original' or so-called 'primitive accumulation' in *Capital* (1990: 873–942). So, labour is forced labour. This is the double bind of capital: without the means of subsistence we are forced to labour, but labour cannot satisfy us, as it is always depriving us of our substance and reducing us to mere survival. In Marx's formulation, under capitalism we find 'the *abstract* existence of man as a mere *workman* who therefore tumbles day after day from his fulfilled nothingness into absolute nothingness' (1975: 336). The worker 'tumbles' from the 'fulfilled nothingness' of wage labour into the 'absolute nothingness' of the time not devoted to '*wage-earning* activity' (289). This latter time is the time of nonwork or unemployment. The difficulty is that moving from the time of labour to the time of nonwork is the oscillation that capitalism forces on us. Freedom from labour does not necessarily lead to freedom, as the time outside of labour is time spent preparing for labour, seeking labour or self-reproducing as labouring subjects.

---

6 For an extreme science-fiction version of this scenario, in which humans have been radically modified into parasitic creatures to survive alien invasion, and the suggestion this mirrors our relationship to capitalism, see Steven Shaviro's (2015: under chap. 3) discussion of Paul de Filippo's short story 'Phylogenesis'.

In the situation of unemployment or nonwork the worker becomes the concern of 'criminal law, doctors, religion, statistical tables, politics and the beadle' (288). The beadle, the overseer of the workhouse, may be considered as the model for the security guard and other privatized regulatory figures of contemporary capitalism. This is, in brief, the experience of labour. It is a binding that is not so easy to escape and one that works through a relation of abandonment, prefiguring the analysis that Giorgio Agamben would develop, in a more hyperbolic fashion, around 'bare life' (1998). What is important is that Marx, unlike Agamben, determines this relation of abandonment through the economic structure and forms of capitalism, rather than treating such abandonment as a largely transhistorical operation of power. In contrast to the dramatic spectacles of life as ontological ruination we find in Artaud or Agamben, Marx works through the historical form of life and labour as a mode of being and also the overcoming of this form of life.

The world-historical drama that Marx traces is a determinate experience of loss and alienation mediated by the experience of labour and the constitution of abstract labour in capitalist society. While the analysis of the early Marx should be read together with that of the later Marx to fully grasp this experience, it does not mean the early account of labour and alienation is inferior. In fact, and this is why we must read him with Artaud, Marx provides an acute account of the experience of loss and of its potential recovery. While Artaud can only seek such a recovery in an idealized outside (Mexico, Ireland)—one that, eventually, fails—or in an idealized internal world purified of organs, Marx proposes a social analysis of alienation and deprivation as it operates through language and the body. This is no less world historical or 'cosmic' than Artaud's drama, once we understand that we live in the 'cosmos' of capitalism, which may determine our lives, in Max Weber's words, 'until the last ton of fossilized fuel is burnt' (1989: 181–82). Of course, Marx rejects in advance the cosmic pessimism of Weber's 'iron cage' or entropic exhaustion, as well as its Nietzschean alternative of the 'great rebirth of ideals'. Similarly, Marx rejects the Nietzschean accents of Artaud's solutions of spiritual revolution and purification that are always somehow beyond the grasp of modernity. The point, contra Artaud, Weber and Agamben, is to delimit and grasp the experience of alienation as one that may be overcome or changed by transforming our material conditions rather than through some miraculous return or rebirth.

Mirrors of Production

To grasp the experience of alienation is a matter of language, but our experience of language is also one of alienation. Our language becomes 'the language our possessions use together' (Marx 1975: 276). This language usurps our usual experience, generating a situation where, as I have already noted, our estrangement from our human essence is so great that 'the direct language of man strikes us as an *offence against the dignity of man*', while the alienated language of value 'appears as the justified, self-confident and self-acknowledged dignity of man incarnate' (276–77). In this distortion of direct language what should be the language of dignity appears as insult, and what should be insulting appears as the language of dignity. These are the reversals we constantly find in the early Marx, indicated by the repeated use of chiasmus, but they are also the reversals of social reality and of language itself, put into the service of the commodity.

Language is subject to the same alienation as labour. What we use to speak and write of our situation of alienation has itself become part of that alienation. This is so to the degree that it is not we who speak of commodities, but commodities that speak of or for us. Language, however, is not completely saturated by the commodity. Before and beyond the language of the commodity lies an 'immediate expression' (277) that would have 'directly *confirmed* and *realised* my authentic nature, my *human, communal* nature' (278). In this situation, employing a fascinating metaphor, Marx suggests: 'Our productions would be as many mirrors from which our natures would shine forth' (278). There is enough here—in these claims to 'immediate expression' and 'authentic nature'—to condemn Marx out of hand as belonging to humanism and the metaphysics of presence. This would be a metaphysics of subjectivity in two senses: an insistence of the metaphysics of subjectivity as a metaphysics of the individual as possessor of property, prior to all division, and a metaphysics of subjectivity in terms of community as immanence and transparency (Nancy 1991).

We can interpolate Derrida's later suspicions from *Specters of Marx* concerning use value here, especially his remark that use value can 'always relate to what is proper to man, to the properties of man' (1994: 188). In Marx's *Capital* use value is an aspect of value and so not strictly opposed to exchange value. It is hard not to suggest that Derrida has missed the point and that use value does not refer to any original 'strict purity' (160). The difficulty remains, however, of the critical function of a notion of what might be beyond use value *and* exchange value. First, we can note that while not referring to a strict purity it is also possible to think of use value as a complex site of subjectivity and immanence which does have a potential critical form (Echeverría 2014). Second, even if use value is to be taken as intrinsic to political economy and Derrida's criticism misguided, his wider point might stand. This would be the argument that Marx resists the spectral and always tries to re-establish an authentic and original point from which capitalism can be criticized. Derrida's analysis, as many have noted, would then disable any notion of a critical purchase on capitalism, except one displaced into the spectral and messianic.

The problem of an authentic and direct language could be seen as anticipating and repeating the problem of use value. The search for such an authentic and direct language would be only the result of refusing to accept the spectral contamination of language and an inability to live with this spectrality. This problem is condensed in the concept of species-being, which refers to this original productivity and relational experience. It is Marx's name for our original relation to nature and to each other, and as such has often been criticized for its humanism and naturalism. Authentic and direct language would be the expression of this productivity and the relations we enter into. The point here is that this original productivity of species-being is not merely a mirror of production, in Baudrillard's sense of a bad mimicry of capitalism. The mirroring of our productions promises a recognition and engagement of communal nature that is contrary to the limits and abstractions of capitalist production. Marx's view of essence is not simply exhausted by the metaphysics of presence or purity. If Artaud posited original alienation as a threat to the propriety and property of the metaphysics of subjectivity, Marx posits an original exchange that threatens the distinction of use and exchange. Marx specifies that species activity is exchange, 'whose real, conscious and authentic existence consists in *social* activity and *social* enjoyment' (1975: 265). We are predestined to exchange, to engage, to find our essence as a primary relationality, which stems from the fact that essence is community. Instead of the mirror of production, we have Marx's many mirrors of production, in which our language and experience communally reflect our natures (Agamben 1999b: 79–85).

Roberto Calasso writes that 'Marx is greedy. He wants *more* of everything' (2018: 243). While this is supposed to criticize Marx for his lack of a sense of limits, we can reread this as the moment of production and relation that exceeds the limits of capitalist exchange. The irony is that Marx's conception of species-being does not imply an original innocence or some kind of blank state to be remade at will, but an original *greed*, an appetite or craving, to produce and to make relations. This is something like what Spinoza means by *conatus*, a striving to persevere in being, which is not simply the capitalist desire for accumulation projected back onto our original being (1930: 301–2). Engels wrote, discussing Stirner's theory of egoism that:

> What is valid is the idea that we have to make a cause our own before we are prepared to work for it, that, in this sense, apart from any hope of material gain, we are communists out of egoism, are human beings—and not merely individuals—out of egoism [...] If we take the living individual being as the basis, the starting-point of our image of the humanity, egoism—not Stirner's 'rational egoism' alone, but egoism of the heart—will be the ground of our love of humanity and give it sound roots. (quoted in Lukács 1963: 131–32)

Egoism feeds into our love for humanity and is not opposed to it. Our egoism seeks out relations with others. We could speak, even, of a primary exchange that is then overwritten by capitalist exchange value, which imposes a relation of value onto this relationality: 'economics establishes the estranged form of social commerce as the essential and fundamental form appropriate to the vocation of man' (Marx 1975: 266). Economics creates a '(second) nature' of competition, immiseration and wealth, which replaces the nature of humans as creatures of exchange and recognition (Lukács 1967). This overlaying is not some natural and destined fall from grace. Capital comes into the world 'dripping with blood and dirt' (Marx 1990: 956); it is an act of historical violence generated primarily out of the separation of workers from their means of subsistence and sustained as a social form by constant and ongoing violence.

One striking confirmation of Marx's view of the complexity and relationality of species-being can be found in what we can call Marx's critique of communism. This involves a shift from questioning the assumption of a simple origin to questioning the notion of ending as 'eschatological presence' (Derrida 1987a: 45). The cliché of communism lies in the supposition that it is a state of transparency, a condition of continuous conscious control over production. In the *Economic and Philosophical Manuscripts* Marx critiques communism as a simple reversal of the capitalist relation to private property. The destruction of private property in 'crude' communism threatens the fact that 'the category of *worker* is not abolished but extended to all men' (Marx 1975: 346). Pursuing a *reductio ad absurdum*, Marx argues this 'wholly crude and unthinking communism' will replace marriage with 'a *community of women*', and so lead to 'universal prostitution' (346). Instead of replacing private property, this kind of communism is a 'logical extension' of private property, expanding it to the community. Prefiguring Nietzsche's analysis of *ressentiment*, Marx suggests this 'envy' results in an abstract negation, a levelling down, which raises labour to the condition of 'an *imaginary* universality' (347). Here, Marx is a critic of communism, prefiguring many of the later criticisms that would be laid at his door.

This is, however, only a first form of communism, and the process of 'the reintegration or return of man into himself' (347), requires 'the complete restoration of man to himself as a *social*, i.e. human, being' (348). This mode of restoration does not seek its proof 'in isolated historical forms' (348), but on the development of the collective and social powers already found in capitalism. For Marx, the basis for revolution is to be found 'in the movement of *private property*' (348), which can then be returned into '*real life*' (349). Rather than calling for an unbinding that would place us somehow beyond capitalism, Marx suggests that it is only through a bond, through the linking with others, through the relation of sociality, that communism can be implemented. This is not to erect the social over humans, which, for Marx, would institute another abstraction (350). Instead, there is a dialectic between the individual and the communal through the recovery of those social powers that capitalism has mutilated and disguised (Henry 1983). Marx's analysis implies a deepening of the complexity of relation as crucial to liberation from capitalism (Williams 2015: 433). This suggests that the way out of the bind to capital is through another bind, another linking that will allow us to develop our freedom through our binding.

What we have restated here is the role of language in Marx as the means not only for grasping the primacy of abstraction and especially the form of abstract labour, but also the means to rupture this form of abstraction. This is partly why we have returned to the early Marx and the problems of alienation and labour. To remain with *Capital* treated only as an analysis of the power of real abstractions is to remain hypnotized by real abstractions. This might well be the small truth of those criticisms of Marx for being bound to capitalism. The irony is that to shake this binding we have to turn to labour and alienation again as ways to work through the forms of abstraction. This is why language not only leads us to the language of commodities and the language of our possessions, an internal language of value spoken between commodities, but also to the direct language that might overturn this monologue of the commodity (which always presents itself as a dialogue or even as dialogic). The commodity speaks to itself and we are forced to join in this soliloquy as we are formed into producers of abstract labour, and formed as commodities. Direct language, in contrast, is an offensive language, which interrupts this soliloquy of the commodity. It offers the promise of a rational understanding of relations that are not subject to the alienations of capitalist value. Direct language is the language of freedom found in our relations to others and the world.

CHAPTER TWO
1901
Freudful Mistakes

James Joyce, in *Finngeans Wake* (1939), ironically noted that if you forget psychoanalysis 'you never made a more freudful mistake, excuse yourself!' (1992: 411). As I will argue, to forget psychoanalysis is, among other things, to forget that language matters. Psychoanalysis is the 'talking cure', a phrase coined by Freud and Breuer's patient Anna O. in English (1974: 83). It begins with a recognition of the power of language in relation to matter. Language, such as the signifier 'arm' in the case of Anna O., determines the symptom, the paralysis of matter in the form of the paralysed arm (Adams 1986). 'Arm' as a signifier dividing the body does not conform to neurological reality, hence this paralysis is not caused by the body but by the word or signifier. Freud, trained as a neurologist, knew the difference, and so knew that language mattered in its effect on matter. These are 'magic words' (Abraham and Torok 1986), which echo in the body and in matter. Language matters not only because language determines the unconscious symptom, but also because language engages with matter and because language itself is strangely material. Psychoanalysis reminds us of this experience of language and of matter. We had better not forget that.

Of course, Joyce wanted nothing more than to forget psychoanalysis. Joyce was angered by C. G. Jung's essay on *Ulysses*, hostile about Jung's treatment of his daughter Lucia, and generally dismissive of the 'new Viennese school' as inferior to the insights of

Thomas Aquinas (1992: 264). He was not the first or the last writer who wished to forget psychoanalysis, while remaining so close to it (Nabokov would be another example). In *Finnegans Wake*, Joyce writes of the 'grisly old Sykos who have done our unsmiling bit on 'alices, when they were yung and easily freudened in the penumbra of the procuring room' (115). The 'psychos', Freud and Jung, do grisly work on young girls in their consulting rooms, pimping them out to their 'unsmiling' theories. In a fashion that has not gone away, the psychoanalytic emphasis on sexuality is returned to sender and, it is suggested, psychoanalysis has the prurient and exploitative interest in sex. Of course, however, Lacan wrote that Joyce 'is the simplest consequence of a refusal—such a mental refusal!—of a psycho analysis, which, as a result, his work illustrates' (1977: *ix*). The revenge of psychoanalysis upon Joyce is that while Joyce may be the one who most forgot, or tried to forget, psychoanalysis, his work is, for Lacan, the greatest illustration of psychoanalysis as an encounter with language and with jouissance. After all, Joyce, like Freud, knew something of enjoyment, of jouissance, as their surnames testify to 'joy' in English and German respectively (Lacan 2016: 146), and they both knew something about language.

Joyce, we might say, forgets psychoanalysis to remember the matter of language in its modes of inscription. Derrida has noted that vast ambition of Joyce's work, which 'circulates through all languages at once, accumulates their energies, actualizes their most secret consonances', and in doing so 'rediscovers the poetic value of passivity' (1989b: 102). The passivity is one before language, before the signifier, in which language appears as such. According to Lacan, this passivity also makes language appear as *lalangue*, a neologism that names the intersection of jouissance and language (2016: 146). Jacques-Alain Miller explains that 'there is a jouissance, which derives directly from the relation to language' (2005: 12), which Joyce achieves. Joyce's writing is a writing that while trying to forget psychoanalysis illustrates the saturation of language by jouissance, the moment of the 'lettering' and 'littering' of language (Joyce 1992: 93; Lacan 2016: 145). Language appears in and through equivocation and homophony (Milner 2017). The freudful mistake is the frightful mistake (through the *lalangue* English) and a joyful mistake (through the *lalangue* German). The frightful mistake is to forget the freudful mistake and so to forget the joyful mistake, to forget that language matters. This is why the path back to psychoanalysis and language lies in the Freudian slip, as the moment that allows us to register that language matters in its frightful and joyful aspects.

This is the path I want to follow here, through Freud, Lacan and the critics of both. My aim is to traverse psychoanalysis, and my references to politics will remain oblique. I do not present 'Marx and Freud in the same incandescent light' as Foucault described Freudo-Marxism, but neither do I want to offer a chastened acceptance of incompatibility (1983: *xi–xiv, xii*). My real debt, not always directly evident in what follows, is to that working through of psychoanalysis and politics pursued by Juliet Mitchell (1990), Parveen Adams (1996), and Jacqueline Rose (1986), which we might call socialist-feminist. For these writers, the incompatibility or stress induced in the relation of the psychic to the social is precisely the point of intervention that sustains socialist and feminist politics. I will register this stress through the relationship of language to sexuality, especially as that relates to the problem of matter. The forgetting of sexuality, which is often involved in forgetting psychoanalysis (Badiou 2007: 68–80), accompanies the forgetting of language and matter.

The Primal Scene of Forgetting

Freud is riding in the company of a stranger in a carriage going from Ragusa in Dalmatia to a destination in Herzegovina: 'I asked my companion whether he had ever been to Orvieto and looked at the famous frescoes painted there, painted by . . . ' (1975: 39). An ellipsis appears, the three dots (. . .) that indicate an omission or falling short. In this case, the omission is the name of the painter, a moment of forgetting, a deficiency at the moment of expression. This elliptical moment might well be understood as the rhetorical figure of aposiopesis, the showing in language of a falling silent, a breaking off. As a rhetorical figure, this usually indicates being overcome by passion, being speechless with rage or feeling. In fact, we could say that Freud's analysis will supply that missing passion to what seems a trivial act of forgetting and sudden falling silent.

Freud has forgotten the name of a painter, Signorelli, who painted the frescoes of the 'Four Last Things' in the Orvieto Cathedral. It is an apocalyptic moment. Freud, however, remembers two other names of painters—Botticelli and Boltraffio (38). He seeks explanation for this in the previous topic of conversation, which had concerned the (supposed) custom of Turks living in Bosnia and Herzegovina of trusting in doctors to a high degree and being profoundly resigned to their fate when terminally ill. They address the doctor as '*Herr* [Sir]' (39). A second repressed thought of Freud's concerns the emphasis these Turks place on sexual enjoyment as the highest value of life—so much so that death is preferable to loss of it. Here we can see an instance of those fantasies of racialized enjoyment that speculate on subjects who possesses full enjoyment and, in this case, who will sacrifice their life for the sake of that enjoyment (Žižek 1990). In particular, this is the continuation of the fantasy of the Orient that fantasizes the Other as a site of enjoyment (Grosrichard 1998). By projecting this enjoyment onto the Other we alleviate our anxiety concerning our own loss of enjoyment and we get to enjoy the phobic rejection of the Other as hypersexualized. While Freud reports this fantasy without comment, we can see here how this fantasy of full enjoyment might actually be our own projection on the Other. In such a recognition we are forced to confront our own enjoyment and our own anxiety at its loss.

Freud, at the time, was also concerned with the news that reached him at Trafoi of a patient's suicide due to an incurable sexual disorder. The fantasy of the Other who might possess full enjoyment and fear its loss is paired with the much closer proximity of the patient who prefers self-willed death over the loss of sexuality. Out of these signifiers—Bosnia, Herzegovina, Herr and Trafoi—we get the substitute signifiers of Botticelli and Boltraffio, while Signorelli disappears. The passion is not random; it is the passion of 'death and sexuality' or their intersection (Freud 1975: 40). The discussion of the Turks and of the patient who committed suicide, as well as the apocalyptic frescoes, sediment the intimate relation of sexuality and death. The sexual drive is what passes to the limit of death or inhabits it, figuring its own later status in Freud's work in the thinking of the death drive. Already, within sexuality, we have the intimation of the death drive at work.

Freud's act of repression is evident in the process by which Signorelli is forgotten. The name is split in two, in which the first part, 'Signor', which recalls 'Herr' and so death and sexuality, is displaced into *Her*zegovina and *Bo*snia. The second part, 'elli' is then the root for the movement from Bosnia into 'Botticelli', while 'Boltraffio' absorbs 'Trafoi' and the 'Bo'. The result is a rebus, a picture puzzle.[1] It is the occasion for one of Freud's famous diagrams, which traces the splitting of the signifier into component letters, little bits of nonsense, which are treated homophonically to generate new signifiers. Here the ideality of the signifier, its capacity to produce meaning, is also intimately related to its materiality, as a sound, which is what produces this movement along the chain of signifiers. The act of forgetting is one that works on the materiality of language to create new, and dissembling, acts of meaning that obscure what has been repressed, and so generate new idealities and concepts.

The moment of forgetting is the moment of the eruption of *lalangue* into language. It is not only the play of the signifier, but also the play of the signifier as a piece of material. This is what Lacan (2016: 145) will call, after Joyce (1992: 93), the letter. The

---

1 Freud, in *The Interpretation of Dreams* (1976: 382), famously describes the dream as a 'rebus'.

failure of repression, in the emergence of the slip, not only reveals Freud's preoccupations with death and sexuality, but also the moment of 'primal repression' which denies the entry of the 'psychical (ideational) representative' of the drive into consciousness and language (Freud 1984a: 147). Each instance of repression speaks to this primary repression and so each later instance of repression also speaks to the earlier repression in which the drive was denied entry into language (Žižek and Schelling 1997). This moment is marked negatively. It is the absence, the hole made in language (Lacan 2016: 21), which reveals the insistence of the drive as paramount. The drive is that uncanny concept 'lying on the frontier between the mental and the physical' (Freud 1977: 83; Dolar 2017: 55–80). In this moment, matter, in the form of the insistence of the drive, of the bodily circuit, penetrates language, to cross Freud's diagram of forgetting with Lacan's of the circuit of the drive (Lacan 1977: 178). It is only via the negative moment, of forgetting, that it becomes possible to remember this primal repression that is the condition of any remembering and forgetting.

I am undertaking this remembering of forgetting in psychoanalysis under the tutelage of Lacan, who has done most to remind psychoanalysis, and us, that language matters. In fact, Lacan draws inspiration from Freud's account of forgetting as a revelation that the unconscious operates through language, through the signifier. It also operates by 'effacement' (27), by the erasure of a signifier that must then be reconstructed. The operation of the unconscious through language is what, for Lacan, constitutes the unique logical form of Freud's unconscious and distinguishes it from the Romantic unconscious of 'the divinities of the night' (24).[2] The unconscious is not the site of 'primordial will' but of the 'play of the signifier' (24). Here is the break with vitalism and all understandings of the unconscious that see it as an expression of the

---

2 It is for this reason that the prophets of the vitalist Romantic unconscious constantly reject the 'mechanical' (we would say logical) unconscious of Freud, from Jung to Ludwig Klages (Lebovic 2013: 53).

drives of life or as some mysterious depth, represented within psychoanalysis above all by Jung. This play of the signifier is not a happy play, because in the phenomena of the unconscious there is always an impediment (25). Lacan states that 'in a spoken or written sentence something stumbles' (25). In this moment, we see 'absence emerge' and 'silence emerge as silence' (26). The slip, once again, is the negative moment that gives us access to the intersection of language with matter.

For Lacan, the incident with the forgetting of Signorelli is one that demonstrates this mode of effacement, of silence emerging, and of the censorship by which the unconscious emerges. In the scene in which the signifier 'Herr' both appears and disappears Lacan sees in this appearance and disappearance of 'Herr' ('master'), the appearance and disappearance of death as 'absolute master' (27; Lacan 2002: 316). Lacan goes on to argue that what we find in Freud is a desperate attempt to regulate desire through the death of the father, through the Oedipal myth. There is a parallel, for Lacan, in Nietzsche declaring god is dead, as this supposed confidence in disposing of the master signifier is perhaps another myth sheltering us from the threat of castration. Similarly, the Oedipal myth may be a shelter against the castrating power of language, seen here in Freud's forgetting of the apocalyptic frescoes of the Orvieto cathedral (27). While Freud is at risk of forgetting castration and language, he at least remains closer to them than those who simply dissolve the problem entirely. In this way Freud still registers the traumatic intrusion of language as castration.

Even more radically, as Jacques-Alain Miller suggests, castration, or the fantasies around it, might conceal 'the true traumatic kernel [. . .] the relation to language' (2005: 15). It is this relation that emerges in Freud even if it is, via the Oedipal myth, repressed by him. Miller's claim that the real trauma lies in our relation to language risks making death, sexuality, fantasy and materiality disappear. Replacing death and sexuality with language threatens to create its own myth, in which only language matters. This is the position of Agamben (1991), for whom the only real relation is our relation to language. Such a speculation remains in the Heideggerian meditation on language as primary. Marc Froment-Meurice argues that for Heidegger 'language and language alone can speak—not the stuff, not the sound of language, not even its mouth' (1998: 63). What we lose is this materiality, the mouth as the site of speech, in which death and the drive will also emerge.

In contrast, in Lacan, we see the attempt to integrate the relation of language, enjoyment and matter. Lacan unpacks the Joycean portmanteau 'freudful mistake' of its baggage of the frightful mistake and, with the German *Freude*, the joyful mistake. What Joyce dismisses as Freud's mistake becomes Freud's recognition of the fright and joy in the mistake, which points towards the 'original fault' of language (Lacan 2016: 5). For Lacan, the fault of language is one that is also the life of language, a particular and peculiar life in which death and life play a central role (128). The life of language coincides with death, or with the uncanny correspondence between the life drive and the death drive. What is forgotten in the forgetting of psychoanalysis is the life of language, in which the drive intersects with and infuses language. This is the moment, as we will see, in which the death drive emerges, precisely within life. Here lies the scandal of psychoanalysis, as a relation to language and matter through sexuality. This moment is also a moment of politics, of sexuality, of the repression of femininity, and the return of all that, traumatically, to psychoanalysis.

Two Ways of Forgetting Psychoanalysis

What does it mean to forget this moment of forgetting? What if we were to forget the drive, to forget psychoanalysis? This often takes the form of an imperative: forget about it; an active desire to forget the psychoanalytic interpretation of forgetting. In this case, forgetting remains, but without the causal form psychoanalysis inscribes, without death and sexuality, and without the drive. This is the moment of resistance to psychoanalysis, which, as Derrida proposes, can take a double form: the usual sense of resistance to psychoanalysis from the outside, and a second sense, a resistance of psychoanalysis, in which psychoanalysis confronts its own internal limit. I want to take two examples of these forms of resistance and forgetting (1998c: *vii–viii*). The first is that of Sebastiano Timpanaro's 1974 work *The Freudian Slip*, which rejects psychoanalysis as an unnecessary imposition of sexuality and the unconscious on to language by suggesting that an understanding of the materiality of language can account for any freudful mistakes. This is resistance to psychoanalysis from the outside, while my second example, Catherine Malabou's 2007 work *The New Wounded: From Neurosis to Brain Damage*, is an example of the internal resistance of psychoanalysis, in which psychoanalysis is pushed to encounter its own limit. Malabou argues that not only can psychoanalysis not account for the traumatic results of brain injury or illness, but also that these forms of damage pose a problem to the psychoanalytic search for meaning in relation to trauma (2012). Let us consider these two moments of forgetting as central challenges to my argument.

Timpanaro provides an almost classical instance of the resistance to psychoanalysis. In *The Freudian Slip*, as his friend Perry Anderson summarizes, Timpanaro demonstrated that slips of the tongue 'were to be explained more persuasively by a standard set of deviations from the lexical norm, "corruptions" of which philologists had developed their own fine-grained classification' (2001). It is the materiality of language, rather than any force of death and sexuality, which is to account for freudful mistakes. Even more classically, Timpanaro's objections to psychoanalysis are also rooted in a personal animus at its failure to cure his neurotic symptoms—agoraphobia and the intense anxiety caused by public speaking. What is noteworthy, although at the risk of wild psychoanalysis, is that these symptoms are symptoms of speaking and of appearing in public. They are symptoms that indicate how language matters in the relation of desire to expression.

In Timpanaro's (1976: 64) account of Freud's forgetting of Signorelli and its replacement by Botticelli, the explanation is that it is merely 'a confusion between words of an equal number of syllables which are also connected by a marked phonic similarity, or even better, by assonance or rhyme'. The explanation of the more unlikely substitution of Boltraffio is, according to Timpanaro, a misguided act of correction. As Freud is now thinking of Botticelli the path of correction lies along Renaissance artists beginning with 'Bo-'. For Timpanaro, language matters, but in the very matter of its blind materiality, in the very literal substance of its own operations which create errors for its users. This is a materialism of language as matter.

Timpanaro's materialism of language is strangely similar to Paul de Man's notion of language as a fundamental material tropology in which 'the prosaic materiality of the letter' disrupts ideology and aesthetics (1996: 90). De Man suggests that language is not an expression of psychic energy, but that the features of the drive and its vicissitudes in psychoanalysis are merely the 'aberrant, metaphorical correlative of the absolute randomness of language, prior to any figuration or meaning' (1982: 299). Timpanaro would not, I think, agree with this largely chaotic conception of language, which would deny the possibility of a coherent materialism. De Man invests language with some of the features of the Freudian drive, whereas Timpanaro prefers a materialism that resists the intrusion of the chaotic. There is, however, a common emphasis on the materiality of language claimed for materialism against the psychic and psychoanalysis.

Timpanaro's scepticism towards psychoanalysis also extends to his understanding of Lacan's emphasis on the primacy of the signifier. While Timpanaro concedes, in a postscript, that this is 'not without interest' (1976: 222), in a footnote he is much more typically condemnatory, regarding Lacan's writing as that of a charlatan and exhibitionist, while suggesting it contains nothing of substance (58n5). The unkind Freudian or Lacanian critic might note the excess of this denunciation, including the accusation of exhibitionism, in relation to Timpanaro's own phobias, but what is also interesting is the suggestion of a lack of substance. We might read this as a rejection of Lacan's materialism of the signifier, founded on negativity and difference, in the name of materialism as the reality of the inscription of language. What risks being lost here, in this resistance to psychoanalysis, is the materiality of psychic reality, let alone the Lacanian Real. In particular, Timpanaro's materialism risks rejecting the relation of language to materiality, in this bodily form. While Timpanaro accuses Lacan of lack of substance and abstraction, his own thought lacks an attention to the body and its relation to language.

Attention to the material body might well be seen as central to Catherine Malabou's argument that we need to take neuroscience seriously to understand the brain's capacities. Using her concept of plasticity, also a term in neuroscience, Malabou argues that the brain offers capacities for change that are not simply consonant with neoliberal capitalist flexibility (2008: 78–82). As plasticity can refer to traumatic damage (as in plastic explosives), Malabou argues the brain can undergo far more radical traumas than are usually considered in psychoanalysis. In line with Spinoza's famous remark about the body, 'they do not know what a body can do', we can say, 'they do not know what a brain can do' (1976: 72). Malabou argues we need to explore these capacities as well as the damage and negativity that is condensed in the concept of plasticity.

Malabou's analysis in *The New Wounded* makes a transition, as her subtitle has it, 'from neurosis to brain damage' (2012: 72). She argues that psychoanalysis relies on a sexual aetiology of neurosis that correlates an external traumatic event with an inner sexual conflict. This involves Freud excluding violent events that affect the brain, such as lesions or brain damage, from the field of psychic life. What psychoanalysis cannot think, according to Malabou, is 'the wound without hermeneutic future' (8), a charge she also repeats to Lacan and Žižek (Malabou 2015). Contrary to the image of a subject already subject to sexual trauma, Malabou posits the new wounded as forms of subjectivity in which trauma intrudes from outside, is senseless, and rearranges the coordinates of personality.[3] In this way, she eliminates the psychoanalytic account of forgetting, which depends on sexual meaning and the drive, from consideration in psychic life. Materiality, this time the plasticity of the brain, comes to replace a materialism of language or meaning.

While we might recognize the truth of this claim in regard to severe forms of brain damage, which do seem to elude meaning in the way psychoanalysis often posits, Malabou argues for the extension of this claim over psychic life as whole (2012: 10). The new wounded becomes every patient in a state of shock, including those without brain lesions, anyone who has suffered a trauma damaging to their neural organization and psyche. By extending this account of damage, Malabou renders psychoanalysis moot and claims the domain of psychic life for the new wounded. While traversing psychoanalysis to the limit of the hermeneutic, both in Freud and Lacan, she ends up restricting psychoanalysis to a very limited field. The difficulty here is not that psychoanalysis might struggle with the physiological forms of brain damage, although one might consider how the work of A. R. Luria (1987), for instance, demonstrates the sensitivity required to grasp the forms and results of brain trauma, including a hermeneutic sensitivity. The difficulty is more that the new wounded is a category that is metaphorically extended to all or most forms of trauma, precisely to exclude the matter of language and sexuality.

To repeat Derrida terms, Malabou's resistance of psychoanalysis comes to coincide with Timpanaro's resistance to psychoanalysis. Malabou's argument is for a materiality of the brain that also constitutes an affective plasticity and so replaces language (and the problem of forgetting) as the key to our psychic life. She exits

3 Malabou is drawing upon Derrida's (1998c: 44) argument that psychoanalysis cannot deal with 'radical destruction' that goes beyond a logic of repression and retention.

from psychoanalysis and into a new domain. Malabou and Timpanaro share a strange symmetry in which the matter of language is displaced and so is psychoanalysis for a new type of matter. In the case of Timpanaro, language has to be understood in terms of its own materiality, so that forgetting and slips are not the result of our psychic life but result from the material nature of language itself. Interestingly, Timpanaro also hoped for a neuro-physiological explanation that would transcend the claims to science made by Freudian psychoanalysis (1976: 95). For Malabou, language and meaning are less important than the brain as a material entity and the effects of changes to that materiality. Forgetting is a matter of the worst, of radical trauma from violence or disease which bypasses language and meaning. So, for Malabou and Timpanaro we have a new materiality that goes beyond the matter of language, and the strange intrusion of matter into language is replaced by a materiality that answers any absence of language.

Nothing Matters

If Timpanaro and Malabou say no to psychoanalysis, saying yes to psychoanalysis is not a persuasive retort. Timpanaro, in an instance of what Franco Moretti called 'feline sarcasm', remarked: 'Western Marxists are those thinkers who are convinced that Freud is always right' (2020: 63). That accusation could be laid my door too. I want to suggest, however, that the path to grasping psychoanalysis, language, sexuality and materiality is instead one that passes through saying no. So, I want to conclude this chapter by turning to Freud's (1984b) late essay on 'Negation', written in 1925. Lacan remarks on this text that it is 'a text which carries speech insofar as speech constitutes a new emergence of truth' (2002: 318). The essay is well known for its opening concerning the moment of resistance. Freud recounts how patients present material in the mode of a negation: ' "You ask who this person in the dream can be. It's *not* my mother." The psychoanalyst's rejoinder is "So it *is* his mother" ' (1984b: 437). Timpanaro singles out this moment as the sign of a

Freudian refusal to consider counterexamples and to take every such instance of negation as an 'involuntary confession' (1976: 56). In this way, according to Timpanaro, while Freud recognizes a psychological mechanism he generalizes it to such an extent that there is no space for denial and refutation within psychoanalysis.[4]

This initial point of denial in Freud's paper opens out on to a discussion of negation that has a wider metapsychological significance as a mechanism of defence crucial to the ego (Lacan 2002: 311). While negation is a refusal or denial, by refusing or denying something we make that very thing appear. Negation is, therefore, a momentary lifting of repression, even if what was repressed is not accepted. So, if we are told 'this is *not* about my mother', we know the mother is what is being repressed, but that does not mean the repressed is accepted, on the contrary it is denied. Lacan notes, with a negation, 'doubtless the ego makes a great many things known to us' (1988: 59). In the experience of negation the affective and the intellectual are separated, but we would add, the material and the linguistic are intertwined. We feel something but do not know it, although the negation ironically connects matter and language at the moment of denial. It is also true that, as Freud had pointed out, the word matter is connected to the maternal (Freud 1973: 193–94; Derrida 1987a: 106). The act of negation is an intellectual function linked to the 'primitive' function of the oral drive. The intellectual judgement of negation corresponds to the judgement of whether I would like to eat this or whether I would like to spit it out. The act of negation is the act of spitting something out, but in that act what is negated appears, it has a presence in the mouth, on the tongue, before being negated, before becoming nothing. If, in forgetting, something is present in the mode of absence—we can taste the absent word on the tip of our tongue—in negation, something absent is made present to be ejected from the mouth—to be spat out. This can obviously include words, as we can spit those out too.

---

4 Freud (1964) would dispute this claim to the infallibility of psychoanalytic interpretation in his 'Constructions in Analysis' (1937).

This intellectual function of negation is also a matter of the drives. Judging refers not only to oral desire, but also, in the polarity of judgement, to the drive: 'Affirmation—as a substitute for uniting—belongs to Eros; negation—the successor to expulsion—belongs to the instinct of destruction' (Freud 1984b: 441). Negation is rooted in these drives, but is also a moment of freedom, through the creation of a 'symbol of negation' (441). While we have a distinction between Eros and Thanatos, we can also see how they remain bound together. Negation is the moment of destruction, a saying no, but also one which reveals matter and the drive. We do not simply enter into the death drive, but into the intimate relation of these drives, between affirmation and negation, binding and unbinding (Laplanche 1976). This is a point reiterated by Žižek, for whom the death drive is the inconsistent repetition that haunts and inhabits the libido (2010). The act of negation is the revelation of that repetition, but also a revelation that bears on the materiality of language as the moment in which language concedes the intrusion of the drive. Negation is a negativity that reveals the positivity of the drive.

Language emerges as the moment of negation that, as Paolo Virno insists in a different register, disrupts agreement and consonance for the possibility of destruction and even evil (2008). It also, I am suggesting, marks the moment of negativity as a materiality that comes to be in the moment of ejection. Language matters in this strange space of the materialization and de-materialization of something and nothing. Forgetting indicates to us the strange presence of absence, which is denied in those materialisms that try to silence language. They negate language, which is to say they make it present but only to say no. For them, language does not matter. Negation points to this persistence of language in the moment of denial. It indicates the way in which resistance and denial of language and of psychoanalysis carries the trace of that denial, of that liminal space in which language matters. Living as we do in the time of materialisms of many types (although few that are historical or dialectical), we also live in the time in which language does not matter. Language has to disappear, to be forgotten, to be spat out. In the face of the circulating abstractions that make up our world the appeal to materialism is to something that denies these abstractions. Yet, the denial that language matters leave us only with a pseudo-concrete sense of what matters. The matter of abstraction is rendered absent by the abstraction of matter.

The matter of language is a matter of the mouth. We forget language, only to remember that language matters: It is on the tip of my tongue; just spit it out! This matter of the tongue and the drive is attested to by Antonin Artaud. Artaud writes of the tongue as a peculiar kind of organ that lives a life of its own in the mouth (1995: 243–44). The tongue is 'an obscene hooker' that is oriented to the teeth for mastication and to the orifice to push food down the throat. It is the mediating materiality that appears as a scandal in the mouth. Speaking in tongues becomes penetration by the tongue, and the tongue 'a chunk of blood sausage' in the mouth in parallel to the penis; this is 'a sex organ / between his teeth' (199). Words and language, as well as a matter of faecality, are also a matter of sex and transmission. This is also why Artaud violently rejects psychiatry, especially in his discussion of Van Gogh as a man 'suicided' by society (2019). Artaud extends his ire to psychoanalysis in his focus on one Dr L., almost certainly Lacan, described as one 'who inserts his sexual prey beneath his tongue and turns it over like an almond as a means of ridicule' (3). All that Lacan can produce 'is the embodied testimony of a filthy debauchery' (4), which is not a bad way of describing psychoanalysis. Delirium, for Artaud, is 'strangle[d] [. . .] with your disgusting sexuality' (4). Van Gogh, and Artaud, are virgins free from sin contaminated by a discourse that would turn their delirium into sexuality.

Artaud is rejecting psychoanalysis in the name of materiality, this time of the physical body. As Artaud states: 'there is no inside, no spirit, outside or consciousness, nothing but the body as it may be seen, a body that does not cease being, even when the eye that sees it falls' (1995: 72). The body is not the sexual body of psycho-analysis, which is only ever a later corrupted body imposed on this original body. In a scene that is not uncommon, as we have seen with Joyce, the tools of psychoanalysis are turned against it. Psycho-analysis is accused of projecting sexuality where none should be found. But while Artaud violently rejects psychoanalysis he also registers, against his will, the strange psychoanalytic notion of materiality in relation to language. The tongue is the way in which the speaking cure registers materiality as an act of language and sexuality, of filthy debauchery.

This materiality of the tongue and mouth appears in psycho-analysis most famously in the 'dream of Irma's injection', in which Freud dreams that he finds in Irma's mouth 'a big white patch' and 'extensive whitish grey scabs upon some remarkable curly structures which were evidently modelled on the turbinal bones of the nose' (1976: 182). Lacan gives this moment an even more grisly appearance, as a moment of the Real (1988: 154). It is a 'horrendous discovery' of a hidden flesh that is 'the foundation of all things' and 'the flesh from which everything exudes'. Here is the Real as materi-ality, as the interruption of language, but it is found in the mouth, in the site of language. The Real, as Lacan would always insist, exists in relation to language as well, as an intrusion, as a littering, which is evident in the nonsensical chemical formula for trimethylamine that appears later in the dream.

It appears that the scene of this dream is related to the real treatment of Freud's patient Emma Eckstein for nasal problems by his friend Fleiss. Fleiss botched the treatment, which was revealed when Ignaz Rosanes, an old school friend of Freud's and a reputable specialist, attended Emma and revealed a large amount of gauze left in the nasal cavity. Freud, present at the procedure, nearly fainted, and when he returned to consciousness Eckstein sarcas-tically remarked 'So this is the strong sex' (Gay 1989: 84). There is the reality of this medical misconduct and the desire to repress this reality. Such a repression is not only a repression of reality, however.

Already, we can see a reversal in the scene of the usual cultural fantasies of male strength and feminine weakness, and who can take the experience of the traumatic Real.

The point here is not simply that we need to supply the material referent of the botched operation. This need to done, of course, but we are not only dealing with Freud's professional anxieties, but also that Freud was overcome by 'the pressure of emotions' (84). This is not to deny Fleiss' misconduct or Freud's cover-up, but it is also not to ignore that such a cover-up fails and remains a site of fantasy. The dream is a product of overdetermination, that crucial mechanism of psychic life identified by Freud and later developed politically by Althusser in his essay 'Contradiction and Overdetermination' (1969: 89–128), which refers to the production of meaning or an event as a result of multiple conflicting forces. In this case, Freud's professional anxieties are also linked to the weird materiality of the Lacanian Real, and to the problem of feminity.

Derrida has also pointed out how this dream involves a number of women, between three and four: Irma, Irma's friend, a governess Freud was treating, and, by omission, Freud's wife (1998c: 8). The dream is a dream of resistance to treatment, to psychoanalytic treatment, and, according to Derrida, a resistance of psychoanalysis itself to moving from three to four, 'from the triangle to the square' (10). It is also the dream in which 'so much pass[es] by way of the mouth' (10). I want stress what passes by the mouth and what is also stuck in the throat—a moment of matter and its relation to language and to the drive. What is at stake is a blocking of speech, a blocking of language, which appears in relation to language and to sexuality, in which the nose and mouth are overlaid. It is a dream, according to Lacan, of 'the quest for signification as such' (1988: 160). It is also, I would add, a dream of this scene of language, matter and sexuality. The relations between these three elements also raises the problem of politics, the four, as the moment of founding. This is not only a problem of the founding of psychoanalysis, but also of these particular and peculiar forms of materialism.

These problems of founding that return to the problem of the maternal as origin. The relation of materialism to language is one, in which matter, of course, gives birth to language, but also language gives birth to materiality. The forgetting of this relation lies, it seems, at the foundation. It is a forgetting that forgets the drive as the emerging force of this relation that joins and dis-joins. Gillian Rose remarks that 'it is at the crux of gender that philosophy—love of wisdom—, the republic, and the legal fictions of personality explode' (1984: 6). Freud offers a testament to this explosion in another form. We might speak here of a speculative matrilineal materialism, which emerges from Engels' *The Origin of the Family, Private Property, and the State* (2010[1884]), that other speculation on founding and origins that has often been treated as phantasmatic. In Engels, the speculative primacy of the maternal is needed to disrupt and historicize the patriarchal family as merely one form of the family. This is a historical materialism that turns to the maternal as the site of history, but also to the disruption of history as unfolding from a simple or single origin. The attempt is not simply to replace patriarchal myths with matriarchal myths, but instead to explore matrilineal materialism as a displacement and revelation of fantasies of origin, of which the maternal is often the figure.[5] These include the fantasies of psychoanalysis itself, which also struggles with this matrilineal materialism in its own forgetting and remembering of the maternal (Sayers 1992; Marder 2012).

In the process of forgetting psychoanalysis, the mediation of language and matter through the drive is forgotten or elided to ensure a process in which nothing gets stuck in the mouth or throat. Psychoanalysis, on the contrary, finds matter in that *nothing* stuck in the mouth, in the matter of language that engages with this *nothing* in the redoubled negation. There is a matter here, a matter of language, which emerges within the conflict engendered by language. This is also a politics, as the cases of Artaud and Irma

---

5 This can be found in the fascination with the thinking of Bachofen on matriarchy and 'mother right' in the early twentieth century (Mali 1991).

demonstrate, a politics that is antagonistic to psychoanalysis. In the case of Artaud, we witness a violent rejection of psychoanalysis for its material emphasis on sexuality, while in that of Irma's dream we see the return of physiological explanation, the possibility of incompetence and even charlatanry. The moment of materiality aligns what we could call a social and professional politics and a calling into question of psychoanalysis. The politics of psychoanalysis includes the psychoanalytic struggle with this politics and its own encounter with the limits of its determination of language and materiality. This is not only true of Freud, but also of Lacan. And yet, the political opposition to psychoanalysis also struggles with the problem of the contract and the institution (Deleuze 1986: 144; Guattari 1984). It struggles to give an alternative form or determination to the relation of language and matter. There is a sense in which the resistance to psychoanalysis might also open a path to language and materiality that forces psychoanalysis to remember politics and the conflict around materiality and language. This is, as I have suggested, an experience of negativity, but one that also returns to the positivity of a politics and an engagement. It does not remain in nothing. Psychoanalysis is a practice as well as a theory and the *nothing* is not simply left as nothing (as Marx had noted with that other nothing—the proletariat). Nothing must be made to matter.

CHAPTER THREE
1916
Pure Values

Languages are mechanisms which go on functioning, in spite of the damage done to them.

Ferdinand de Saussure,
Course in General Linguistics

We can credit the discovery of the great abstractive and expropriative force of language to Ferdinand de Saussure. The innovation of his *Course in General Linguistics* has now, perhaps, faded into accepted common sense. Its account of the sign as composed of the signifier—the material sound or inscription—and the signified—the attached concept or meaning—and of the relation of signifier and signified as arbitrary, finds a place in all introductions to theory. Either it has a historical curiosity, as a moment on the way to structuralism or poststructuralism, or it seems to have been absorbed into the study of language, as if its famous analysis of meaning as differential made little or no difference. It seems we can safely say goodbye to the disputes occasioned by Saussure. The issue of linguistic imperialism, the determination of thought by language—also associated with Wittgenstein and Whorf & Sapir—is left behind for the safe ground of matter. Language is only significant, it now seems, when it speaks of matter, and its failure to speak of matter leaves it as one tool among others. This dismissal of language and the resulting obscurity of Saussure's work are the reasons I want to return to Saussure. It is not simply a matter of antiquarian curiosity, but a sense that these debates, especially around language and abstraction, are far from settled. The singular abstract force of language, discovered by Saussure, is a trauma for thought that is not so easily healed by invocations of the salve of matter.

I pursue the path of this force of abstraction by reconstructing the work of Saussure as the inscription of a force of negativity within language. This provocation of Saussure's persists, even if today we often shelter from it. The very simplicity of his intervention lies in positing language, abstraction, matter and determination together as a central problem. It is the negativity and abstraction of language that invites its determination and relation to matter. The disruptive force of language as abstract produces the desire to inhabit that force, but also to render it concrete or determinate. This is a problem that will preoccupy modernism and the avant-gardes, although, as we shall see, they both inherit and resist Saussure's own formulations of abstraction and negativity. It is in this struggle with language that we can see the abstract force of language.

Is Saussure's treatment of language as a system of pure values just another mirror of capitalism? This is a recurrent problem, posed to Saussure's theory and to those theories indebted to his work that use it to try and break the ideological image of reality. This is the problem of poststructuralist thinking about language that has led to a turn to the material. If the poststructuralist account of language is too close to capitalism, especially in the form of abstract value, then we can escape this by turning to the material. Certainly, Marxist critics had already argued that Saussure risked mirroring capitalist ideology, a point made by Voloshinov (1973: 58–61), and later, for structuralism more broadly, by Guy Debord (1995). There appear to be two risks in Saussure's linguistic thought. The first is that we treat the signifier as part of a transcendental system of differences. This appears to mimic how capitalism operates as a system conditioning reality through differential expressions of value. The second is that the signifier is immanent, is immersed in relations with other signifiers and other expressions of difference. Now it appears as caught up in reality and in capitalism as a system of differences, as just another expression of difference. In either case the risk is that there is only one language and that is the language of commodities.

In contrast, I wish to stress that Saussure's grasp on the negative and abstract force of language provides a model for how we can also grasp the power of the real abstractions of capitalism. This does not exhaust language in an identity with capitalism, but it also does not suppose that language forms some saving faculty or power so indeterminate as to remain beyond or before capitalism. This would be the late Heideggerian position in all its left and right mutations. Here language and the poetic are redeeming powers that are secreted within the dominance of the technological (Heidegger 1977: 28). Language is what saves us from the abstract by forming the concrete and, as has now been confirmed, Heidegger identifies the abstraction of technology with Judaism in an obviously anti-Semitic fashion (2016). The concrete is given a particularly malignant form as an ethno-national and linguistic community. Even outside of this toxic formulation, the desire to traverse language to find some concrete materiality remains common. The new materialisms deny abstract capitalist value and the abstract power of language in the name of concrete forms of matter. If, for Heidegger, language could be the path to the concrete, today the path is by way of matter. In both cases, what is lost is an idea of language that is intimately related to abstraction and negation, but also as an access to a form of the concrete that is not merely the inversion of capitalist abstraction.

This is not to deny the abstract force of capitalism, which is real precisely in its material form that produces abstraction. My aim is to take the measure of these real abstractions through Saussure as a necessary traversal in analysing the determinations of language in relation to matter and abstract value. Language does not save us through its indeterminacy and mystical materiality, which is a false form of the concrete as undecideable and unnameable. Instead, the negative and disruptive force of language offers potential for the determination of forms of abstraction and for grasping the relations of language and matter.

The Moment of Difference

To offer an introduction to Saussure might seem superfluous, considering how familiar the basic tenets of his work have become. Guy Debord often insisted that the most recent past has become obscured, covered with lies and banalities, and in the case of Saussure we could say familiarity has bred contempt or worse, indifference (1998: 14). That is not to say that excellent commentary does not exist (Culler 1976), but that the scandal of Saussure has been largely buried or minimized. Here I do not want to offer a detailed analysis, but to pursue the abstractive force of Saussure's account of language. This is already to point to an irony as Saussure did not consider the analysis of language to be a matter of abstraction. The linguistic sign, as the fundamental unit of analysis, was not an abstraction for Saussure but a real and concrete element (2000: 101). I do not want to deny this stress in Saussure, which is central to the scientific ambition of his text, but I do want to indicate how this concrete emerges as a result of abstraction. The aim is to re-establish the coordinates of Saussure's intervention as vital to grasping the capacity to traverse abstraction and to engage language and matter.

The crucial unit of linguistic analysis is the linguistic sign, which consists of a signifier (the material or phonic element) and a signified (the concept or meaning). These are the concrete units of analysis. The problem that Saussure pursues is of the identification of such units and of the seemingly trivial problem of how we grasp any particular unit in language. Our experience of language is of a flow of words—how then do we identify particular words or linguistic units and how do we make sense out of this flow? The famous answer offered by Saussure is that identity is dependent on the differences between signs. Identity is the expression of difference. We can show this visually with the example of fonts; while fonts present a letter in very different ways materially we recognize that letter by its difference from all other letters in the alphabet. There is nothing intrinsic to *t* as a letter,

66

which can be expressed as 't' or 'т' or 'ŧ'. Instead, it is the cross form of *t*, in its difference to *y* or *r* and so on, which gives it its identity. The linguistic sign is a unit that gains its identity from its differences to other units in the linguistic chain. Saussure (107) suggests that 'the mechanism of a language turns entirely on identities and differences. The latter are merely counterparts of the former.' If we take the signifier 'cat', the signified is something like 'four-legged furry feline', which gains its identity from its difference from other signifiers: 'dog', but also 'kitten', 'tiger', and so on to all other potential and actual signifiers in a language.

While the linguistic sign is the concrete unit, this concrete effect is the result of the structure and system of a language. The unit gains its meaning and value through its place in the system. While we might start with the linguistic sign, we always have to think about this sign in relation to the system or structure of language. The system is the starting point. This is why Saussure makes the analogy to chess. Chess is a system of rules for the movement of pieces on a particular board (a system that itself changed and modified over time). The identity of an individual chess piece is not dependent on its materiality (hence the diversity of chess sets), but on its difference from all the other pieces. Out of this system a great diversity can result, but the identity of pieces and determinate arrangements on the board refers to this system of differences: 'just as chess is based entirely in the combinations afforded by the various pieces, so too a language has the character of a system based entirely on the contrasts between its concrete units' (105). This is all usefully summarized in one of the great theoretical statements or even slogans: 'in a language there are only differences, *and no positive terms*' (118). We can see why the emphasis on the concrete results from the greatest emphasis on difference and negativity. Difference comes first: 'Difference is what makes characteristics, just as it makes values and units' (119). It is difference that is productive of identity and meaning while remaining nothing in itself except difference.

This difference or negativity forms the system, it is not simply an absence or chaos. While the linguistic sign might be a peculiar nothing it has a form that organizes chaos into value and meaning. Saussure argues that linguistic signs articulate both thought and matter, which without this organization would remain in meaningless flux or flow. Marx and Engels call language 'agitated layers of air' (2011: 44); for Saussure language is not only this materiality but also the division of matter and thought that emerges in the linguistic sign. Here, of course, the difficult question of any proto-organization in this flux emerges, and the relation of language to thought and nature.[1] It is difficult to imagine language as a system of differences emerging out of the flow of sounds unless some organization and some differences between sounds are already present.

We can imagine this proto-situation of matter and language as something like what Hegel (quoted in Hamacher 1998: 117) called 'the night of the world', as a 'pit' of images that lack organization in which 'a bloody head suddenly shoots out, there a white shape, and they disappear again as suddenly'. This is the moment when we look someone in the eye and see this swirling vortex of images. It is a gothic moment, a moment of the phantasmagoria, which was a kind of proto-cinematic show using magic lantern effects to stage ghostly and demonic illusions. The night of the world is also the moment of pre- or proto-language, on an unstable cusp of the entry into speech. In Hegel this moment gains organization through the mechanical linguistic process of naming, itself a meaningless process that organizes meaning. Once again, as with Saussure, we do not and cannot simply remain in negativity,[2] but must abide with its transformation into meaning. Yet, negativity and difference are crucial to this process, and language is an abstract articulation that in its emptiness structures both thought and matter into meaningful units.

---

1 This is the question, of the relation of language to nature, that Julia Kristeva (1984: 83) answers with the concept of the *chora*, borrowed from Plato's *Timaeus*.
2 The emergence of negativity is what obsesses Bataille (1990: 9) and this is why Bataille chooses to focus on this passage as a moment of negativity that resists inclusion.

This determination of meaning by the system takes the path of the determination of value. Value in linguistics, as it is elsewhere, is determined by the differences between units and the institution of a form of equivalence to allow comparison (Saussure 2000: 113). We can get a sense of the value of something by comparing it to something else, but at the same time we need a common ground for the comparison. Linguistic signs are values that differ, but signs that can also be compared to identify them as different values through the system of language. The system is an organization of differences, but as such an organization also allows us to see signs as equivalent.

Value is differential and relational, and it is no surprise that Saussure will use the metaphor of money to explore this. Money is a form of value that allows us to compare all other values, and so linguistic signs can be compared through the medium of the system of language. The role of money as abstraction will be our focus in the next section; here it is enough to remark that the linguistic sign as a positive entity with meaning and value is formed out of the structure or system of differences and its play. The well-known arbitrary nature of the sign, the fact that the sound or the written element of the sign have no intrinsic link to the concept, is strictly related to language as a system of pure values determined by differences. It is the differences that relate together to ensure that this arbitrary connection is sustained and rendered positive. The arbitrary is translated into the necessary connection of signifier and signified, which is why we cannot use the arbitrary nature of the sign to simply impose or generate new signs by forcing new connections. We are never in the position of Lewis Carroll's Humpty Dumpty in *Through the Looking-Glass* (1871), who claims to be able to choose what a word means as the master of language. Instead, the system of language is the master, deciding what a word means, but this system is also unstable and shifting. Its dependence on negativity and difference makes it a system that can transform.

Saussure's radicalization of the arbitrary nature of the sign into the system of difference without positive terms is often thought of as the quintessential modernist or avant-garde gesture and linked to those moments which it preceded and anticipated. Modernist and avant-garde experimentation with collage and the fragmentation of language seems to attest to the fundamental negativity of language and to the possibilities of expropriating language from nature and sense. This can be carried out for its own sake, as a reference internal to language, but also as an offensive against the ideological sedimentation of language. The first path is the pure experimentation with language as a form, found most definitively in Mallarmé. Here the 'words of the tribe' must be purified or purged to recover or produce a new language. The second, political (or leftist), path, can be found in the Russian Futurists, Brecht and is synthesized with Saussure in the early work of Roland Barthes. Here language must be purged of ideological abuses and returned to direct communication. These are unstable divisions, as the first is often as political as the second and the second as experimental as the first. We might better speak of tendencies to purification and politics that emerge in the field of engagement with the negative and abstract force of language.[3]

While there is a clear link in modernism and the avant-garde to Saussure's treatment of language as a system of differences without positive terms, rupturing the 'natural' link of sound and sense, there is also anxiety and rejection of Saussure's conclusions. Encountering language as a system of difference, modernists and the avant-gardes often hope to forge a new concrete link between signifier and signified, sign and referent. The recognition of the force of abstraction and expropriation in language, as we have seen with Artaud, is often accompanied by the desire to establish a new concrete mode of expression resistant to the abstraction all around us. Ezra Pound, for example, turned to Ernest Fenollosa's study *The Chinese Written Character as a Medium for Poetry* (1936). For

---

3 Jacques Rancière (2011) discusses the entanglement between gestures of purification and politics in Mallarmé.

Fenellosa the alphabetic language uses symbols that are arbitrary, whereas the Chinese characters for 'man sees horse', offers 'a vivid shorthand picture' (1936: 8). Instead of an 'algebraic figure' dependent 'upon sheer convention'—virtually the Saussurean definition of language—we have 'natural suggestion'. In short, the characters embody what they signify materially. Certainly, this is something of a fantasy of the Chinese language; the contemporary Chinese poet Yang Lian (quoted in Balso 2014: 73) declares that 'Chinese is abstract through and through'. The point is, however, the desire for the concrete within the abstract. The modernist and avant-garde gesture aims at a traversal of the abstract and differential elements of language to establish the concrete and the material. The use of myth by modernist writers like T. S. Eliot, James Joyce, Mary Butts and David Jones is another instance of the desire to re-establish connection and the concrete. In all these cases there is an awareness that the connection between language and matter is broken, but this fuels the attempt to re-establish a new concrete connection within language and between language and reality.

In Saussure we can see this struggle also take place in his later work on anagrams. Saussure believed he had discovered encrypted patterns in Indo-European and Latin poetry. In a sense, this both denies the arbitrary, stressing a motivated use of language, and reinstantiates a materiality into the process of language.[4] This other Saussure becomes linked to the poststructuralist moment of a concern with materiality and language during the 1970s—'the irruption of the signifier on the scene of writing' (Lotringer 1979: 2). The aim was not to abandon the Saussurean insight into the expropriative and abstract force of language, but to engage with that as a material practice. It was a repetition of the modernist or avant-garde moment carried out with a deeper degree of awareness of the issue of abstraction and the difficulty of the return to the natural and the concrete that was part of that legacy.

---

4 For a contemporary instance of this re-motivation of the sign, this time towards a mathematical materiality, see Quentin Meillassoux's (2012) discussion of Mallarmé's poetics, especially his poem 'Un coup de dés', as driven by a numeric structure.

We can draw a schematic distinction between the two avant-garde moments which conveniently run through the work of Roland Barthes. The first is the ideological questioning of the passing off of the sign as natural, which Barthes analyses in *Mythologies* (1957). In this case, the natural is displaced by the sign, but there remains the possibility of a concrete link between language and referent, especially in the form of history, which would refute the ideological sign. The second moment, embodied in the later work of Barthes and the avant-garde of the 1970s, adopts a material practice within language or 'writing', taking up, often loosely, a term developed by Jacques Derrida (1998c: 61). Here we have again the war *on* language and the war *of* language, in an unstable configuration.[5] There is an attempt to recover a true language, but then a more despairing war on language as such that can only be carried out by means of language. The difficulty remains, however, of giving determination to this practice of writing and not dissolving it into an undifferentiated negativity or play of forces. In this sense Saussure bequeaths us a problem of abstraction. This is one that is intensified by the parallel between this system of pure values, on the one hand, and the abstraction of language and capitalism as a system of empty values, on the other.

Under the Sign of Exchangeability

Roberto Calasso notes the parallel between Saussure's notion of the system of language as a differential structure and the form of capitalist exchange:

> *exchangeability* arrives on the market, and quickly changes the whole aspect of reality. That same power that was already active in the 'arbitrary nature of the sign', in the practice of convention, in every gesture of substitution (x *stands for* y), but which had not yet had the impious presumption to present itself as an independent entity, now asserts itself. (2018: 252)

---

5 As Jacqueline Rose (1986: 229) reminds us these shifts in modernism and the avant-garde also often turn on the materiality of sexual difference.

Saussure's analysis of language as a system structured by value seems prescient and overtaken by the force of exchangeability, which rewrites language as a model of capitalist exchange. A seemingly neutral linguistic analysis would either predict future capitalism or find itself as the ideological image of capitalism. Calasso was not the first to notice this overlap and the difficulty has not been exhausted.

This problem of science and the models proposed by science in relation to capitalist society is also not new. Marx excoriated Malthus for a view of overpopulation that was proposed as scientific but was, for Marx, ideological (1990: 766–67). Malthus represents not the science of population, but the capitalist loathing of the mass of workers on which it depends. Here scientific pretensions are deflated on the grounds that they merely represent an ideological form making scientific claims. More broadly, Marx's reading of the science of political economy was a critique predicated on the fact that such a science was both the most truthful model of capitalist society we have and a model that replicated and reinforced the features of capitalist society. Here the tension is more nuanced, as a materialist reading is required to recognize the truth of political economy in Smith and Ricardo, but also to demonstrate how that truth is limited to a particular historical moment and functions as an ideological justification. A similar problem occurred with Darwinism, a science that modelled itself through political economy, especially the work of Adam Smith (not only the *Wealth of Nations* (1776) but also the *Theory of Moral Sentiments* (1759)) (Pichot 2009). Darwinism promises to Marx and Engels a model of secular science as grasping historical change at the level of biology, while also forming an ideological image of bourgeois society in its model of individual competition (1956: 156–57). In each case, the difficulty lies in the relation of the scientific model to its mirroring or replication of features of capitalist society. This is evidently also the case with Saussure. Is Saussure's model of language simply an image of the abstract forms of value in capitalist society? If not, this leaves the more difficult question of the relation of the model to capitalist society. It is a question that has received wildly different answers that can help us trace the relation between language and abstraction in capitalist society.

Saussure's own 'abstract objectivism' attracted the censure of V. N. Voloshinov, in his pioneering 1929 work *Marxism and the Philosophy of Language*. For Voloshinov, Saussure made the system of language determine human activity, allowing no space for struggle (1973). In the place of Saussure's 'objectivism' Voloshinov sought to mediate the psychological and the sociological through the concept of the sign. In particular, Voloshinov emphasized that the sign was social and could be 'accented' in different class forms. There were not different class languages nor was language saturated by class, instead the ideological sign was a site of conflict and struggle expressed through this 'accenting' (15). This was and remains a valuable corrective to Saussure. It insists on the element of class, struggle and materiality, which can disappear in other critical readings of Saussure's system. There is an ironic risk, however, of according the sign such centrality that problems of referentiality and materiality are rendered mute. The materiality of the sign comes to stand for materiality itself. Certainly, Voloshinov insists that the sign 'reflects and refracts another reality' (10), but the equation of ideology and sign does not always do justice to the tension of this relation. This is why we remain with Saussure to think through these configurations. Voloshinov's criticism of Saussure does not directly fall on Saussure's notion of value and its relation to capitalist value. Instead, for Voloshinov, the fault of Saussure is not so much that he mirrors capitalist society but that his 'abstract objectivism' is symptomatic of the oscillation of bourgeois ideology between subjectivism and objectivism. It is perhaps telling, something to do with the intensifications of capitalism and capitalist value, that the critical discussion around Saussure and capitalist value would emerge not in the 1930s but in the 1970s.

Alberto Toscano has described '73 thought (*la pensée soixante-treize* as opposed to *la pensée soixante-huit*, '68 thought) as the crucial moment of the mediation of the system of capitalism as totalizing, which succeeds and mutates the utopian moment of May '68 thought (2012). We pass from language as cultural revolution, in the broad sense Jameson gives this concept in his periodization of the '60s, to the problem of language within capitalist counter-revolution (1984). In this latter moment, Jean-Joseph Goux has done the most to probe the relation between language and capitalist value. Goux argued that the rupture that Saussure introduces between language as naming and language as system is 'rigorously homologous to the qualitative economic rupture which decisively privileges, in theories of exchange, the logic of banking capital over the logic of commercial and industrial capital' (1990a: 23). Goux is not simply speaking about causality, in which innovations in currency exchange cause Saussure to read language as if it were capitalist value. Instead, Goux prefers to think in terms of homologies and socio-symbolic regimes. He suggests that the Saussurean reading of language as a system of pure values is homologous to late capitalism, and that the mutations of the thinking of the sign also follow the mutating developments of capitalist value.

The collapse of language into this play of values signals, as Goux notes by reference to Sartre's 1938 novel *Nausea*, a parallel collapse of materiality. In *Nausea*, the narrator Roquentin famously experiences the vanishing of words and sees the roots of a tree in their brute materiality, as a 'black, knotty lump, entirely raw' (Sartre 2000: 186). Goux argues that this is not simply the emergence of a nature or reality beyond the play of language in a turn to a real object or the earth to ground the play of values. Instead, the experience is one of an arbitrary and gratuitous relation of language to matter, in which matter turns into horrifying stuff (we can think of the parallel with Hegel's night of the world and Lacan's Real) (Goux 1988: 24). The disruption of language does not lead to the recovery of matter but a chaotic collapse of language and matter into pure play. We remain within the capitalist regime of value, in which everything can be transformed into value and the levelling of sign and matter is merely part of this process of value extraction (Povinelli 2016: 20). That is why the problem of determination remains one between language and matter. To void or abstract language itself into a pure negativity is not to reveal the positivity of matter, but to lose matter in a pure negativity. In the rush to have the concrete we lose the very thing we desired by discarding the seemingly abstract means. This suggests that contemporary solutions that leap to matter in itself remain more closely within the space of the turn to language than they imagine.

Goux, however, also implies a powerful homology that weakens Saussure's scientific claims and implies that language becomes equated to the structures of capitalism. This argument can be repeated for all further mutations of language and literature. The increasing power of the real abstractions of capitalism, the increasingly virtual forms of money ('cash, cheque, charge', in Goux's (2012) terms; we can add tapping the card and cryptocurrency), are all paralleled in the increasingly unstable and deconstructed understanding of language. This would precisely map the shift from structuralism to poststructuralism around the abandonment by the United States of the gold standard in 1971 and the rise of speculative finance. It would also map that transition we briefly traced from the avant-garde of the 1920s to the avant-garde of the 1970s: a crisis of the sign leading to a crisis of materiality and the very capacities of politics energized by the original avant-gardes. Goux's suggestion of the equivalence of theory and finance has been repeatedly used to criticize the limits of theories dependent on the sign. A more recent example is Michael Tranter's (2004) provocative suggestion that Jacques Derrida's notion of writing, which emerged out of a deconstruction of the stability of Saussure's system, should be likened to the invention of neoliberal economics by Milton Friedman, which destabilized Keynesianism. Here temporal homology, the emergence of the notion of writing in the 1970s along with neoliberalism, is used to mount a damaging critique of the turn to writing as merely an intensified registering of the dynamics of capitalism.

In these moments the abstract and expropriative force of language is given over to capitalism. Certainly, within Goux's claims to trace homologies the tension remains over the inability to articulate any other economy. All that Goux can do is gesture towards the power of difference and the feminine as articulating an 'other' economy to language, the father, the phallus and money (1990a: 6). Here we have the revenge of indeterminacy, mysticism, and materialism, which had also afflicted the utopian moment of the adventure of the sign. While we have suggested the disruptive possibilities of a matrilineal materialism, this is a materialism that is not opposed to relation, determination and totality. In Goux's hands, such an Other economy becomes as ungrounded as the speculative forms of finance to come. For example, the turn to the general economy of Bataille, which Derrida (1978: 251–77) engages with as a potential to deconstruct and rupture the restricted economy of capitalism, is troubled by what Goux would later note as the parallel between general economy and speculative capitalism (1990b).

A similar criticism could be returned to Goux. The realization of the closing horizon of capitalism, which we could add had been evident to many long before this 1970s moment, creates the abstract attempt to escape into an Other economy. The very power of the homologies disables any critical determination of the relation of language to materiality and abstraction. It is the precision of the cartography that is part of the problem, seemingly finding what it always wants to find in a one-to-one mapping (Derrida 1992: 110n1). Such a totalization recalls Baudrillard's (1994: 1) retelling of Borges' (2000: 181) fable of the cartographers of the empire, who create a map so perfect it coincides with the territory. For Baudrillard this perfect map becomes the allegory of the sign disappearing into simulation, in which we lose any sense of the outside. Goux, however, retains the outside, which is accessed through the leap to a phantasmatic Other economy. These two modes of thinking mirror each other, as the more we present the system as totality the more the exit from that system requires a speculative leap to the outside. In Goux's analysis the notion that language and abstraction can be traversed and transformed is lost. The notion that the sign can be accented and contested, as proposed by Voloshinov, is replaced by the monologue of capitalism speaking to itself or a sudden leap outside altogether.

If language becomes more and more similar to the force of capitalist abstraction then the desire to escape from language becomes more and more radical. The totalizing system of abstractions is increasingly contrasted with the Nietzschean or Weberian breakout of the iron cage of modernity and our grammar, in the form of new gods, paganism or Dionysian excess (Descombes 1980: 183–86). What is lost is the contradiction in capitalist abstraction, its own constant relation to labour and matter that is denied by it trying to form an abstract system. In terms of language, this contradiction is denied when we see language as a pure abstract system and so see language as parallel to the capitalist fantasy of a system of self-engendering abstractions that create value. The very pure values that Saussure presents might help us unlock the friction-free dream of capitalism as a pure system of value. This is the fantasy of capitalism itself as a pure autotelic system that can engender its own value (Žižek 2006: 60). If Voloshinov could indicate the tension of Saussure's thought in relation to class struggle, while risking dissolving all into language, Goux indicates the tense relation of the abstraction of language to real abstraction, while risking dissolving all into economy. This is the tension I aim to maintain by taking the force of abstraction and difference in Saussure's system as seriously as possible.

Illiterate Capitalism

Criticisms of Saussure have directed attention to the limits of the system of language. In this way they parallel Hegel's criticism of Kant: positing a limit to reason sets up a relation of reason to its other and so creates a new possibility for reason that remains unrecognized. In a similar fashion, Saussure's drawing of a limit to the system of language as a system of 'differences without positive terms' illegitimately confines that difference within the system. This, I think, is the substance of Derrida's (1976: 60) deconstruction of Saussure, which summarizes and radicalizes all previous criticisms of Saussure, from Benveniste to Voloshinov. What we have so far traced is the limit of that system in regard to matter, history, and the homology with capitalism. I have already tentatively suggested the necessity of remaining with Saussure's insistence on abstraction as against a sudden jump out of the system into another economy or another language. If, however, Saussure has appeared ideological due to an unthinking reproduction of capitalist abstraction I now want to consider the argument Saussure does not go far enough. From this perspective, proposed by Gilles Deleuze and Félix Guattari, Saussure is accused of reproducing the ideological forms of capitalism by his emphasis on structure, which mimics capitalism's restraint of the forces of production. If, so far, the tendency has been to chide Saussure for being too abstract, now it appears that Saussure is not abstract enough.

This argument is made by Deleuze and Guattari in their 1972 work *Anti-Oedipus*. Celebrated by Foucault (1983: *xiii*) as a new book of ethics, denounced by Jacques Derrida (quoted in Peeters 2014: 241) as 'very bad book' that 'has been welcomed by a very broad and very dubious sector of opinion', I want to turn to one moment of this sprawling work. Deleuze and Guattari, analysing 'Capitalist Representation', proclaim that 'writing has never been capitalism's thing. Capitalism is profoundly illiterate' (1983: 240). Their aim is not to write another jeremiad on the waning of a culture of literacy, but rather to gauge the way in which capitalism has unleashed a particular regime of representation that transforms the problem of language. The issue is not only of how capitalism has historically transformed the potentiality of language; Deleuze and Guattari also launch a polemic against those structuralist and poststructuralist currents that maintain the hegemony of the signifier, even if for subversive effect. For them, the retention of the Saussurean model of the sign retains a transcendent function of language as dominant over representation. This is true even of those currents that try to delink the signifier from the signified and have it float over the field of representation—as in Lacan or, in a different way, Derrida. Deleuze and Guattari argue that this delinking does not grasp the immanence of language and, relatedly, does not grasp how capitalism operates as an immanent axiomatic.

For Deleuze and Guattari, the signifier remains a transcendent regime, a despotic control over codes, which resists immersion in the immanent flows of what they call 'nonsigns' (241). To undertake this criticism, they turn to the Danish linguist Louis Hjemslev, who tried to develop a linguistics that was immanent to itself and would resort to no other discourse, especially psychology. Hjemslev writes that linguistics 'must attempt to grasp language, not as a conglomerate of nonlinguistic (e.g. physical, physiological, psychological, sociological) phenomena, but as a self-sufficient totality, a structure sui generis' (1953: 2). The irony here is that Hjemslev is even more systematic than Saussure, but for Deleuze and Guattari this creates a 'purely immanent theory of language' (1983: 242). It is for this reason that, as they put it later, Deleuze and Guattari consider 'Hjelmslev, despite his own reservations and vacillations, to be the only linguist actually to have broken with the signifier and signified' (1988: 523n28). Hjemslev's project is a purification of Saussure's (Derrida 1976: 60), a deepening abstraction, and this is what makes it, for Deleuze and Guattari, a theory that resonates with capitalist reality.

The importance of this theory is that for it there are only flows of content and expression, or a 'pure field of algebraic immanence' (Deleuze and Guattari 1983: 242), which composes language. Deleuze and Guattari conclude that Hjelmslev created 'the only linguistics adapted to the nature of *both* the capitalist *and* the schizophrenic flows: until now, the only modern—and not archaic—theory of language' (243). This converges with their analysis of capitalism as a particularly equivocal social formation, which deterritorializes social and linguistic coding and sedimentations, thereby constituting an immanent social form, while binding these fluxes and flows, reterritorializing them through axiomatics. In contrast to the desire to find another economy, here the aim is to identify a single economy of desire of which capitalism forms a limited part. The fact that the primary logic of desire is deterritorialization, which is unleashed by capitalist flows, means that it can never be finally reterritorialized. Capitalism makes its own gravediggers, not in the form of the proletariat but in the form of desire.

In regards to language, capitalism unleashes a language of nonsigns and a crisis of historical sense, which it struggles to control:

> The language of a banker, a general, an industrialist, a middle or high-level manager, or a government minister is a perfectly schizophrenic language, but that functions only statistically within the flattening axiomatic of connections that puts it in the service of the capitalist order. (246)

Deleuze and Guattari aim to unleash this schizophrenic language further, beyond that axiomatic of connection and sense that makes it serve the generation of value. Capitalism is identified as a senseless regime, but one that uses sense, uses connections, to generate value everywhere and anywhere. What Saussure did, according to Deleuze and Guattari, was construct language as a transcendent system and he could not grasp what ruptures and escapes that system. In a similar fashion, capitalism appears as a system, but is in fact the pulsation of these decoded flows.

The result is also an identification of the abstraction of language with the abstraction of capitalism itself conceived as a point of rupture. Of course, the difficulty remains that this rupture appears within capitalism as a mysterious force or moment and the splitting of the excess of schizo-language from the language of the capitalist manager is difficult to achieve (see Chapter 8). It might be that the writing of William Burroughs is, in part, testimony to this particular 'identity of opposites', and of the implosion of language as control and resistance. In that sense, parallel with Goux, Deleuze and Guattari represent, at this point, the risk of an identification of the abstraction of language with the real abstraction of capitalism. Of course, they still try to split the difference by retaining the force of language as nonsign beyond capitalism, but this appears as a romantic opposition that accompanies the bourgeois view of language as sense 'right up to its blessed end' (Marx 1973: 162). The antithesis of sense and nonsense, or sign and nonsign, cannot think dialectically beyond the limit it has set itself. We are left in an alternation of literacy and illiteracy, transcendence and immanence, restricted and general economy, which founders at the moment of its collapse into this identity.

Deleuze and Guattari grasp a particular limit of Saussure's thinking and their reflections on language will try to draw out capacities of language through a pragmatics that works against the illiteracy of capitalist language (1986). The truth of this and other criticisms of Saussure lies in the limit Saussure places on language as a system. What is problematic is the way in which the system is exceeded or overturned by the appeal to an outside that would escape negativity and come to lead a purely positive existence. This is the problem of the 'other economy' we found in Goux, but is one which haunts many post-Saussurean interventions.

Instead, I have argued that we need to seek within the account of difference and negativity the capacities to overturn the capitalist subsumption of language. While Deleuze and Guattari do seek these possibilities inside capitalist language, they treat those possibilities as the positive expression of a force and so create another economy. Deleuze and Guattari also suggest the rupture of sense, the nonsign, will deliver us from capitalism, risking the celebration of the collapse of sense and reason. I am suggesting that the possibilities of liberation lie inside in the negativity that offers the means for determinations of language against capitalist language. This involves not the turn to immediate affirmation, but a negation of the negation that can discover the direct language that lies obscured in the language of the commodity. This is to refuse to see all language as fatally contaminated and to add another lamentation about the decline of language. Instead, it is to trace the historically shifting conditions and struggles that occur over the accenting of language itself within struggles for emancipation.

Traversing Language

It is the very abstraction of Saussure's account of language that allows it to grasp how abstraction penetrates our lives and how abstraction can be a mode of thinking. It is not only that Saussure's discussion of language as system of values mirrors the form of capitalism, but also that the development and aggregation of capitalist abstractions can be regarded as preconditions for Saussure's thinking. It is not possible to think outside of this condition of abstraction, and that condition is intensified as a lived experience by capitalism. The relation to capitalism is not only a negative one, in which capitalism is an epistemological obstacle to a true account of language, but a positive one in which the abstractions of value allow us to form an understanding of the abstractive and expropriative force of language. It is, however, true that capitalism also limits such an understanding by naturalizing this abstracting force and treating it as a source of productive value. In that sense, the perennial suggestion by critics of Saussure that his conception of language is of prison house lacking a referent outside itself, has its kernel of truth. Capitalism integrates everything within its field of value, as Saussure's model of language integrates the sign as an internal relation to other signs. This is where the relation to capitalism becomes illuminating, in that the outside posited by capital is always exists in relation to capital and to the force of abstract value (Walker 2016). An outside is permitted only as a moment in the cycle of value and as secondary to it, without its own reality, it is the outside *of* capital.

That is why, while overturning the image of structuralism as a pure and unhistorical system—one possible image of capitalism— Deleuze and Guattari replace it with an immanent thinking of flux and flow, another image of capitalism. In that sense they lose the full possibility of thinking through abstraction by collapsing language into immanent flows. This is the alternative that Marx traced in bourgeois thought, between the naturalization and lack of historicity of that mode of thinking and its romantic alternative, which is in the final analysis its complement and companion (1973: 92–93). That is why I wish to step back from this alternative. In a sense, Saussure's abstract account of language is rooted in capitalism and is true to a certain loss of the historical forms and sense of language. Without wishing to engage in a romantic nostalgia for the past power of language, we can see that the abstract power of language increasingly renders it abstract from historical forms and experiences. The dialectic between language and history that Hegel and Gramsci attempted to keep alive is under threat. We could and should add that new global possibilities emerge, such as the development of languages online that mediate between national languages and dialects. These confirm Gramsci's insight into the complex relations between dialects and national languages, but now repeated at the global level.

This situation, in which history and language are put into a relation of crisis, is also the fading or crisis of a certain philological imagination—one grounded in the capacity of language to write or experience its own crisis or loss (Brennan 2014). We have seen an ecological catastrophe in the loss of so many languages and that capitalist illiteracy noted by Deleuze and Guattari, in which language is both excessive and empty at the same time. The account of language by Saussure might even be criticized as ratifying this loss in abandoning any historical dialectic. This situation is presaged by Nietzsche and his own particular adaptation of philology. What Nietzsche represents is an awareness of history that emerges out of this crisis of language and a stress on the need for history and an awareness of the failure of philosophers, especially, to recognize history (1968: 35). It is the force of abstraction and the crisis of sense that does not simply lead away from history but back to it. The difficulty, however, is that Nietzsche's way back to history produces an image of it robbed of any direction, rationality, or sense. The rediscovery of history produces a new image of history as a series of chaotic impositions of forms of the will-to-power. Nietzsche writes in *On the Genealogy of Morals*, that the history of a thing or custom can 'be a continuous sign-chain of ever new interpretations and adaptations', driven by chance (1969: 77). Here historicity, a philological attention to the sign, coincides with history's randomness. The concrete, or seemingly concrete, rein-troduction of history is bought at the cost of an abstract conception of perspectivism that robs that history of sense (Lukács 2021). Foucault, directly inspired by Nietzsche, will confront a similar dif-ficulty (1977a). In these cases, we can see both the detaching of language from history and an attempt at re-joining the two that itself reinforces the processes of abstraction that operated the initial severance.

Instead, I am suggesting the abstract force of Saussure's analysis opens the problem of historicity and relation that is not dependent on this sense of randomness or simply reproducing the structure of abstract value. This is why I have integrated Voloshinov's account of accenting, which I think is precisely an engagement with par-ticular historical forms of relation between word and thing, language and materiality (Hall 1996: 40). This is also to mark a limit of language, in which language itself calls for its own placement in a totality that includes our own understanding of the historical existence of language itself. The possibility of what Marx called 'direct language', which can name these types of relation and totality, is something that has to be historically articulated out of the crises of language and matter that we confront. It is the return to Saussure, and the problems of his work, which suggest the need for abstraction to grasp historical relations and the limits of abstraction as a force that nullifies the historical and totality.

CHAPTER FOUR

1937

Corporeal Joins

David Jones, the Anglo-Welsh modernist poet and painter, is an unlikely figure to feature in any rehabilitation of materialism. Jones, the exemplary hieratic modernist, obsessed with grail myths and legends and reactionary in politics, would seem to offer more of a case study of what Marx called the 'flight into the misty realm of religion' (1990: 165). In fact, Jones' own engagement with religion was focused on the need to connect the sign with matter. In the preface to his 1952 epic poem *The Anathemata*, Jones stated 'the artist deals wholly in signs' (2017a: 112), while in his earlier great poem of the First World War *In Parenthesis*, written in 1937, he affirmed 'the validity of material things, and the resurrection of this flesh' (Jones 1961: 118). These concerns go together, in that the dealing with signs is one that concerns engaging with the validity of things. Jones' own Catholicism—he converted in 1921—drove his aesthetics towards the resurrection and incarnation, in which the word (*logos*) and flesh are fused.

Jones is an obscure figure and remains so. Even as modernism is becoming firmly historicized, with a concomitant emphasis on the dense materiality of its embodiments—evident in the focus on the modernist magazine, modernist material culture, and modernism as media—Jones remains largely unassimilated. Despite repetitive attempts to canonize Jones, his works remain notoriously difficult.[1] It is this difficulty that interests me. Certainly, the

---

1 Elizabeth F. Judge (2001) makes the quirky suggestion that it was Jones' relentless annotation of his poems that, by explaining too much, blocked his becoming a canonical modernist.

appropriation of modernism by philosophers and theorists has often been to a restricted canon: while Joyce had his place in the celebration of the materiality of the signifier, to be displaced by Woolf and more completely by Samuel Beckett, Jones, along with Wyndham Lewis,[2] is a recalcitrant figure for theoretical appropriation. This is not only a political matter, with Jones and Lewis being more overtly reactionary, but also a matter of abstraction and language. Joyce's linguistic excess and Beckett's minimalism have been taken as more conducive to thinking language than the strained and violent attempt by Jones to bridge sign and reality.

The bridging of sign and reality is one that makes Jones an almost hyperbolic figure of the modernist desire to invest the art work with a sacred status; Lewis might be the figure of the symmetrical desire to de-sacralize the art work. Such a sacralizing desire risks, as Jameson argued, a convergence or merger with the Heideggerian tone of 'contemplative solemnity' (1994: 89). First, we should note that Jameson displays his own persistent interest in the Heideggerian tone, which is evident in his study of Raymond Chandler. While Raymond Chandler is not a high modernist, and was notoriously hostile to modernist pretension, Jameson makes a surprising turn to Heidegger to understand Chandler's fiction. Jameson argues that a historicized Heideggerian account of death and Being is central to understanding how Chandler's writing pursues 'the end of the world' in a revelation of death and Being (2016). Jameson's supposition is that by historicizing Heidegger's ontological claims, by treating them as simply symptomatic or reflective of modernity, then one becomes immune to the problems of Heidegger. This seems to me naive, not least because of its own failure to engage with Heidegger's periodization and historicization of modernity. Instead of a materialist Heidegger, we risk being left with a Heideggerian materialism—in which death and Being retain their privileges despite their historicization. The irony is that Jones, who is much closer to Heidegger, might provide a better departure from the Heideggerian reading of the poetic, modernity, and abstraction.

---

2 The exception being Fredric Jameson's (2008) study of Lewis.

Jones is certainly very close to Heidegger in his reactionary politics and in a parallel understanding of technology. Heidegger's 'A Question Concerning Technology' and its concern with technology as *Gestell* or 'en-framing' is similar to Jones' (1993: 140) concern with the problem of 'the utile infiltration'. For Jones, utility triumphs over the artistic deployment of signs and true making is surpassed by mass production. Both, in different ways, would share a belief in Nazism as one possible solution to this problem of technological domination (Heidegger 1959: 199; Wootten 2003). Jones' own reflection on the work of art, 'Art and Sacrament' (1955), produces a strangely mutant British Heidegger, in which his examples of making are the very British cake baking and cricket, rather than Heidegger's pottery or his 'clear-eyed peasant' (Badiou 1999: 53). Jones' own epochal history from 'pillar to pylon' is also strikingly similar to Heidegger's narrative of the forgetting of Being, from Socrates to technology as embodied Nietzschean nihilism (2017b: 9). To read Jones with Heidegger is an almost irresistible temptation.

Here I want to turn to a more unlikely figure, Donna Haraway. Haraway could not, by most measures, be further away from Jones in terms of politics and even style. Yet, Haraway remarks that 'my soul [is] indelibly marked by Catholic formation' and notes how this is one factor in her fascination with 'the corporeal join of the material and the semiotic' (2016: 107). It is this join, I want to suggest, which also fascinates David Jones. While Jones places this join under the sign of the sacred, something reinforced by a Heideggerian reading, his poetic practice also places this corporeal join at the intersection of language and matter. It is this that makes reading Jones with Haraway a crucial as a way of displacing the problem of language from the sacred, as we find in Heidegger, and towards a materialism that thinks the relations between language, matter, and history.

My focus will be on Jones' poem *In Parenthesis* and the ways in which war shapes a thinking of the relation of language to materiality in modernity. Walter Benjamin wrote of how, in the First World War,

> A generation that had gone to school on a horse-drawn streetcar now stood under the open sky in a countryside in which nothing remained unchanged but the clouds, and beneath these clouds, in a field of force of destructive torrents and explosions, was the tiny, fragile human body. (1968: 84)

These unleashed forces of technology created a new *physis*, a new technologically mediated nature, replacing what we know as nature (Benjamin 1979: 104). Benjamin also notes how the violence of war created a poverty of experience, which damaged the possibility of transmitting this experience of violence (1999). The First World War was the exemplary site of the emergence of technologized nature and broken experience. Jones' poetry, a delayed writing of his own wartime experience, is a reflection on this new nature, on the difficulty of transmitting his experience of war, and on the extension of war into our life and experience. Our reading of materiality in Jones can also double as a reading of our moment as one of a 'new geography of violence', which shapes our experience of nature and social life today in the time of climate crisis (Parenti 2011).

The War-Shape

Jones was the longest-serving poet-soldier on the Western Front, spending 157 weeks at the front line. The experience shaped not only his poetry but also his life, resulting in a series of catastrophic mental breakdowns. In one of his critical essays, Jones noted that his wartime experience 'had a permanent effect upon me and affected my work in all sorts of ways' (2017a: 28). War is not only the obvious subject of *In Parenthesis*, which tells of Private John Ball from his entry into the military in 1915 to the battle at Mametz

Wood in 1916, but, in one sense, of all of Jones' art. Jones was not only concerned with capturing the experience of the First World War battlefield as one of 'sudden violences and the long stillnesses' (1961: x), but also what he would later call 'the world-enrolments / that extend the war-shape' (1981: 57). The war zone lost cohesion in a conflict that dug down into the earth, drowned in mud, fought in the air, involved constant artillery barrages, and in which the air itself was poisoned (Sloterdijk 2009). The shapelessness of war would be a central way in which the extension of the war-shape would reproduce itself into the postwar world. Jones' ability to grasp this material rearrangement of the world in warfare would also be vital to his ability to grasp the reproduction of war in its proliferation across the world.

Aesthetics and art had to take the measure of this shapeless war-shape (Jameson 2013: 240), but were also enmeshed with war. This is a commonplace of modernist studies, focused on what Lewis (1982: 9) called the 'men of 1914', but for Jones there is a more profound relationship between art and war. In a suggestive aside from a discussion of modernism, Jones proposes what we could call a military aesthetics:

> Yet it would be interesting to know what relationship there is between Cézanne's painful and glorious mastery of mass and recession and the troop-dispositions of the Franco-Prussian War—not much one tends to think, and yet, I wonder, it may be the affinity is more than appears. (Jones 2017a: 101)

This seemingly casual remark leaves the suggested affinity as an undeveloped speculation. It is, however, developed in Jones' poetry and painting, which interrogates the relationship between the logistics of war and the logistics of perception (Virilio 2009; Bosquet 2018). Troop dispositions and the forms and movements of the battlefield will become the concern of a poetry that tries to shape this incoherent and chaotic experience. The very delay and difficulty Jones experienced in writing *In Parenthesis* suggests the struggle involved in trying to use language to express these forces and dispositions, themselves rendered enigmatic by the war space of the First World War battlefield.

Jones' work is an exemplary instance of the deployment of what Alain Badiou (2012) calls 'the figure of the soldier' in poetry. Badiou argues that with the mass citizen armies of modernity we witness a transition from the singular figure of the warrior to 'the democratic and collective figure of the soldier'.[3] The soldier becomes the embodiment, for Badiou, of the inhuman dimension of risking death for the collective and so the figure of 'an immanent mortality'. It is also a Christian figure of sacrifice, heroism, and collectivity, represented in poetry by Gerard Manley Hopkins. Badiou's analysis provides an insightful framework in which we can read Jones' poetry. We can also, however, contrast Jones' antiheroic perspective with Badiou's retention of the heroic being-toward death, which risks a reactionary and Heideggerian emphasis on war and death as limit experiences.

For Jones, the soldier, in the form of 'the tommy', was a trans-historical representative of the collective, from the Roman Empire to the battlefields of the First World War. He particularized this generic soldier in the figure of 'Dai Greatcoat', an alter ego cum idealized soldier who served from Ancient Briton to the Western Front (Jones 1961: 79–84). Jones' stress is on sacrifice and the collective, as he makes ironic use of the soldier's song 'Old soljers never die they / Simply fade away' (84). This fading is resisted by Jones' poetry and painting, although its own evident struggle to give material form to such a figure indicates the perpetual risk of such experience fading away. In Jones' poetry, the soldier does not incarnate Badiou's notion of the heroic encounter with death or an immanent mortality. In fact, Jones, who felt as a soldier he was 'grotesquely incompetent, a knocker-over of piles, a parade's despair' (xv), might well confirm Foucault's (1977b: 164) insight

---

3 Georg Lukács (1962: 24) suggests the role of mass military experience in the emergence of realism as a literary form.

that, in modernity, 'the soldier is above all a fragment of mobile space, before he is courage or honour'. Instead of the heroism and encounter with mortality Badiou supposes, Jones implies something much more spatial and even comic. Here the figure of the soldier is certainly that of a Christian collective, but one that remains mobile and abstract—a figure, again, of this shapeless shape of war.

Like his modernist influences, Eliot and Joyce, Jones made extensive use of myth or legend, especially, in his case, the Arthurian romances. Before focusing on the use of myth to connect bodies and language, I want to turn to Jones' use of the materiality of language to probe the battlespace as a space of corporeal joins. This is a space that is already material and semiotic and we may see it as equivalent to the space of proto-language. The battlefield, by smashing matter and fragmenting language, recreates the experience of the child trying to connect words to things. *In Parenthesis* makes use of a peculiar prose poetry, a form that is itself shapeless, collective, and resonant with mythic elements. It is also, in common modernist fashion, supplied with its own footnotes detailing the dense materiality of its own textual references, which accumulate alongside the material confusions of the battlefield.

In Parenthesis traces the relation of the material and the semiotic through the fragility of the body and of the material world. The battlespace is one that is churned and fractured, with explosions resulting in 'overturned far throwings'. The ground, the Heideggerian earth, is thrown into the air and returned as 'heaped on, heaped up wastes'. Trees, which form a constant reference point for Jones' painting, are 'leper-trees', diseased, 'rownsepykèd out of nature', stripped of leaves (Jones 1961: 39). It is the tree that is the mythic figure of the Christian cross as one instance of the corporeal join of the material and semiotic. But this cross is now shattered into fragile remnants and dispersed across the battlespace. Trees are also metaphoric for the shattered human bodies of the Western Front. We have the imagery of 'the spilled bowels of trees' (31), in which the trees parallel the traumatic wounds of humans. Jones (quoted in Fussell 1977: 145) would write that 'wounded trees and wounded men are very much an abiding image in my mind as a hang-over from the War'. This recurrent imagery, casually presented as a 'hang-over', is, in fact, a vital mediation of language and materiality.

The battlefield offers a fusion of nature, the human and the technological, in which the corporeal join of language and matter is both shattered and remade. The violent rending of the tree—coincidentally, used as an example by Saussure to demonstrate the notion of the sign as signifier and signified—disrupts the unity of the sign as well as reality. The poet does not simply repair this damage and re-establish the sacrament of sign and referent, but also registers the fracture and corporeal joining in all signs. Jones' battlefield is a field of waste, in the quite literal sense. We have the familiar barbed wire, 'thin / ribbon-metal chafing', but also margarine tins sailing like little boats in the water collected in shell holes, 'their sharp-jagged twisted lids wrenched back' (Jones 1961: 39). The tearing and wrenching of the object is, again, mimetic of the violence suffered by human bodies. In the peculiar object-world of the Western Front we find a mirrored piling-up of the tech-nological and the natural, the deadly and the banal.[4] This object-world, as throughout In Parenthesis, is one that follows a logic of disposal and junk, of what is thrown away, in what Jones ironically calls 'a perfectly sanitary war' (43).

This is an irony at the expense of the human labour that con-stantly works on this natural environment to create the unnatural warscape of World War I. Splintered trees, trenches, liquid mud, a whole shattered world, are the result of a constant labour: 'trench warfare and attrition meant daily rebuilding what was daily

---

4 On Jones' sympathy for objects, see Robin Ironside (1949: 14). Paul Fussell (1977: 154), in his criticism of In Parenthesis, says the frontispiece image and by implication the poem is 'too crowded' with objects and so 'too much'. This excess, we would suggest, is the point of the poem, which overwhelms the reader.

destroyed, merely to stay alive, and if possible, to interrupt the life-sustaining labour of the enemy' (Riede 2015: 691). The sanitary war is also a result of the reparative labour to constantly clean and repair this damage as a means of sustaining violent conflict. Jones' soldiers spend their time cleaning and trying to tidy this object-world of violence. In Jones' poetry the material joining of the corporeal and semiotic is not merely the interaction of human and nonhuman objects in some neutral field of chaotic collisions, but a mediated and mediating process of fusing and defusing the material and the semiotic in relation to the creation and destruction of forms of nature. Jameson remarks that the dialectic of war is one of 'abstraction versus sense-datum', which 'dictate dilemmas of representation navigable only by formal innovation' (2013: 256). This is Jones' situation and solution, in which he confronts the state of nature as it is transfigured into a war that is a constant labour to render life as brutish and short. The paradox of Jones' poem is its own attempt at a labour of integration, the constitution of a tradition, which also encompasses this violent world making and which would falter into psychic crisis for Jones himself (Riede 2015: 693). In the end, Jones too is placed in the position of the soldier collecting and repairing fragments that themselves sustain the conflict. Eliot's fragments 'shored against my ruins' are here the broken signs that Jones has tried to repair into a coherent and mythic whole (1983: 79). The necessary failure of this task is a mimetic repetition of the soldier's labour in this sanitary war and a registration of the sign making that tries to render this state.

The Place of Enchantment

The unification of the corporeal join of the material and the semiotic is carried out by myth and sustained by a particular myth of historical continuity. It is will be this sense of historical continuity—from the soldiers gambling over Christ's robes, to the tommies of World War I, and then to British soldiers serving in Palestine—which will create in Jones a sensitivity to historical fragmentation and crisis. While myth or even fantasy are called upon to do the work of repair they stand witness to the wound in experience. Also, in the desire to establish continuity and connection the experience of trauma and fragmentation is itself extended. Within *In Parenthesis* Jones links together the material and semiotic 'Waste Land' of the Western Front with the suburban interzones of his London life. The object-world of waste and junk is matched by the 'untidied squalor of the loveless scene spread far horizontally', which is 'sordid and deprived' and a place 'where waste-land meets environs and punctured bins ooze canned-meats discarded, tyres to rot, derelict slow-weathered iron-ware disintegrates between factory-end and nettle-bed' (Jones 1961: 75). The edgeland between the garden and the railway line, the place of the factory-end, the various in-between spaces, are rendered as mimetic to the junk-space of the battlefield. Once again, we have an extension of the war-shape in the form of an extension of the shapeless series of objects, in which, again, tins feature prominently. This awareness is ecological, but an ecology of violence and waste, in which barbed wire and metal tins on the battlefield are rendered equivalent with rotting tyres and discarded cans. Jones' remark in the preface to *In Parenthesis* that 'even while we watch the boatman mending his sail, the petroleum is hurting the sea' indicates this ecological awareness that emerges from this sensitivity to historical damage (*ix*).

While this might seem another instance of reactionary ecology, what concerns me here is Jones' claim that 'many newfangled technicalities' require 'a new and strange direction of the mind' (*xiv*). This direction is one attuned to the violent materialities of world making and unmaking, and is even sanguine about this violence. Jones is not simply fighting 'the extension of the world-shape' of war, but rather tracing how it unfolds across time and space. His own experience of war has become prefigurative of our experience, including of the difficulty in transmitting that experience. In his writing we find an acute reading of this violence and chaos, but this is the condition of the reactionary re-establishment of continuity and place. There is a particular conception of history at work here.

This is a history of mutation, of 'adaptations', 'fusions', and 'trans-mogrifications', 'but always / the inward continuities / of the site / of place' (Jones 1993: 154). Jones registers fragmentation and instability, depicting history as a 'great confluity and dapple, things counter, pied, fragmented, twisted, lost', in parallel to the fractured materiality of the Western Front and to the language of Gerard Manley Hopkins (2017a: 46). Jones would agree, albeit for different reasons, with Jameson's dictum that 'history is what hurts' (2002: 88). This is also a history of continuity as spatial, of site and of place. In this way history is admitted but also collapsed into a mythic, even structuralist, conception of a repetition that does not fundamentally alter the ways things are. Jones' use of myth predominantly partakes of the organic conception, of repairing the sign and creating a stable link, but it also inhabits the repetitive and structuralist mode of myth as resolution of contradiction in spatial forms. Continuity, mythic continuity, is one of eternal recurrence mediated by site and place, in which the fundamental figure is the battlefield.

This conception of history as mythic battlefield demands a certain labour, a certain quest, to make whole, or to engage with this abstract violence. We wander, as Jones puts it in his 1974 work *The Sleeping Lord*, through 'the tangle of world-wood' finding 'mutable and beggarly elements' with which to 'give back anathema its first benignity' (2017b: 60, 61). The role of the poet, as we have seen, is one of repair and reparation, but one that also refuses to heal or escape this mythic cycle of sacrifice and violence. Hence, we have the antinomy of continuity and violence, concrete and abstract, but always with a desire to join together that can never succeed. Drew Milne has noted that we can read Jones' work as a 'mosaic of mythopoetic delusions fragments, providing perspectives on reality despite itself' (1996: 261). Milne also suggests that Jones' 'alienated aesthetic affords more specific insights into poetic and historical problems'. In a manner akin to Jameson's reading of Wyndham Lewis, Milne reads Jones as attentive to the experience of alienation and fragmentation, not despite but because of his reactionary tendencies.

What is vital, however, is to move further into the problems and potentials encoded in the corporeal joins that Jones poses. We could say that if he sees his role as fusing history and myth then the element which makes this suture possible is fantasy. This is not fantasy in the derogatory sense, as escapism or flight into the imaginary, but fantasy as the articulation of the join between history and myth. In the preface to *In Parenthesis* Jones remarks of the 'Waste Land' of the Western Front that 'it was a place of enchantment' (1961: *x*). With this strange suggestion, the profound material violence of war and his own suffering become transformed into something wonderous. Jones does not shy away from the vision of the battlespace as a space of enchantment, especially in the section of the poem devoted to the battle at Mametz Wood, where Jones himself was injured. Jones' own fascination with the matter of Britain, and with Arthurian and Celtic myth, is obviously central to this poetics of enchantment (Whitaker 1997; Jones 2017a: 202–11 and 212–59). He was also happy to cite J. R. R. Tolkien as a source for *The Anathemata* (Jones 2017a: 132). Tolkien, in his preface to *The Lord of the Rings*, defiantly rejected any allegorical reading of his work as some recounting of the Second World War or industrialization. Tolkien did, however, note that 'by 1918 all but one of my close friends were dead' (2005: *xxii*). Tolkien's novel and Jones' poetry are both marked by what Ernst Jünger called war as 'inner experience' (2021).

The notorious accusation that fantasy literature is simply escapist is in this case certainly misplaced. There is escape here, a flight into myth to record experience, but also the mediation of a broken experience through the appeal to fantasy and myth. Jones turns to fantasy, as he explicitly states, to render a battlespace of 'sudden violences and long stillnesses'. It is also the condition for his suturing of history and myth, language and matter, into a new continuity that would sustain a future making. This continuity is reactionary in its fusing of one long history, or mythic history, of decline, corruption, and the loss of sense. The translation of war into history, while insightful, also renders history into the chaos of war as perpetual violence. These tensions of myth and making condense in the closing description of battle in *In Parenthesis*.

The battle of Mametz Wood took place on the 10 and 11 July 1916 and was part of the battle of the Somme. The Welsh 38th division, of which Jones was part, took heavy casualties, with 565 killed, 585 missing, and 2,893 wounded. In Jones' recounting Mametz Wood becomes a mythical place of violence and death: 'But sweet sister death has gone debauched today and stalks on this high ground with strumpet confidence, makes no coy veiling of her appetite but leers from you to me with all her parts discovered' (1961: 162). The virgin soldiers 'may howl for their virginity', but in Jones' vision sexuality and death are integrated in the sister's vulgar seduction of the virgin soldiers. We can see how the mediation of history and myth is one that has an essential relationship to sexuality, especially in the form of a literal femme fatale.

The kitsch misogyny of Jones' mythic vision of death is also something that reveals the explicit sexuality at work in myth. Jones, despite his sometime self-presentation as monkish and nonsexual, is not coy. This is evident in the erotic female nude of 1929, which Jones forbade from exhibition in his lifetime (Bankes and Hills 2015: 80). It is also evident in his recurrent use of Petra Gill, later Petra Tegetmeier, as muse and model, as well as of Prudence Pelham in a similar role (Sinclair 2002). For Jones the mythic is sexualized in the female figure; it is especially embodied in the mythical figure of the lady or goddess that owes a particular debt to the tradition of courtly love in the figure of Guenever, subject of a 1940 watercolour. Jones' figure of the lady repeats the inaccessibility Lacan had noted, but also a leering intrusion when translated into sister death (1992: 171–90; Žižek 2005: 89–112). The battlefield is not a wholly male or homosocial space, but one inhabited by the mythic form of the feminine, as well as by a feminization or literalized castration of the masculine.

In the space of the battlefield those who 'impinge less on space' and 'nourish a lesser category of being' are left temporarily safe from death's attentions (Jones 1961: 162, 163). To be saved is a matter of burrowing into the earth and minimizing one's being, almost fusing with nature. This parallels the way in which Jones does not abandon materiality with myth, but tries to fuse matter with myth as an act of survival. The mythic elements are themselves rendered material and the material rendered vulnerable. Again, this is fused with sexuality, and so material vulnerability is rendered through sexual desire, need, and violation, although of the male body. It is a matter of an experience of space and volume in which soldiers sheltering from machine-gun fire aim to 'reduce our dimensional vulnerability to the minimum' (177). In the desire to fuse with the earth as matter (and as mother, as we have seen), the soldier finds that: 'The inorganic earth where your body presses seems itself to pulse deep down with your heart's acceleration' (167). Here matrilineal materialism is a mimetic pulsing of the inorganic earth with the speeding heart of the soldier. Thrusting oneself into the earth is not only a sexual act, but a strange protection against emasculation and violation by the feminine sweet sister death.

These material matters are not only fusions with the earth, but also the disintegration of the material; in the no-man's-land of the night, 'material things are but barely integrated and loosely tacked together' (181). This obviously recalls the 'Nighttown' episode of Joyce's *Ulysses*, with its phantasmagoria of sexual experience in Dublin's red-light district. The experience of fantasy is that of suturing which also conveys these transformations and sudden violences that shift the relation of matter and sign. Fantasy as genre—also, as it does in the present—seems to unlock an experience of sudden violence and catastrophe (Lanchester 2013; Steyerl 2016). Jones renders the landscape of war mythic and suggests how that landscape can lend itself to mythic forms. In this way his work traces the extension of the war-shape into our experience of abstract violence in the landscapes of late capitalism (Tsing 2015; Gordillo 2014). The experience of sudden violence and long stillness echoes in our experience of ongoing crisis and strange inertia. Our quests for work and survival traverse strange lands of emptied buildings, abandoned retail outlets, digitally mediated visions of protest and war, deserted cities under lockdown, and a multiplicity of face masks. This sense of static crisis engages not only the experience of the past, but also the extension of the war-shape into the muted class struggles of the present. We live the contemporary war-shape as a shapeless experience, exacerbated by the conception of the world as global battlespace (Croser 2007).

Jones traces, against his own ostensible reactionary aims, how capitalist real abstractions bind together with matter to penetrate all forms of life. We live in a fantasy landscape in which nature is no longer apparently natural. What Lukács (1971: 64) called 'second nature', 'the nature of man-made structures' which 'has become rigid and strange' and 'is a charnel-house of long-dead interiorities', has become fused with nature or surpassed by new virtual and digital forms of third nature (Foster 2018). Today, the abstractions of digital technology merge with human-made structures and with nature itself. Jones' poetry and painting, in their own ethereality and unworldliness, capture something of this experience. Fantasy articulates a peculiar realism of real abstractions, at least in the mode in which Jones deploys it. Certainly, Jones casts this situation in a reactionary form, just as there are no shortage of such reactionary forms in the present moment. Yet, the aesthetic fragility of his own writing, in his poetry, renders these reactionary forms in ways that might offer other articulations of the corporeal joins of violent abstractions. Writing out of his faith in labour as a redemptive and sacred joining of the sign to matter, Jones' poetics resonate in their strangeness, their fantasy elements, across our landscapes of enchantment where dissolution afflicts the form of nature.

This is why I have chosen to dwell with David Jones. It is also because Jones' poetics also resonates and disrupts the Heideggerian meditation, with Heidegger's own peculiar translation of the front experience into philosophy (Losurdo 2001). In fact, it is Jones' own thinking of the dense materiality of war that offers an engagement which relates matter to abstractions and does not simply reinforce the heroic communal destiny of being-toward-death. This is not to absolve Jones of the reactionary elements we have noted or to engage in the quixotic struggle to separate a good Jones from these bad elements. It is precisely the reactionary nature of Jones' work that results in this registration of materiality and language through the abstract. To simply force a translation of this work into acceptable terms has not been my aim, although I have wanted to see possibilities in Jones that are not limited by his reactionary commitments. What we are left with, in the difficulty of Jones' work that resists assimilation, is something that can give shape to the shapeless war-shape that still remains dominant.

CHAPTER FIVE

1968

Cosmogony of Revolution

Diane di Prima's *Revolutionary Letters*, first published in 1971, are exhortations, instructions, reflections, analyses, provocations, meditations, and speculations that are all directed towards revolution. Directed can be read in a double sense: directed towards making the revolution happen and directed towards guiding us in a revolutionary process. In this the *Letters* remain somewhere between the performative—exhorting the revolution, or what Robespierre (quoted in Koselleck 2004: 12) called 'the particular duty of hastening its pace'—and the constative—describing the revolution in motion. Di Prima wrote these poems primarily from the 1960s through the 1970s, although they extend to 2003. These poems were also performance works; as the Last Gasp edition of 2007 notes 'Diane read the early poems on a flatbed truck in New York City and later performed them on the steps of City Hall in San Francisco with Peter Coyote and the Diggers'. They call to be enacted, both in themselves and as ways of triggering or encouraging revolution. The poems belong to that moment of the 1960s or, more precisely, to what Fredric Jameson has periodized as the long '60s (1984). This is the time of a general cultural revolution (broader than the Maoist concept), or what Jameson calls 'the adventure of the sign' (194–201). Di Prima's inspiration was far from global Maoism and she drew on her grandfather, with his anarchist wisdom, and an eclectic range of revolutionaries and writers: Oscar Wilde, Trotsky, 'big/dumb Kropotkin', and others (di Prima 2007: under 'April Fool Birthday Poem for Grandpa').[1] I have chosen 1968 as the dating for this chapter as the usual sign that condenses the long '60s, but this should not disguise the longer temporality or di Prima's long commitment. Of course, that revolution did not succeed but the *Letters* provide a singularly rich and dense conceptualization of this revolution that did not arrive at its destination (Derrida 1987c).

Di Prima's anarchist revolution, which forms the heart of her adventure of the sign, is one of immediacy and transparency. The aim is to put an end to the need for mediation. It is a war on all the abstractions that separate and alienate us and which must be destroyed: money, the media, synthetic foods, schools, and the 'plastic constructs' that are our own selves under capitalism (#22). The process of the revolution involves dismantling of all these separations and constructs, while the course of the revolution is determined by the success of these activities of dismantling separation. Language is at once part of this force of separation and abstraction and also the medium in which it must be addressed. The simplicity of some of the *Letters* should not deceive us. While not taking modernism's path of deliberate difficulty, di Prima is waging her own war with and on language. The *Letters* inhabit a point of struggle with the resources that language offers and with those constructions of language that prohibit or impede revolution.

The *Letters* now stand as testaments to the failure of a particular vision of revolution, but they also embody the hopes of that revolutionary moment. They incarnate, as Dale Smith has suggested, a 'heavy optimism' (2013). Heavy, a very '60s slang word for intense or serious, can also be read in terms of the weight of all the inertial forces arrayed against the revolution, and optimism as the confidence and belief of being in a revolution that will take its course. It would be a failure of imagination to read such a stance as naïve, or to dismiss it in the name of a maturity that serves as a disguise for cynicism. Instead, we must return to the *Letters* as a

---

1 All further in-text citations of di Prima's *Revolutionary Letters* will include the letter number preceded by '#' sign.

meditation on the possibility and necessity of revolution that is fully aware of past, present and future failures. They would not attend so closely to the process of revolution or constantly intervene in that process if they assumed revolution was a foregone conclusion. To project naivety back into the *Letters* prevents us seeing how they make us aware of the crushing weight of abstractions that can render even our language mute. At the same time, these poems were written. There is a refusal to inhabit muteness and silence, difficulty and the rebarbative, which makes di Prima's work exceptional with regard to the usual histories of poetics, especially of modernism, as well as to the typical documents of the war on and of language. This is a political war on and through language, a return to something more like the simplicity of Brecht or Blake, but with the anarchist insistence on spontaneity and directness.

My reading aims to take seriously this heavy optimism as a form of working in the process of revolution and does so by reading the letters in an impersonal way. This may seem strange. The *Letters* are intensely personal demands from di Prima to us. They appear as intimately material, in the sense of being attuned to materiality, to revolution, to nature (as we will see), and in the very character of their demands. The *Letters* were also originally intended as live performances, inhabiting the insistent interpellation of one body by another, and the poems retain this element. Why adopt an impersonal reading, which would seem to conform to the sanitizing procedures that govern interpretations of modernism as a self-contained and subject less art? The reason for this impersonal reading is faithfulness to di Prima's own faith in the process of the revolution, of which her and the poems are simply a part. Di Prima (quoted in Dale Smith 2013) also proposes her own impersonal mode of reading: 'Archetypes have their own drama: a vast uncharted cycle of *Comedia dell'Arte*, which they play out through us, without our informed consent. And with, ultimately, no concerns for human purpose'. Such an archetypal approach is influenced by Jung, although in a critical way, as we see in her ironic treatment of the figure of the 'imaginary Jungian scholar' in her exploration of female deities and archetypes *Loba* (di Prima 1998: 83, 94, 165). In fact, *Loba* is written in parallel with the *Letters* and this suggests that we read these projects as parallel reflections. While I will focus on the *Letters*, we should be aware of this parallel, and the reflection it develops on the role of the archetypal. We can see di Prima's poetics as a divine comedy, the comedy of the revolution as turn and return, as a cosmic cycle. Di Prima's poetry offers an 'impersonal lyricism' (Balso 2014: 78), in which the poem fuse into one. She offers the conceptual personae of revolution (Deleuze and Guattari 1994: 61–84).[2]

Turn, Turn, Turn

In a late letter, #75, written in the early 1980s and subtitled 'RANT', di Prima suggests 'You cannot write a single line w/out a cosmology / a cosmogony / laid out, before all eyes'. Poetry, according to di Prima, cannot be written without a theory of the origin of the universe. There is a truth to this, in that all thought and poetics pre-suppose a cosmology and a thinking of totality. We are used to the banal sense in which writers create worlds or engage in world build-ing, but here we are speaking of an act of creation that participates in the creation of totality itself. Di Prima is unusual in assuming this totality as a task for writing. If we are speaking of revolution then we are also speaking of the cosmos, and thus the *Letters* are a cosmology or cosmogony of revolution. This is a conception of revolution as origin, as birth of the universe. Poetry, and the revol-ution, are acts of creation, of the creation of the universe, but also acts that trace and operate within that creation. This is not simply the word as divine Logos[3]—'in the beginning was the word'—but the word as dependent on a cosmology or cosmogony. To read di Prima requires that we take this cosmology seriously precisely as a cosmology of revolution.

---

2 This convergence between Deleuze and di Prima could be explained by their common Jungianism (Kerslake 2004).
3 On the issue of the translation of the word 'logos' in the New Testament, see David Bentley Hart (2018: 549–51).

The power of the poetic word lies in its intimate relation with revolution. Poetry and the revolution remake the world and so repeat the initial act of cosmological creation. It is not so much the old battle between poetry at the service of the revolution, or the revolution at the service of poetry, but a new equation of poetry with revolution. In di Prima's formulation: 'IF THE WORD HAS POWER YOU SHALL NOT STAND / AMERICA' (#40). Cosmology, revolution, and poetry, together form this impersonal power that is part of the course and flow that overturns. Both poetry and revolution are works of imagination and both form a whole. Our experience, however, is of a war on the imagination, the 'only war that matters' (#75), which has split poetry from the revolution, impoverishing both. The role of the poet is to repair and make whole what has been divided. Poetics is an act that remakes the cosmos in the image of this unity and everything we do, whether we are 'plumber, baker, teacher', is a poetics in the sense of a making or remaking of this unity (#75).

I want to insist that we read di Prima's *Letters* as a revolutionary cosmogony. This use of the term might be considered a retrospective imposition of the spiritual on the material urgency of the early *Letters*, which are often practically oriented. The appeal of these poems in the present moment has often been predicated on this practicality and urgency. For Joshua Clover, di Prima's *Letters* 'comprise the great modern georgic' and a 'simple lesson' in the practicalities of revolution (2016a). Here what is important are those *Letters* of instruction, which tell us the lessons of revolution, such as 'hoard matches, we aren't good / at rubbing sticks together any more' (#3). This contemporary reading returns to di Prima's anarchist and insurrectional vision and fuses it with the contemporary theory of communization, which envisages the immediate possibility of communist measures, and with invocations of the 'riot form' as an exemplary mode of contemporary struggle (Clover 2016b). Di Prima becomes the poet of urban insurrection, and this has resonated with our time of riots and uprising in the period since the global financial crisis of 2008. While true to a central element of di Prima's project, such a vision risks shearing di Prima from her cosmological impetus. While we have the apparently 'simple' letters of insurrection, these form part of the cosmological vision of the ebbing and flowing of revolution.

This cosmogony is not only a positive vision of overturning but also a vision of war on all the separations imposed on us by capitalist society. The *Letters* explore the necessity of the destruction of a whole range of separations. So, in letter #9, we are called to 'destroy the concept of money', and di Prima suggests that we reconsider Ezra Pound's suggestion of a money voucher that only operates for a limited time. Di Prima joins that current of left Poundianism that tries to deploy Pound's poetic thinking about the money and economy detached from his anti-Semitism and fascism (Prynne 2016: 123–31). Pound's thinking of money and value rests on a desire to reconnect sign and matter, money and value, developed through an anti-Semitic identification of Jewishness with abstraction (Rabaté 1986: 183–241). While the dissident left reading of Pound is aware of this, it tries to engage with Pound's introduction of political economy into poetry. Di Prima's fascination with the notion of self-voiding money, a money that will self-destruct, attempts to avoid the naturalizing tendencies in Pound that drive his anti-Semitism. Such a strategy is, however, risky. It may be both naïve about money, considering the risk of reintroducing capitalist forms of value into revolution, as well as naïve about the risks of reproducing Pound's claims about real value. This is one of the animating tensions of di Prima's poems, as they try to wage war on abstraction but struggle to find a real concrete content for revolution.

To smash the power of money is not enough. The point of the cultural revolution of the 1960s, broadening out from the Maoist concept, was the pursuit and overturning of all forms of power and oppression. In the same spirit, di Prima also targets other forms of mediation: 'SMASH THE MEDIA, I said / AND BURN THE

SCHOOLS' (#11). Here it is those ideological state apparatuses, subject of Althusser's famous analysis as the key ideological forms of contemporary capitalism, which are treated as separations that require immediate destruction (2008). Once again, we have the desire to annihilate separation that risks the loss of all mediation in its desire to overcome any division. Following this logic to its end point di Prima argues the revolutionary is perhaps the last and final mediation to be destroyed by the revolution: 'for every revolutionary must at last will his own destruction / rooted as he is in the past he sets out to destroy' (#12). This logic is pursued to its end, through all the plastic constructs, to the destruction of the I as the final barrier. This is reminiscent Stirner's assault on all forms of abstraction, which he called 'spooks' or 'ghosts', including the final abstraction of identity itself (2013).

This logic of antiseparation is in keeping with the insurrectional forms of anarchism and also converges with a range of 1960s tropes of revolution that critique the spectacle as general form of capitalist dominance through the separation of life from its activity, especially as articulated by Guy Debord (1995) and the Situationists. Separation, for Debord, is the fundamental act of power, which will find its fullest and most complete realization in the reign of the spectacle as a form of abstraction. In the spectacle we contemplate our separation from our own activity and even participate in our own alienation as spectators. As we have seen, di Prima figures these separations as plastic constructs, as fake abstractions that conceal real relations of domination.

Di Prima's analysis is also similar to critiques of technology as a force of separation and violence linked to capitalism, such as Herbert Marcuse's (2002) influential *One-Dimensional Man*. Here technology becomes an autonomous force of utility, reducing the world to what is useful as an expression of 'instrumental reason' (Horkheimer 2013). In Marcuse this is explicitly linked to capitalism, while other theorizations tended to treat technology, in a Heideggerian vein, as a force in its own right. Di Prima works more towards a critical understanding that treats technology as one among multiple forms of capitalist separation. In the face of such separation and violence, which separates us from the cosmos, revolution is an act of re-joining with this flow from which we have been alienated. In both cases, in the notion of separation or instrumental reason, the risk run is a totalization of such forces into ahistorical abstractions, which dissolves their historical force and modes of articulation into one transhistorical narrative of the fall.

We are not only separated from each other, but also from nature. Di Prima shows an awareness of the ecological as a political matter. So, di Prima suggests a concept of revolution in which 'we will all feel the pinch' and that 'the "necessities", luxuries / will have to go by the board' (#17; see also #34). Contrary to contemporary correlations of revolution with wealth or richness (Ross 2015), di Prima proposed a concept of revolution as sacrifice. Such a position can always be read as coterminous with a reactionary loathing of consumption and the masses, a reactionary anticapitalism. In di Prima, however, the aim of sacrifice resonates with its particular social moment, of the postwar American consumer society. The difficulty remains, however, of grasping sacrifice in a register that does not become another critique of mass society or technological modernity.

Certainly, di Prima offers a defiant rebuff, *avant la lettre*, to those who call us to embrace the powers and forces of capitalist technology and abstraction as the means to achieve a postcapitalist society. This is not surprising, as di Prima was writing at the initial flowering of cybernetic theorization that would develop out of the 1960s moment. She suggests that we repudiate cybernetic and futurist visions of revolution, as a cybernetic civilization will be unable to 'show us our root / our original face' (#33). We have to 'turn off the power, turn on the /stars at night' (#34). Those who premise revolution on 'science fiction utopia' are 'the enemy' who are willing 'to sacrifice the planet' (#19). This repudiation still carries a force against contemporary currents of techno-utopianism that draw on this earlier moment, but it is vulnerable to the charge of regression and mysticism in its celebration of the pretechnological.

If the revolution is one against the despoliation of nature, it is also a natural process. This is the cosmogony of revolution that emerges once we have destroyed all the separations. The revolution is natural, both in the sense of a return to nature and in the older one of the revolution as cyclical, particularly in regard to astral bodies. Koselleck notes that 'revolution, at first derived from the natural movement of the stars and thus introduced into the natural rhythm of history as a cyclical metaphor, henceforth attained an irreversible direction' (2004: 23). Di Prima returns to this notion of revolution as return and away from the sense of irreversible direction. Letter #41 is a key statement: 'Revolution: a turning, as the earth / turns, among planets'. This turning is also a turning from the dark to the light, to a dawn, and so revolution turns and returns. The turn is also a turn to the beginning, to the root, as it is not 'western civilization, but civilization itself / is the disease which is eating us' (#32). We have to ask 'how far back / are we willing to go?' (#33) The future revolution will result in a new tribal society in which our 'great-grandchildren' will be new 'American aborigines' (#24). Revolution will return us to the state in which 'MAN IS INNOCENT & BEAUTIFUL' (#36), and 'left to themselves' people will return to the 'touch of love' (#4). The origin of the universe is in question in the process of writing revolution. The return is one to a cosmic order of birth and death, of return and revolution. This is the final whole to which Di Prima's work speaks: a defence of the power of imagination as the core of the revolution.

These conceptualizations of separation, totality, and nature, which I have treated separately, are all linked together. We are separated from nature, which is the original fall, and we then need a total revolution of all relations, including our relations with nature, to return to an unseparated and natural relation to time and nature. They key problem here, which is where di Prima joins currents of primitivist and anticivilizational thinking that blames civilization itself as the cause of our ills, is to account for the original moment of separation and to return to the previous nonseparated state. It comes as no surprise that one of the major thinkers of anti-civilizational primitivism emerged from Adornonian critical theory and another from the Situationist milieu.[4] In both cases the tendency to posit an original fall—in Adorno forms of mythic rejection of nature, and in Debord the separation imposed by power—license going further and further back to find a moment of innocence. Deleuze and Guattari remarked sarcastically that 'Psychoanalysis is like the Russian Revolution; we don't know when it started going bad. We have to keep going back further' (1983: 55). Instead, primitivist and anticivilizational critiques take this logic seriously, going back further from when the Russian Revolution went bad to when the Neolithic Revolution went awry. Beneath the cobblestones, the beach; beneath capitalist mediations or the mediations of civilization, nature; such conceptualizations are familiar enough objects of critique (Derrida 1976). This impulse is undeniable in the *Letters*, albeit one not much discussed in contemporary appropriations of di Prima. She is making a particular use of the 'savage' and of the critique of civilization as a means to recover or return to forms of integrity violently disrupted by civilization and capitalism,[5] but the result can be a mysticism of the pristine origin and fall that places the revolution outside of history.

The completion of the cosmogony of revolution is one of return, of revolution as a return to other forms and logics oppressed by reason and science; 'to seek help in realms we have been taught to think of / as "mythological" ' (#45). We must 'Seek out / the ancient texts: alchemy / homeopathy, secret charts / or early Rosicrucians (Giordanisti)' and 'LOOK TO THE 'HERESIES' OF EUROPE FOR / BLOODROOTS' (#59; di Prima 1991). These heretical forms of knowledge posit another tradition: one which

---

4 John Zerzan (1998), derives from Adorno and the Frankfurt School, and Fredy Perlman (1983), derives from the Situationists.

5 For a savage critique that uses the state of nature against biopolitical and philosophical imaginations of this state see Federico Luisetti (2016). For a general defence of savage thought, see Eduardo Viveiros de Castro (2014).

rediscovers the whole and which grounds the current revolution (of the 1960s) in a longer process of heresy and revolution as a series of struggles for totality and wholeness. Here di Prima is comparable not so much to Guy Debord, but to another Situationist, Raoul Vaneigem. After falling out with Debord, Vaneigem would pursue revolutionary thought through recovering a mystical vitalism from the heresies of the past (1998). Di Prima also wants to re-establish a longer tradition of knowledge, and we must 'Rewrite the calendar' to discover and recover a new sense of history and time (#59). This is di Prima's intuition of a necessity for totality that can overturn the plastic construct of capitalism, that feigned totality. The difficulty is that it takes the form of a return to hidden knowledge that denies rationality and celebrates myth in ways that deny the critical power of knowledge.

In the contemporary reception, di Prima is often purged of her cosmology and her primitivism, despite these modes of thinking still being prevalent in New Age movements and amongst radicals. The di Prima of the riot form is the di Prima of the insurrectional letters at the expense of this 'other', cosmological, di Prima. My point is not simply to rehabilitate this other di Prima, as I am sceptical of this strain of primitivism as a solution. In fact, in our moment, we witness some oscillation between concepts of revolution that embrace the technological and the revival of forms of mysticism and occultism. We also often see strange fusions, in which technological capacities are geared to the generation of new mythologies or forms of mysticism. This is a kind of internal oscillation. We are not, therefore, necessarily beyond di Prima's moment, nor have we successfully integrated a thinking that can avoid such divisions or oscillations (Fluss and Frim 2021). In the case of reading di Prima, we need to integrate the cosmological mysticism that risks being antiscience and hostile to reason because we need to understand how the turn to myth embodies a particular understanding of revolution as cosmological. That does not mean we have to accept the antiscience position as such. We do, however, need to understand the hostility to reason and science to understand what is at stake in this particular adventure of the sign, this form of cultural revolution, which aims to overturn mediation and abstraction for a new integrated poetics.

The Course of Revolution

What, then, is the course of the revolution? The *Letters* trace the course of revolution as return, but they also follow the waning or ebbing of revolution as the long '60s come to an end and the counter-revolution begins. In fact, the *Letters* offer a complex temporality of revolution, not least because di Prima concertedly questioned logics of the revolution which understand it as unfolding, as simply another step within the modern. This temporality of simple progression is one that belongs to bourgeois revolutions, which, according to Marx, 'storm quickly from success to success' (2010: 150). Di Prima links this conception of time as linear progress to science, in which if 'we submit / to a system based on causality, linear time / we submit, again, to the old value' (#51). Linear causality is rejected to open up the problem of revolution to alternative temporal modes. This is the refusal of a scientific cosmogony, whose only purpose is 'to drain / hope of contact or change' (#63). Again, we have notes of antiscience and an opposition to teleology itself driven by a desire of return. Yet, the complexity of time registers tensions and potentialities within this primitivism.

Certainly, return and revolution, as the revolving of astral bodies, are one of the primary forms of this alternative temporality. This cyclical temporality, of the turning earth, is a return that is also a disruption. It has to differentiate itself from the cyclical form of capital and the cyclical form of defeat: 'History repeats itself / only if we let it' (#62). The question of turns and returns is a complex one. Deleuze remarks of Nietzsche's eternal return that it is not just a matter of a return of everything, but a selective ontology in which what returns is only the active (1983: 72). Similarly, di Prima's return to an aboriginal state is not just a return to the past, but the return to a new future. In this future making of the aboriginal we will contrast the new 'American aborigines' with 'the affluent / highly civilized Africans' who will now be trading for American artefacts (#24). In this imagined future the return is one of reversal, in which America has returned to its aboriginal state to repeal the long history of American violence, to overcome and obliterate the particular settler-colonial logic of the United States. Although, of course, such a vision risks obscuring the experience of indigenous peoples, those native Americans who were the actual 'American aborigines', or even repeating their erasure by settler-colonialism. Africa, by contrast, has embraced a technological future, in a quasi-Afrofuturist vision, which gives restitution for the despoliation and violence inflicted on that continent and its people. While aiming at a restitution, a recovery, and a rearrangement of American imperial power, at home and abroad, such a return as reversal is still haunted by the settler violence it tries to exorcize.

Di Prima's poetic turning is also not a turning in the sense that Heidegger gives it. In the case of Heidegger absolute domination by technology, as a form of danger, creates the possibility of a saving that can transcend technology's limits (1977: 36–49). The turn is a turn to Being (and of Being itself), which in its absolute subsumption by technology is somehow revealed as a possibility irreducible to technology. In Heidegger's writing, technology is something like a necessary evil, which by pushing Being to its point of greatest danger, where it will be completely forgotten and enframed, also opens the possibility to transcend technology. While not simply an antitechnology, Heidegger's vision lends itself to a thinking of Being and the turn that denies the form and possibilities of revolution. Heidegger's turning is the simulacral revolution of the transcending of technology, which the Nazis did not complete (1959: 199). It is a revolution or turning against the emancipatory project and process of revolution. While it might share superficial similarities with some movements in di Prima, it must be distinguished. The temptation of the Heideggerian reading of poetry, as we have seen, is a recurrent one. Di Prima's turn opens up a multiplicity of times, suggesting a turning back for America and an advance for Africa, a turn as a reversal of positions and not simply the escape from technology or some vision of poetic or fascist mastery.

The *Letters* also attend to the course of revolution as one that is explicitly transitional. In letter #10 di Prima suggests that 'These are transitional years and the dues / will be heavy'. These dues include a recognition that 'Change is quick but revolution / will take a while', which is an important reflection on the temporality of '68 and of the tendency to mistake change for revolution. The immediacy, then, that di Prima demands is one that recognizes revolution to be a slow process of dismantling and an organic process of growth. The *Letters*, as an evolving process, are themselves the form of this slow and organic process of paying dues and taking the time of the revolution. In summary, then, we could argue that di Prima's poetics is a vision of what Luigi Pintor calls retractive revolution: a revolution that 'restores inner rhythms and inner restraints, abolishing clocks', and understands 'the gestures that brush living things and inanimate ones, and say more than the articulate words we are proud of' (2013: 113).

The thinking of the time of revolution as a transitional time suggests that the revolution will not be easy. In contrast to di Prima's images of return to primal innocence, or the recovery of a future state 'aboriginal' state, we can read her work as struggling with language, with signs and representation, to present revolution as a complex space of rhythm and restraint. While she can easily conform to what I called the war on language—trying to exit the sign and language for a fusion of sign and referent, or even mute fusion with reality—I also want to suggest her writing attests to that war of language, an internal struggle. There is something valuable in di Prima's attempt at direct address and a certain simplicity of language, which is allied to this belief in the reality of revolution. At the same time, this simplicity comes under the pressure of events, of the recognition revolution does not storm to success in the linear manner of the bourgeois revolution.

The insurrectional revolution will be one that obeys its own temporality, that of growing from a seed. The revolution is organic not, as conservative polemics often claim, an instance of what is antinatural. This organic revolution is, however, not simply something that grows without tending and without activity. The practical dimensions of the *Letters* are part of this cosmological vision of the course of revolution. This is also embodied in the form of the *Letters*. Letters are urgent, but can be slow, they demand and they report, they beg and they cajole. They ask for a reply, for a correspondence, they go astray, but they inhabit a temporality that has now largely passed. The range of poetic interventions in the *Letters*, from advice to cosmology, suggest the scope of revolution that engages all and everything. This is, in the end, a cosmic process in which the cosmos is at stake.

The *Letters* are didactic; they are lessons in revolution. Certainly, they reject various errors that would put the revolution off course, from cybernetic utopias to the rejection of violence. At the same time di Prima also notes that:

NO ONE WAY WORKS, it will take all of us
shoving at the thing from all sides
to bring it down. (#8)

The course of revolution retains this unpredictable element, veering off course and taking multiple paths. The return is not simple and neither is the process of insurrection. Di Prima rejects the idea that we put bodies in the line of fire, a sacrificial logic of militancy and masculinity. She suggests that we study the Sioux and their ghost dance (#45), a revolution of despair, apocalyptic and millennial, as a lesson that we should not repeat (Davis 2003: 23–31). The struggle against power should not be suicidal, but involves maintaining and preserving our capacities for struggle. Revolution is a matter of repetition, but repetition that learns.

This revolution, as I have already suggested, is not my revolution. In fact, what I have called the other di Prima is, precisely, an insistence on this cosmological vision of revolution by word and deed, or the fusion of both. It is a magical and mystical revolution. Despite the contemporary and continuing interest or fascination with the magical, the mystical, and the occult, it is remarkable that this side of di Prima's work is not better attended to. It is worth remembering di Prima's words from a text considering the work of the alchemist Paracelsus: 'The whole of modern criticism has as its aim the softening of the statements of poets, alchemists, philosophers, into something symbolical and therefore twice removed and digestible without effort and without faith' (1991: 30). I remain a modern critic, although I have tried to take seriously di Prima's own effort and faith. Di Prima is insistent that such secularizing readings rob the work of its power, as once you learn magic you must also learn to believe if not 'you undercut / your power' (#46). The cosmogony of the *Letters* is one predicated on this belief, on this sense of power of the word in its materiality. While this can be read as the expression of the performative dimension of language, of the power of certain words to make things happen, such an easy turn away from the cosmological fails to take di Prima's own thought seriously.

Revolution Redux

Di Prima's *Letters* have returned in the present moment, although they have not arrived at their destination. The revolution has still not run its course, although the old mole may still be grubbing. At present, the cosmological and mystical return in the usual fragmented and kitsch forms, if not in the service of reaction. The sense of the cosmological is not often truly felt, although it sometimes remains in fugitive forms. Di Prima's heavy optimism is hard to recapture, but perhaps worth considering in relation to all the various leaps to immediacy that can be traced in the poetics and other writings of the riot form. At the same time, we should not read a simple optimism into di Prima—a happier, better revolution from which we have fallen away. Di Prima, in an appreciation of the Swiss alchemist, notes that 'the world into which Paracelsus was born was at least as complicated as our own' (1991: 26). While it might seem as unutterably distant, the world into which di Prima was born and wrote is also at least as complicated as our own. The innocence of revolution has not been lost, and di Prima's own thoughts and meditations on the complex course of revolution as return suggest we should not suppose or project onto her writing an ease that we cannot feel.

At the same time, I obviously maintain a critical relation to this desire to end all separation, a desire that can fly too close to the war on language and the demand to destroy all abstraction. The leap to the concrete can shoot too fast, and result in magical constructs and fabulations in the negative sense—a fanciful wishing away of actual conditions. Marx remarked that 'As a rule, the most general abstractions arise only in the midst of the richest possible concrete development, where one thing appears as common to many, to all' (1973: 104). It is also worth noting that for Marx such a development was to be found 'in the most modern form of existence of bourgeois society—in the United States'. Di Prima, as a poet writing from that site, the place of plastic constructs, lives in the density of those forms of abstraction. The reaction against them is obvious and necessary, even if the transition through them becomes difficult and problematic. These are not surprising developments. The burden that is placed on us, a heavy burden no doubt, is to dialectically think both thin abstractions and the rich concrete together, especially as those thin abstractions have not ceased proliferating. We cannot and should not contrast the thin abstraction to a rich other world.

To simplify dramatically, di Prima's cosmogony is one of a return to a moment or form of life before abstraction. The totality is intuited and established, but it risks remaining outside history, on its edge, unable to develop. This is countered by her attention to the process of revolution, but this process needs attachment to a developing history. If di Prima searches for a life before abstraction and a future exit from abstraction, the current adoption of the *Letters* tends to celebrate them as a revolutionary war on abstraction. The focus of readings like that of Clover are on the immediate aid the *Letters* offer to the process of overturning abstraction. This is not incorrect, in fact, it is central to di Prima's poetics. The difficulty is that in leaving aside the broader cosmological claims on which di Prima rests some of the complexity, ambiguity, and tension of the *Letters* is lost. We lose the sense of the need for spiritual revolution and lost tradition, which runs alongside appropriations of existing technologies. We also lose the sense of the *Letters* as documents of defeat as well as defiance, of holding on as well as breaking through. Contemporary readings could be taken as valuable correctives to the more problematic and even embarrassing elements of di Prima's primitivism, especially for the modern critic (or modern revolutionary). And yet, the cosmological desire of the *Letters* also attests to a desire for totality beyond the limits of capitalist civilization, even if that might be mistaken for civilization itself. They also attest to the difficulties of revolution and transition, which the martial forms of contemporary revolution, at least in the riot form, risk disavowing (Clover 2016b). The *Letters* are a work of revolution that inhabit the course of a revolution that went astray and failed, one that we live after.

There is an irony here. We might be returning to the *Letters* to find a seemingly simpler and more hopeful time, a time when revolution was on the table. That sense of immediacy and imminent revolution is then supposed to resonate with our moment, which, while less hopeful, wants to reclaim the necessity of urgent revolution. Today, it is suggested, the density and complexity of capitalist abstraction, the overwhelming material reality of capitalist society, demands an absolute break. More than that, it is argued that the unsustainability of contemporary capitalism, its inability to guarantee a liveable life, might provide the condition for a new revolutionary leap. This hypothesis, formed from various and conflictual currents of communization theory, insurrectional anarchism, and material experiences of conflict, converges with di Prima's *Letters* in the desire for an immediate practice of revolution. What I am suggesting, is that di Prima's impersonal poetics contains more complex lessons and more challenges, in part by thinking through the failure of revolution as immediacy. Of course, to celebrate complexity for its own sake can easily be an ideological gesture. That is not my aim. Instead, to return to di Prima, to read di Prima, is to explore the possibilities and problems of revolution. It is to suggest that our return to simplicity is not just naïve, but also does not offer a simple solution. Instead, the desire to create a direct language is one we should pursue, and that includes grasping when a simplicity falls short. Direct language involves complexity and simplicity, involves notions of integrity and wholeness, as well as difference and dispersion, insurrection and the slower work of retractive revolution. This, I think, is the impersonal lesson we can learn from di Prima.

CHAPTER SIX

1794 / 1982
British Sounds

Perhaps the factory has no language but only makes sounds? When Marx descended into the 'hidden abode of production' in *Capital* (1990: 279), he entered into a realm where the working class was 'stunned at first by the noise and turmoil of the new system of production' (390). It would take time until the class 'had recovered its senses to some extent, [and] it began to offer resistance'. The factory is a site of the systematic derangement of the senses, a place that scatters our wits, and is antithetical to language and sense making. To read the language of the factory is to read the absence of language. Marx writes of the factory:

> Every sense organ is injured by the artificially high temperatures, by the dust-laden atmosphere, *by the deafening noise*, not to mention danger to life and limb among machines which are so closely crowded together, a danger which, with the regularity of the seasons, produces its list of those killed and wounded in the industrial battle. (522; my emphasis)

The class struggle takes on a tangible and deafening form. It is a battle in which the aural violence of capital is realized on the body and realized as noise.

Marx would rely on reports by factory inspectors to grasp the nature of this new assemblage that epitomizes the violence and despotism of capitalist production. These reports provide the language of the factory in the absence of the language of the workers. Marx's materialist reading of the hidden abode of production is a second-hand reading—a reading of a reading—which is an abstraction necessary to capture this primary experience. Marx, famously sat in the reading room of the British library, analysed the forces of abstraction in their materiality through a process of reading and listening to what was said and what was not. What these reports record is 'the voracious appetite of the capitalists for surplus labour' (349). The factory inspectors scrupulously list the various extractions of extra time carried out by the mill owners, 'a petty pilfering of minutes' (352), as they put it. They also report the medical effects on workers, who are 'stunted in growth, ill-shaped, and frequently ill-formed in the chest' (355). The inspectors and commissioners provide a catalogue of abuses and violence. This is the record we have of the violence of the factory, the language which replaces or interprets the sounds of the factory.

And yet, Marx is also dialectically attentive to the powers unleashed by the factory, including the powers of the working class. The task is to read the factory not only as a site of alienation, but also of objectified powers that must be reappropriated. In the *1844 Manuscripts* Marx writes: 'it can be seen how the history of *industry* and the *objective* existence of industry as it has developed is the *open* book of the essential powers of man' (1975: 354). Marx aims to make this book legible, to return us to the capacity to read in industry our own powers. But what if that attempt to read is overcome by sound? This is one way to read the struggle over the factory and the struggle over the language of the factory—a confrontation between language and the materiality of sound. If, according to Alain Badiou (2014a: 145), 'capital has always written the factory', then how can we write and read the factory otherwise? It might not only be that capital has written the factory, but also that the sound of the factory destroys writing. Gilbert Simondon asserts that 'all the prestigious colour photographs of sparks, of fumes, all the recordings of noise, sounds, or images, generally remain a use [*exploitation*] of technical reality and not a revelation of this reality' (2017: 236). Simondon inadvertently echoes Brecht's earlier remark that 'a photograph of the Krupp's factory or AEG reveals next to nothing about these institutions' (Brecht quoted in

Benjamin 2015: 92). Photographs might be inadequate, language is compromised, but here I want to turn to poetry.

Poetry is a form that works on the materiality of language as sound. It approaches the noise of the factory to make use of that sound and to read those powers in the book of the factory. Certainly, I am not suggesting poetry simply replaces photography or analysis. Poetry can be read together with and as an analytic intervention as much as a practice of sound. There is something, however, in the attention of poetry to the materiality of language, of language as sound, which does accord it a privilege in grasping the relations of language, materiality and abstraction at work in the factory. I explore this writing and reading of the factory through two poets, William Blake and Leslie Kaplan, and through a temporally divided structure. This chapter is also divided between the birth of the factory and what it would be too easy to call its end, but is more accurately termed its displacement and silencing. Badiou notes that 'the factory, so to speak, is anti-Hegelian (2014a: 142). If for Hegel time is the presence of the concept, here time, devoid of all meaning, succumbs to exteriority'; of course, Hegel was well aware that 'factories, manufacturing, base their subsistence on the misery of one class' (1983). If the factory lacks time, as well as language and meaning, then perhaps it must be treated in a divided way to give it a relation to language and meaning that is not exterior. The factory is an exteriority that is intimately inside our societies, and it is this relation that is obscure. Blake and Kaplan are not the only voices or sounds at work here. There is the Soviet modernist Andrei Platonov, Jean-Luc Godard's film *British Sounds* (1969), Nanni Balestrini's 1971 novel *We Want Everything*, Pietro Perotti and Pier Milanese's 2014 documentary *Senzachiedereper-messo* [Without asking permission], and the theoretical reflections of Jean-François Lyotard, Alain Badiou, and Maurice Blanchot on factory writing. In all this we have a small but precious corpus of writing on the factory. The spacing of these moments, the range of writing, are all crucial to capture and determine the concentration of powers that compose the 'factory site' (Badiou 2006).

Forging the Factory

The factory is the site of machines. It is the machine, both actual and figural, which is the key to grasping the productive forces, and so *a fortiori* the factory. Marx, in *Capital*, noted that it is with the machine that alienation and inversion is fully achieved. The 'automaton' is 'the shape of capital, of dead labour, that dominates, and pumps dry, living labour-power' (Marx 1990: 548). The reactionary German Romantic Adam Müller wrote, in 1816:

> Man needs a many-sided, even an all-rounded, sphere for his activity, limited and restricted as this activity itself may be [. . .] But if the division of labour, as it is now being practised in the big cities and the manufacturing and mining areas, cuts-up free man into wheels, cogs, cylinders and shuttles, imposes on him one sphere of activity in the course of his many-sided search for one object—how can one expect this segmented segment to be adequate to the full and fulfilled life or right and law? (quoted in Avineri 1968: 55)

Here the machine is a device of fragmentation and segmentation, a figure of the division of labour that reduces or divides humans into a mimesis of the machine. Humans are machines. This reactionary Romanticism, driven by a desire to return to unity, to wholeness, to a mythical past, is a movement that Marx will definitively reject. Marx's reading of the powers of the factory is a reading of alienation and fragmentation, but also of new powers and new possibilities composed within the factory.

To read this dialectic of alienation and new powers we must turn away from the nostalgia of reactionary Romanticism, its feudal socialism (Marx and Engels 1973), and towards radical Romanticism. Here the machine and the factory compose powers as well as alienate them, and the factory must be read as a new world. I will focus on the British poet, engraver and radical, William Blake.

Blake's *Songs of Innocence and of Experience* (1794) offers a dialectic between these 'two contrary states of the human soul' (1967),[1] but this dialectic also encompasses the new world of manufacturing. The *Songs of Experience*, in particular, reflect on the forging of the human soul out of a series of productive processes. In fact, Saree Makdisi argues that Blake is the poet of production, whose work is dominated by processes of making (and making noise): 'think [. . .] of all those hammers, anvils, bellows, tongs; think of all the measuring, stretching, pulling, cutting, fracturing, compassing' (2003: 263). Robert Essick (quoted in Makdisi 2003: 263) remarks that 'Blake may be our noisiest poet'. Blake is the poet who brings together production and noise, production and poetry, and new sense of production that can exceed capitalist production.

Blake notes that human powers are subject to the violent division and fragmentation of the forces of *ratio*: science, philosophy and the forms of capitalist labour. This is evident in Blake's poem 'London' (plate 46), from his *Songs of Experience*:

I wander thro' each charter'd street,
Near where the charter'd Thames does flow,
And mark in every face I meet
Marks of weakness, marks of woe.

'Charter'd' refers to the power of charters and corporations to dictate the flow of humans through streets and the flow of nature, particularly in the form of the river Thames. We witness here the enclosure of life, its containment, separation and subjection to the forces of capitalist production in 'Marks of weakness, marks of woe' (Linebaugh 2014). This form of enclosure reaches into the soul of the individual, in the 'mind forg'd manacles' Blake sees as chaining the psyche (plate 46).

---

1 All further in-text citations of Blake's *Songs of Innocence and of Experience* will reference the respective plate number in the 1967 facsimile edition edited by Geoffrey Keynes.

Unlike the reactionary Romantic anticapitalists, Blake does not simply decry the imposition of *ratio*. Blake's work is not simply nostalgic for some prior state of innocence, but concerned with forging a dialectic between innocence and experience. This is evident in 'The Tyger'. The tiger is the tiger of wrath, 'wiser than the horses of instruction' of *The Marriage of Heaven and Hell* (1794) (Blake 1975: *xix*, plate 9), which incarnates a primal energy and violence. The tiger is a force beyond *ratio*: 'What immortal hand or eye, / Could frame thy fearful symmetry?' (plate 42) The fearful symmetry of the tiger's powers exceeds the geometric powers of *ratio*. The violent force of the tiger is also the force of the revolutionary masses: the French people, according to the London *Times* of 7 January 1792, had become 'more ferocious than wolves and tigers' (quoted in Erdman 1977: 195). Blake traces a revolutionary eruption of energy, 'burning bright', which overturns the existing order.

This insurgent force is also a force forged and made—manufactured. The tiger is not purely natural or excessive, an abstract potentiality, but a force that emerges through industrial processes:

What the hammer? what the chain,
In what furnace was thy brain?
What the anvil? what dread grasp,
Dare its deadly terrors clasp! (plate 42)

It is the hammer, chain, furnace and anvil that are invoked as the sources of the tiger's energy, even if they escape imagination. This is a force of excess within and over the industrial process.

For J. H. Prynne, the tiger 'seems created from burning and hammering' (1993: 25). Prynne reads the poem as a metaphor of the blast furnace, dependent for its fuel, charcoal, on 'the forest of the night' (26). Blake's poem is one of 'violent metallurgy' (27), hammering out and smelting signifiers to create a new image of production. In the words of Barthes, borrowed by Prynne, this is language as 'incandescent metal' (31). In particular, Prynne suggests, 'Blake's active, working outlook was in these terms profoundly ambivalent and transitional: to tap energy and to break free required the directed battery of the individual metal-forger's hammer' (29). Prynne's reading confirms that Blake is a poet of production and, more particularly, industrial production or proto-industrial production. The forces and forms of this poetic are not simply or only a mystical vitalism, although this should not be denied, but also of the powers of life constantly transformed into noisy motion.

Perry Anderson remarks that Blake 'had an acute feel for dialectical opposition, but much less for surpassal or synthesis' (1980: 170). Similarly, although in a more celebratory fashion, Maurice Blanchot declares that Blake 'wants to unite contradiction in himself not to resolve it or surmount it but to maintain it in its constant tension' (2001: 30). These negative dialectical readings of Blake do not do justice to the dialectical moment in his poetry. The tiger is the moment of synthesis, and not only of opposition or tension. This is evident as the tiger integrates, dialectically, with the lamb, Blake's symbol of innocence. The integration of ferocity and innocence is evident in the strangely benign appearance of the tiger. In particular, the tiger synthesizes the powers of production and revolution, making these powers legible within the chartering and symmetries of *ratio*. This is a poetics of production that dialectically reads the scene of the beginning of the factory, in which the channelling or capture of the forces of energy—human and carbon—unleashes powers that cannot be controlled. This is the primal scene of fossil capital. In Blake, the potentiality of revolution is discerned in the figure of the tiger as a figure of production that dialectically integrates innocence and experience, the oppression of industrial production and the possibility of revolution.

Blake conceived his own engraving and poetry as a violent process of making: 'by printing in the infernal method, by corrosives, which in Hell are salutary and medicinal, melting apparent surfaces away, and displaying the infinite which was hid' (Blake (1975: plate 14). In the case of the tiger, David Erdman makes explicit the cosmo-political stakes of Blake's vision:

> The creative blacksmith who seizes the molten stuff of terror and shapes it into living form on the cosmic anvil must employ dread power as well as daring and art, but the dread, Blake hopes, will be sufficient unto the day. The climax of the forging is a mighty hammering which drives out the impurities in a shower of sparks, like the falling stars children call angels' tears. (1977: 196)

Hammering does not only involve pounding the industrial worker into machine shapes, the forging of humans into segments, but also the dialectic that forges an insurgent force that exercises deadly terrors against *ratio*. Blake creates a dialectic between class struggle and the productive forces, a synthesis of violent making and unmaking.

Blake's tiger finds a later echo in Andrei Platonov's novel of Bolshevik modernism *The Foundation Pit*, written in 1930. In the novel, set on a collective farm, we encounter 'the unknown proletarian', a bear, who is hammering at the forge and growling 'some happy song' (Platonov 2009: 127).[2] The bear, inspired to become a shock worker by party slogans, hammers violently at iron, 'expending all his furious, speechless joy into the zeal of labour' (128). The peasants are frightened that this violent, accelerated, labour will destroy the molten iron, shouting 'don't torment matter!' (130). The Stalinist politics of production—taking place, as they did, under the most primitive of conditions—torment matter in an act of cosmic violence.[3] Stalinist shock production was notoriously inefficient, wasteful and environmentally catastrophic. Annie Epelboin argues, in her notes on the text, that the bear 'wanting to force open the doors of the future, [...] threatens to return the world to primordial chaos. Wanting to force the pace, to accelerate time, [...] [he] shows us that time is reversible' (222). The violence of shock work, the

---

2 Oxana Timofeeva (2018: 151–81) discusses the 'poor life' of Platonov's animals.

3 On the artistic expressions of 'shock work', see Owen Hatherley (2016).

attempt to punch through time, reverts matter and humanity to a primal state of chaos. Platonov's acute reading suggests that the legibility of the book of industry can become an illegible chaos and violence, a hammering that does not hammer out the future, but instead one that begets destruction. The very attempt to master and control production unleashes a destructive effect that shatters development into regression. If Blake reveals the forces that arise at the emergent moment of the capitalist factory, Platonov traces the destructive forces that emerge as the attempt to revolutionize production turns towards a Stalinist politics of production.

Georges Bataille, writing of Blake, noted that 'everything within him came to a halt before the necessity which entails laborious activity in a factory' (1985: 96). We might dispute Bataille, however, by saying that Blake does not simply remain before the factory but also sees the possibility of forging the soul that lies within the factory. Powers of humans and nature (especially carbon) are captive in the factory, which will reconfigure those powers and, against its intent release revolutionary forces. Those forces, as we see in Platonov, can regress into chaos in response to the Stalinist storming of production. Here the legible powers of production become unreadable and the revolution regresses to the mimicry of capitalism. We might add that in capitalism such powers have also been rendered illegible and uncontrollable in a mode of production concerned primarily with the generation of surplus value at all cost. In Blake there is a dialectical tension maintained between poet and production, worker and capital, precisely at that moment of the making of the English working class (Thompson 1991). Blake's poetry is a poetics of forging and sound that attempts to render this new industrial soundscape into a radical new poetics.

Flights from the Factory

In the factory sound drowns language. This is made evident in Jean-Luc Godard's film *British Sounds* (1969), which begins with the extreme noise of the car production line at Ford in Dagenham. The tracking shot down the line, which mimics the long tracking shot of Godard's earlier *Weekend* (1967) along a line of stalled and wrecked cars in an apocalyptic traffic jam, is now a shot of production that encompasses sound. If *Weekend* is the image of the car abandoned at the end of the world, this is the image and sound of the making of the car as model of capitalist production. These are the British sounds of the drill whine, of shouting, hammering, sawing and banging. In the film this industrial noise is the basis, which will have to be transformed into language, of the spectre of communism haunting Britain. It is central to Godard's tour of what Tariq Ali called *The Coming British Revolution* (1972). This was a revolution that did not arrive, although in 1974 the miners would topple a Conservative government in Britain's own '68. Godard's transformation is one from British sounds to language, in the form of interviews with the workers, and then a shift out of the factory and to occupying students. These are competing sounds: the din of industrial production that threatens to drown out the sound of class struggle, which Godard's film tries to render as audible. It lives, however, with the hope of revolution displaced from production.

This flight from the factory is echoed in Nanni Balestrini's *We Want Everything* (*Vogliamo Tutto*) (2016[1971]), a fictional memoir of a factory militant at the Fiat Mirafiori factory in Turin. What is striking is how little is actually said about the factory in the novel. This text is structured by the refusal of work, especially as enacted, primarily, by internal migrants from the Italian South to Fiat in the Italian 'hot autumn' of 1969. The text, however, regards the factory as a Dantean inferno. Contrary to the spatial precision of Dante's text, this hell is inchoate and lacking focus. Attention is given to struggles over the work process in the factory, but the primary focus is on urban militancy and the flight from the factory. This is certainly true to the social and political experience of the time and the text tells the story of the galvanizing effects of a militancy addressed to immediate demands rather than political abstractions. The language of the text is not one of sound but of slogans and the militant possibilities of language, of emergent speech and demands that come from the workers. The difficulty remains, however, of the occlusion and displacement of the factory, subsumed under a politicization that was certainly real and active but that also struggled with the inscription of the factory as site and suppressor of struggles. Godard and Balestrini trace a necessary movement of militancy that departs from the sounds of the factory that drown out possibilities of politics and articulation, but it is a movement that struggles to engage with the factory as a site that can itself be transformed. The division of factory and the social is rendered but not escaped.

In a more concrete form, such an emergence of competing sounds is also traced in the 2014 documentary *Senzachiedereper-messo* [Without asking permission] by Pietro Perotti and Pier Milanese. The film concerns the militant experience of Perotti in the Fiat Mirafiori factory in Turin from 1969 to 1985, the same factory as in Balestrini's novel. Perotti made his own documentary films in that period, silent due to the technological limitations of the time, and participated in the aesthetics of protest by making various puppets and figures for demonstrations. At issue, however, is also noise. Perotti recalls the noise of the factory, simulating it by making sounds with his mouth: the sparks of welding, 'zin, zin, zin'; the grinders, 'zzzzzz'; the small metal presses, 'tum, tum, tum', like machine guns; the medium presses, like mortars, 'bom, bom, bom'; the big presses, with their deep noise, 'badaboom, badaboom, badaboom'; the shrill noise of machine tools, 'iiiiii', like animals or birds. In response, to call protests over this deafening noise, the workers took to banging steel drums, using hub caps as makeshift cymbals, or blowing whistles. This would continue into the marches and protests outside the factory, bringing the noise of the factory out into the streets. In this case we witness a war of noise, a battle to exceed the sound of capitalist production with a new militant sub-jectivity. The advantage of this film is that it also traces the moment of the destruction of the factory, with mass lay-offs in the early 1980s. Once the biggest factory in Europe, now Fiat Mirafiori remains in limited operation. The factory has been displaced, not by revolution, but by capitalist reorganization and counter-revolution.

This sound of the factory is explored in all its density and ambiguity by Jean-François Lyotard. In his 1974 book *Libidinal Economy*, Lyotard has insisted that the worker desired the experi-ence of the factory and 'enjoyed the mad destruction of their organic body which was indeed imposed upon them' (1993: 111). The libidinal economy of capitalism is also a libidinal economy of the worker and of production, not only of consumption. We have got used to the notion that commodities embody desire, or the insight of the early theorists of marginalist economics, such as William Jevons (1970), that price embodies a desire. What is less evident is that the labour-power commodity embodies a desire and libido. Lyotard's disturbing vision forces us to think what is at stake in the mad destruction inflicted on the organic body of the worker.

This mad destruction is also a matter of sound. For Lyotard the worker's ear is in question; drawing on a study by Dr Alfred A. Tomatis of a worker who sat next to an alternator functioning at 20,000 hertz and could not hear this sound Lyotard speaks of the 'hysterical treatment of a fraction of the auditory body' (1993: 111). As with Freud's case studies, in which hysterical paralysis freezes a part of the body, here the worker nullifies their own ear in a kind of paralysis of sound. The infernal din of the factory—the sound that threatens to drown out thought and sense—is nullified in the configuration of a new body that composes both mechanical and physical elements. This is, according to Lyotard, evidence of 'the extraordinary dissimulated-dissimulating force of the worker' (111), but this is a force that does not destroy these conditions but lives with them.

The worker emerges in parallel with the hysteric as a figure of simulation and dissimulation, tracing a strange body invested with libidinal forces that constitute a new experimental arrangement. This is Lyotard's further provocation. Not only does the worker desire to enter the factory, contrasting all those images collected by Harun Farocki of workers hastening to leave the factory (2006), but once in the factory the worker creates a new libidinal body out of sound. This turns on the worker's ear, as an example of such an experimental intensity, as much an avant-garde production with its particular hysterical insensitivity as the sensitivities of Nietzsche's ear (Derrida 1985). In one sense this seems to celebrate the worker. The worker is as much a radical figure of modernity as the Freudian hysteric or the avant-garde artist, combining the capacity of the hysteric for bodily transformation with the capacity of the avant-garde for transforming the experience of modernity into art. And yet, this praise is profoundly ambiguous, leaving the actual worker, and their suffering, behind as they come to be inscribed as the cutting-edge figures of a new libidinal world of pure intensities.

For Lyotard, we cannot speak of alienation. There is no alienation from a previous state of self-possession or an essence, only a series of displacements and new investments of libidinal forces that temporarily coalesce into bodies and arrangements. It is no surprise that *Libidinal Economy* lost Lyotard so many friends on the left. In that book, we do not have a dialectic of alienation, but rather mutations of libidinal intensity in which suffering cannot be measured or is instead tracked as another modulation of desire. This profound transformation of bodily experience is further explored by Lyotard in his 1977 work *Duchamp's Transformers*, where the factory becomes the site of an avant-garde experience of mechanical acesis (1990: 14). The result of the worker being in the factory was the creation of a body that exceeded measurement, which was beyond the usual tolerances of the human, and which constituted an inhuman body. The worker inhabited, or needed to inhabit, a new sensibility, so the workers would not be the passive victims of the industrial environment but actively develop a new 'mechanical asceticism' (15, 16, 17). Lyotard retains from his previous commitment to radical communism, in his role in the group

Socialisme ou barbarie, a refusal to condescend to the worker as victim. He also retains a suspicion of socialism as a palliative that relies on the suffering of the worker to make moral and political claims for restitution. Now, however, these commitments take on the hue of capitalist apologetics: industrial battle is drowned out by industrial immersion.

In different ways, all these texts form a response to the global struggles of 1968 and the exodus from the factory. They interrupt or punctuate our two moments and stand witness to the desire to flee the factory, but they often occlude the factory as a chronic site of struggles. Lyotard's reflections stand at the limit of this kind of narrative, in which we are called to the factory not so much as the location of struggles but as a site of absorption and experimentation. Here, life is not transformed by fleeing the factory, but the factory is transformed into a machine that forms the life of a new avant-garde. It remains, however, another flight from the factory in which that experience of production is flattened into the pulsation of libidinal intensities. Now, the factory forms the closed horizon and resistance is only legible as mutation or as the hysterical silence that emerges in libidinal transformation. The flight from the factory would be solidified by the forces of de-industrialization in the capitalist heartlands, so that new landscape of struggles became harder to read, hear or sound (Neel 2018).

Factory Inferno

Leslie Kaplan's work *Excess—The Factory* (2018[1982]) is a descent into hell. The poem is arranged in circles, echoing Dante's *Inferno*, and draws on Kaplan's own experience as a Maoist *établi*—one of the many Maoist militants who went into the factory for purposes of political agitation after 1968 (Jason E. Smith 2013). The two years she spent working in factories would result in the book of poetry being produced ten years later, which was only recently translated into English. Kaplan's factory hell is one of space and matter, not sounds. While the poetry is delicate and exists in what seem to be fragments, the factory appears within this space of the poem as a saturating presence of matter; as Kaplan puts it, 'You are in matter that expands, fat matter, plastic and stiff' (2018: 99). In an interview accompanying the English translation Kaplan notes that her previous experience of teaching working-class students how to read drew her attention to 'the material difficulty of environment' (2017). The materiality of language and the lived environment of the factory are a similar experience of material difficulty for the working class. Materiality impinges on space and on language, leaving no room for expression. My pairing of Blake and Kaplan does not imply a symmetry between them. Kaplan's factory is not the noisy, clanging scene of forging of Blake's proto-factory workshop. Instead, we move from the possibilities of matter to an accumulated inertia, from the beginning of the factory to its end, but an end that does not end but persists in endless repetition.

The factory occupies all space. It is almost the parody of externalized space 'outside of / time' (Kaplan 2018: 13), which Badiou identified as the signature space of the factory (2014a: 142). For Badiou, this exteriority is one that writers on the factory struggle to capture, precisely because they are militants and not workers. Factory language should be mimetic to the factory, without the subject, compact and limited. While it would be too simple to absolve Kaplan's poetry of these problems, we would prefer to say it tries to confront this exteriority as space and engage this space as one with a subject. We do not have the choice between militant subjectivity and the supposed objectivity of the factory, but enter a space that requires a new formation of subjectivity. To create this involves working with how the factory occupies space, an occupation that has 'become waste' (Kaplan 2018: 15), a sticky space, in which time is congealed in things. It is not surprising then that 'You eat caramels, your teeth are stuck together' (16). The factory is also a space of the subject, but one gummed into silence. In the factory 'Thought is sticky' (55), and 'Matter is really strong' (30). The mediation of language between thought and matter is one rendered sticky and forced to engage with the strength of matter that resists being said. It is not so much the ear of the worker, although that is involved, but also the mouth. The mouth is rendered silent. Kaplan is aware of her own exteriority to the worker, due to her position as a militant, but tries to express this silencing of the worker.

If the sticky lies on the side of thought, we find on the side of matter 'Parts and scraps, the factory' (18). The factory occupies space, but it is waste, scraps and remains that fill up this space: 'Disarticulated and full, the factory' (47). Kaplan's language becomes these scraps and fragments, with modulated repetitions across the circles of hell. This is a language at its limits, because Kaplan's factory is not a factory of language or noise but a factory of silence: 'Never a cry. The factory' (51). In the factory 'Space is silent' and what is experienced are 'Holes of noise, holes of noise everywhere' (56). The silence of the factory is a silence of space and this space is punctured by holes of noise. It is a reversal of Saussure's schema of meaning, in which language is material sound punctured by silence that provides the differences that generate meaning. Instead, the factory is a fullness of silence in which noise is a negativity that disrupts meaning. This reversal is a parody of language and a mimicry of the work of abstraction that generates abstract labour through the disciplining of bodies. Abstract labour is not only the result of the exchange of labour for money, but is also the result of this silent space punctuated by noise that organizes the body into repetitive abstract tasks geared to the generation of value (Braverman 1974).

The factory is a *coincidentia oppositorum*, composed of 'the silent and noisy texture of space' (56). Silence punctuates space and organizes it, but so does noise. This is the alternation or combination of silence and noise in the material texture that composes factory space. The noise appears not in the external space, not in what is being made in the factory, but in the body. This is all part of the life of the factory, in which the often mute and inert presence of the factory is also the presence of life. The factory moves, it is facing you and forms are made in the factory and by the poet. This is the difficult mimesis for the poet, as in grasping the factory as site of production they are forced to contend with the fragility of their own production. Kaplan tries to write this language of the factory within the resources of language in general, so as to delimit it, while also staying very close to it. The attempt is made by Kaplan to produce the language of the factory, as a language of silence and noise, in a parallel fashion to Marx's attempt to mimetically speak the language of the commodity. If the language of the commodity is the discourse of exchange rendered possible by the abstraction of value, then the language of the factory is the discourse of the production of value by alternations of silence and noise. In this language there is never a cry, the actual language of the body, but only the persistent alternation of silence and noise in the production of value. The language of the factory is a language that renders the worker as an abstract unit, their labour as interchangeable on the line, an anonymity in which the labour of the worker infuses the commodity with value. The language of the poet has to produce this scene of production, repeat it even, but somehow also not simply mimic it.

In this language of the factory we not only have silence and noise, but also recurrent sound. This is not the sound of the factory, that din which we have heard faintly as it is registered in a language that strains to contain it. The sound that recurs in *Excess—The Factory* is the jukebox song '*Those were the days, my love, ah yes those were the days*' played in the café before entering the factory. This song is a refrain, which occurs several times. 'Inside the café, there's always that music' (17). It is constant, compared to the silence or noise of the factory. 'At the café, music. It's nothing' (42). This is a sound that is also nothing, another sound that does not seem to register, in a strange parallel to the silence of the factory and the holes of noise we have a music that is nothing. The nothingness of the music leaves this sound as something that is not simply a relief from the noise and silence of the factory, but almost another imposition of a sound that is nothing. If we were to suppose that music is some relief from the factory, one of those utopian dreams of popular culture salving the suffering of labour, we might also say it is another instance of that labour, a constant presence.[4]

The song traces the outer limit of the factory as an opposition to the regular exchange of noise and silence that composes the breathing of the factory. It is a nothing that marks itself out from the noisy and silent nothing of the factory in which production takes place. This might be simple enough to mark as the space of consumption or self-reproduction, but Kaplan's text does not only mark an opposition but also a continuity. The factory space comes to dominate all space, including that of its supposed opposites. The constant music of the café may try to ward off the noise and silence of the factory, but it also engages and reproduces them. This is the social factory, in which the factory form and factory language come to permeate social space and our existence (Tronti 2019: 12–35). Yet the social factory does not dissolve the problem of the factory within it, as hell. The equivalence of factory and social space can reduce the singularity of the factory in a false or confused equivalency (such as the edu-factory for the university, which might better be called the edu-office). If we are to grasp this continuity we must also grasp its striations and differences.

Maurice Blanchot argues that Kaplan's work is at the extreme limit of language and perhaps is more than poetry (2010: 131). The excess of the text, for Blanchot, is an excess over language—an excessive language. Words are too little and too much to grasp the experience of all the circles of hell that make the factory. What is left is infinity in pieces, a fragmentation that is an infinite repetition of the discontinuous in language. Certainly, this speaks to the capacity of the poem (or writing) to work with silence and noise

---

4 My experience of a factory, a brief one in a packing plant, was of the constant sound of the radio, including the raucous sing-along to 'We've gotta get out of this place' by The Animals.

and with the peculiar space of the factory as sticky and excessive. The infinity and repetition here are, however, the material repetitions of the factory engaged in what we have called factory language. It is an image of the factory that speaks of itself and of the image of capitalist production as something infinite in its continual realization of surplus value. This is, however, not be mistaken for reality or even for the excess the text traces unless that text would remain only mimetic of the factory. Badiou calls factory writing to a particular mimesis of the factory and Blanchot argues that Kaplan's writing is an instance of mimesis as excess. We are insisting that Kaplan's writing or poetry is not only a mimesis of the factory or an excess, but also the search for a language distinct from factory language. This is an infinite and broken language, Blanchot is astute on this, but it is also one that tries to intervene in the mimetic factory language and to gesture towards another language. It is a language that tries to trace or delimit factory language as the production of a subject caught within the factory and unable to speak of it meaningfully.

Here is the outer limit of legibility and the loss of productive powers. The factory does not appear as a site to be seized or transformed, but risks appearing as a purely negative sign. This can risk serving the occlusion, dissolution, displacement and transformation of the factory. It can serve the flight from the factory. In contrast, we have insisted here on a factory language that is not simply mimetic, as much in Blake as in Kaplan; a language attuned to dialectical contraries, their tensions, and the possibilities to sublate and transcend them. This is why we have suggested that Kaplan's factory language is a language that does not give up on the subject or simply oppose subject to object. Instead, the materiality of language traces a silence, the holes, the gaps, the fractures, which result in the production of the real abstraction that is abstract labour. This is the difficulty that Kaplan's poetry confronts without reserve.

Factory Nostalgia

The writing of the factory has to respond to the fact that although the factory appears as an invisible site in fact, according to Badiou, 'it has always been caught in writing—albeit in the void' (2014a: 144). While the apparent problem is one of silence and invisibility, the actual problem is a particular kind of noise, visibility and writing—what we have called factory language. The factory speaks in such a way as to render illegible the politics of the factory and to speak itself as a site of production, perhaps hellish, but necessary. Behind its walls, safely enclosed, is the violent making of a language of exchange vouched safe only to those who enter the factory as workers. This, at least, is part of the illusory force of the factory that takes very real forms. In that sense to write the factory, to make poetry out of the factory, is not to respond to silence but to language and to sound. This is what we have stressed. Factory language might appear or indeed be a violent experience of deafening sound. Blake's noisy poetics of production sound the early experience of the factory as site of violent making and the revolutionary forces unleashed in that forging. It is difficult not to read Kaplan's poetics as splintered and quieter, a writing in which those energies appear mute or integrated into the texture of the factory. We have tried to refuse that arc by tracing how both poets recognize the forging of a poetics, a making or a production, in mimetic tension with the factory. What they write is another language, something like what Marx called direct language, which can only be direct through this cooperative mediation of the factory site. To stay with this language and not to simply flee the factory is what leaves us with this uncomfortable factory poetics.

Badiou, in his reading of French texts on the factory, identifies another risk: the risk of factory nostalgia. This is to remain within the limits of the Fordist compact and a certain vision of the working class that refuses to track the mutation of the factory. This leaves us echoing its aporia: 'If the factory oscillates between pre-inscription and the unsayable, this is because it is caught in the trappings of its function as a machine and subtracted from its true essence, which is to be a political place, a production of truths' (145). We would remain in the factory and trapped in its sticky space, remain with a vision of the working class that denies its heterogeneity and complexity—one organized within the global space of the factory. Certainly, we have the attention devoted to Xu Lizhi (Nao Project 2014), the poet and Foxconn worker who committed suicide at the age of 24. This contemporary engagement with the poetics of the factory is, however, only one instance—vital, but one that itself engages with an experience across time and space.

Here I have traced two interventions, along with a range of other moments, which all write the factory. They do not represent a closed sequence, but they do represent a particular and selective intervention in a particular and limited historical experience. As such the aim is not nostalgia for the factory as site of the compact working class, nor nostalgia for a particular moment of associated militancy—themselves complex, heterogeneous and fragmented phenomena. Rather, my aim has been more limited and modest: the tracing of a particular factory language in its appearance and fragility. Badiou argues that the counter to nostalgia is not only grasping the displacements of the factory site but also rendering the factory a political place by a new writing that is attentive to the 'the new forms, punctual and scattered, of political consciousness' (145). The political consciousness we have traced here might appear limited or to oscillate between the revolutionary and the resigned. Again, the aim is one not of nostalgia but of a certain work of memory, of a working-through. While the factory might have been displaced, rendered invisible, or constructed in new global forms, the living past of the factory is still something that we struggle with the language to speak of and to. It is sound, as shattering and traumatic experience, that marks that difficulty here as well as the struggle to find a language beyond the texture of factory language as both noisy and silent. These punctual and scattered moments are points that organize a language that aims beyond the factory experience. They aim to speak of the factory as though it were a reality that could, finally, be left in the past.

CHAPTER SEVEN

1985

Spliced Substantives

The cyberpunk moment was a moment of the fusion of technology and the human, in reality and in fiction. 1984 saw the launch of the Apple Macintosh personal computer, with its famous advertisement deploying the imagery of Orwell's *1984* disrupted by a hammer-throwing woman as symbol of antitotalitarian freedom. It also saw the British Miner's strike, in a parallel that could not be scripted, which demonstrated the violent recomposition of labour in the capitalist heartlands. The same year, in another instance of synchronicity, saw the publication of William Gibson's cyberpunk science-fiction novel *Neuromancer*, prefiguring the fascination with virtual reality, the internet and the figure of the hacker. Finally, 1984 saw the release of James Cameron's science-fiction film *The Terminator*, with its vision of a future in which machine intelligence would plot the destruction of humanity by use of a time-travelling cyborg assassin. One year later, in 1985, Donna Haraway would publish 'A Cyborg Manifesto' in *Socialist Review*, trying to capture the cyborg for a left-feminist project. Her intervention would launch a wide range of projects aiming to rework and reinvent technology, which would parallel the emergence of the new computing and digital platforms. Haraway opened a pioneering inquiry into science and matter in ways that would also influence and even begin the turn against language in the name of a new materialism.

This cyberpunk moment, later reconfigured into the digital turn and multiple interrogations of digital technology (Galloway and Thacker 2007), would also transform the status of language. The displacement of language by this moment was already evident in the work of Jean Baudrillard, who marked the transition of language from writing to code (1993: 57–61). While the cyberpunk moment might, in retrospect, be seen as the launch moment for the new materialisms, it was also the moment in which language shifted from sign to digital code and into new modes of inscription. Where once we might have associated the digital code with the moment of the virtual, so evident in the *Matrix* cycle, today we see the integration of the digital in the material. The haptic interaction with technology (the 'swipe'), the material integration of technology in everyday life, and the use of technology to render the material in various ways suggests the intimate relation of the material to the digital (Breu 2014; Galloway 2014). The convergence of language and matter remains within the cyberpunk moment, even if the role of language has been eclipsed in the material turn.

To return to Donna Haraway is to return to the cyborg moment as a complex site in which shifting patterns of labour, technology, language and imagination play themselves out. Haraway has been a central figure, if not always sufficiently acknowledged, in the turn to science and matter (2016: 3–90). Certainly, Gilles Deleuze is probably the most philosophically influential figure for the contemporary new materialisms and posthumanisms, but Haraway, alongside Bruno Latour, has done most to conceive the potentials of science and technology, and also to sustain an interrogation into the relationship between language and matter. Her primary concern has been, as she puts in in 'The Companion Species Manifesto', 'the corporeal join of the material and the semiotic' (2016: 107). While it may appear that we face a choice—matter or language—for Haraway and Latour matter is a matter of signs that are themselves material. Haraway and Latour share a common Catholicism and, as we have seen with David Jones, this leads to an interest in the sign as material sacrament.[1] In an interview, Haraway states 'there's the material semiotics of Catholicism, which is the word-made-flesh part' (268). She, Latour and Jones, all agree that 'for much Catholic theology, both official and popular, incarnation is a centrally compelling and highly charged mystery' (Moon 2012: 134), and that this incarnation can help us understand the relationship of sign and matter. While Haraway and Latour focus on science, they are both concerned with how science incarnates language into matter, and while posed in a secular mode this activity retains its theological undertones.[2]

The importance of this stress on incarnation and the material sign is that it retains the problem of thinking through the relationship between language and matter. The difficulty is that it tends to think this relation in the mode of a fusion that integrates matter and language as a mystery. The joining of language with matter tends to abolish the thinking of their relation for a new thinking that treats matter as if it had absorbed the features of language into itself. Matter becomes indeterminate, like the acrid wavering of language, and matter is treated as if it could speak itself, as if it had taken over the function of language. The poststructuralist understanding of language as an indeterminate form of material alterity is transferred into matter. We could add, in a similar fashion, that qualities associated with the human (rights, resistance, refusal, intractability, etc.) have also been displaced to matter and objects (Latour 1987). Matter absorbs language and the human, and the relations between

---

1 Henning Schmidgen (2014) offers an excellent account of the theological components of Latour's account of matter. For the explicitly theological reading of Latour, see Adam S. Miller (2013).

2 We might consider the effects of different religious 'callings' on the later 'calling' to particular theoretical or philosophical orientations (Weber 1989). Hal Foster (2017: 176n28) also makes a passing remark about the influence of a Protestant formation on adopting antifetishtic criticism. Hegel's (1977b: 153) discussion of Kantian and post-Kantian philosophy offers an explicit reflection on Protestant thought as one driven by a 'yearning and a grief', which it cannot resolve.

language, humans and matter are obscured by this fusion. While it may well be that matter is more complex than we imagined, this kind of thinking risks collapsing the relations between language, humans and matter, into matter as a mystic or theological substance. Therefore, Haraway's work forms an important site, in which left politics, materialism, science and language are all in play. At the same time, however, it remains problematic and requires a working-through that can avoid a mysticism of matter and a displacement of the critical tools required for grasping the present.

Material Semiotic Ferocity

The cyborg is the fusion of human, or animal, and the technological. In Haraway's hands it is used to both think matter as fusion and to trouble notions of purity that often dominate our political thinking. It is not so much a matter of the reality of the cyborg, but the use of the cyborg as an 'ironic political myth' that is important (Haraway 2016: 5). This is not a political myth we should accept as fact, like the toxic myths of nation or state, but an ironic use of an image or myth to disturb such constructions. Irony is, for Haraway, 'about contradictions that do not resolve into larger wholes' (5). The cyborg is a figure of unresolved contradictions, of 'fruitful couplings' (7), which never cohere into a whole. This refusal of 'larger wholes' and totality is made in the name of the hybrid and the dissident, symbolized in the cyborg as myth. The difficulty is that the cyborg remains a kind of totalizing myth, even if it is presented in an ironic fashion.[3] In Haraway's words, 'the cyborg is our ontology; it gives us our politics' (7). The cyborg speaks the nature of our Being, and so speaks our politics, which could not seem more totalizing. There is a tension between the cyborg as figure of plurality and disruption and this disavowed expression of the cyborg as totalizing figure. This tension runs through Haraway's work in multiple forms.

---

3 This can be compared with Hegel's (1993: 69–75) analysis of the inflation of the self in Romantic irony.

The cultural and political use of myth for an emancipatory project dates back, at least, to the project of the 'Oldest System Programme of German Idealism' (1995[1796/97]), with its claim to a new mythology of reason. One of the tensions of Haraway's use of myth lies in the claim to deploy myth in the cause of reason and socialist politics. Haraway believes she guards against the risk of the myth as irrational by treating myth as ironic. Such an ironic myth cannot sediment into a fully blown myth that we are called on to accept. The difficulty is, however, that the celebration of myth as irony suggests the myth as an instrumental fiction that needs to bear no relation to reality. While ironic myth might not become substantial it can remain as a self-contained fiction. Haraway becomes close to the Nietzschean invocation of myth. In *The Birth of Tragedy* (1872), Nietzsche uses myth as a mode of cultural reinvigoration and to reinstate cultural hierarchy; myth, for Nietzsche, is a useful fiction and useful as a fiction that destabilizes claims to reality and reason (1999: 108). While Haraway is far from Nietzsche's reactionary agenda, her own treatment of myth does not tease out the relationship between myth and reality (Fluss and Frim 2021). This leaves her vulnerable to the inflation of myth at the expense of reality, in which the cyborg becomes a fluid and motivational myth that circulates in ways that are detached from reality and from Haraway's socialist intentions.

The great scholar of myth Károly Kerényi distinguished between 'technicised myth' and 'genuine myth', in which the former referred to the instrumental use of myth for political purposes while the latter referred to inspired contact with the divine (Cavalletti 2014: 3).[4] Haraway flouts this kind of distinction by not only adopting an instrumental use of myth for socialist politics but also deliberately adopting a contemporary technological form for that myth; this is technicized myth with a vengeance. It is part of her deliberate defiance of the notion of 'genuine' myth, and instead

---

4 The work of Furio Jesi (2021a; 2021b) is one of the richest discussions of the potentials and problems of the left use of myth.

the embrace of the hybrid and technological cyborg. Such a defiance is also another way to understand Haraway's animus against feminist theologies that try to recover such 'pure' or 'genuine' myths. The most famous line in the manifesto is the last: 'I would rather be a cyborg than the goddess', which suggests not only the replacement of one myth by another but also the parody or disruption of myth as something serious (Haraway 2016: 68). The difficulty is not that Haraway disrupts the category of myth by a resort to a deliberately impure and constructed myth. The problem is if we imagine an acknowledgement of this construction is enough to resolve all the difficulties. In fact, treating myth ironically or as fiction might leave myth further detached from reality or might even imply that it can create reality. Myth might become what the Cybernetic Culture Research Unit (CCRU), another instance of cyberpunk theory, called 'hyperstitions'—fictions that create a new reality (2015). In this case, the myth takes on a constitutive role and the notion that myth might engage with reality recedes (Fluss and Frim 2021).

The problem lies in the selection of a myth, in this case the cyborg, and later, with Haraway's 2003 'Companion Species Manifesto', the critter, which is supposed to represent some force of difference and capture and condense a reality. While aiming at fusing together sign and reality, such a myth risks creating a false fusion and a myth that takes itself for reality. Marx and Engels, in *The German Ideology* (1846), chided philosophers as:

> knights-errant setting out in search of a word which, as a *word*, formed the transition in question, which, as a word, ceases to be simply a word, and which, as a word, in a mysterious superlinguistic manner, points from within language to the actual object it denotes; which, in short, plays among words the same role as the Redeeming God-Man plays among people in Christian fantasy. (2011: 449)

This is the risk of the word cyborg. Haraway is aware of the risk, and uses the notion of irony to immunize herself. The ironic myth, however, conceals its mastery and still plays the role of the incarnation and fusion of world and reality 'in a mysterious super-linguistic manner'.

The cyborg is a synthetic figure, in a double sense: synthetic as a fusion of human and technology, and synthetic as the gathering together of science fiction, medicine, reproduction, production and war. Such a synthesis is a denied synthesis, however, as Haraway disputes synthesis, mediation and wholeness. This is evident in her discussion of labour, when she refers to unalienated labour as one of the 'seductions to organic wholeness' (Haraway 2016: 8). In contrast to the complex role of the organic and inorganic in Marx's text (Foster and Burkett 2000; Butler 2019), we have another flattened image of unalienated labour as undifferentiated wholeness or imposed totality. While Haraway is attentive to the shaping force of the Cold War and its inheritances, here we see the hangover of Cold War anti-communism (2016: 51). In this case, the anti-communist imaginary of communism as nostalgia for an impossible unity and as the desire to 'immanentise the eschaton' as Eric Voegelin put it (1987: 188). The argument is that communism aims at unity and transparency, or begins from a supposition of unity and transparency, in the unalienated. This cliché is then supported by the claim that this unity is one of a metaphysics of labour, a charge that has regularly been used to criticize Marx (see chapter 1).

The problem of alienation is one that does deserve careful treatment, but the difficulty remains that Haraway disposes of this problem too rapidly, concerned, as she is, by notions that alienation implies a prior purity. It is the hybrid cyborg that is supposed to complicate such origins and trouble notions of labour and alienation. Haraway notes that the socialist-feminist expansion of the category of labour is itself flexible enough to be a tool of analysis that can be analytically rethought. Beyond an antinomy of alienated and unalienated, there lies a mapping of the forms of alienation.

Some of the most important discussions in the manifesto concern this mapping and the new gendered and racialized divisions of labour emerging within and through the new configurations of capitalism and technology. Haraway's sense of future trendlines was distressingly accurate:

> A major social and political danger is the formation of a strongly bimodal social structure, with the masses of women and men of all ethnic groups, but especially people of colour, confined to a homework economy, illiteracy of several varieties, and general redundancy and impotence, controlled by high-tech repressive apparatuses ranging from entertainment to surveillance and disappearance. (2016: 44)

This perceptive analysis is, however, not fully integrated with the possibilities of thinking labour and alienation beyond such binaries and the bimodal social structure that itself encourages such thinking.

Instead, Haraway labour as dangerously ontological, humanist and humanizing: labour is the root of an 'unintended erasure of polyvocal, unassimilable, radical discourse made visible in anti-colonial discourse and practice' (25). While she is correct to draw attention to the importance of anticolonial discourse and its critique of labour, at the same time she does not consider the long and complex relation of Marxism to anticolonial practice (Brennan 2014). Instead, as with the myth of the cyborg, we have another celebration of difference that does not fully engage with the complex and differential experiences of labour, but which instead paints Marxism as the flattening of such differences. There are historical forms of Marxism that do present problematic images of labour as salvation and redemption in ways that do not engage with the complexity of its global history. But, the difficulty I am indicating is that in her myth making Haraway risks a different kind of flattening out that treats Marxism in a clichéd fashion and also treats the thinking of totality as a naive organicism.

While celebrating the power of myth as a means to think about difference, Haraway constantly wards off Marxism as bad myth making. The problem with Marxism lies in its claims to 'organic' wholes, rationality and totality, which, for Haraway, threaten the work of difference and are themselves mythic. This is evident in her dismissal of dialectics: 'dialectics too is a dream language, longing to resolve contradiction' (52). Dialectics is a bad dream because it aims to resolve contradictions. The difficulty is that this leaves us with dreams that cannot be fulfilled and the result is a text that is itself dreamy, in the sense that it cannot connect its own myths and dreams to reality except in the mode of mythic fusion. It might have been worth tarrying longer with the problem of the dream, dream language and the material language of desire, which remains at that intersection between Marxism and psychoanalysis. In the desire to avoid resolution, wholes, and totality at all costs, the manifesto is both symptomatic and problematic.

Coded Texts

Language is not abandoned by Haraway, but remains central to the problems of power and resistance. The power of domination is the power of *'the translation of the world into a problem of coding'* (34), which is the power to impose a common language in which resistance disappears. The rendering of the world as fungible is found in the translation of the world into code. For Haraway, poststructuralism is useful in drawing attention to this problem of rendering the world as code, but it remains fatally complicit with it. Poststructuralism is an ally for its undermining of unities and proliferation of difference, as we have seen. The difficulty is that this difference remains textual, and Haraway argues we have to move beyond this into technological reality.

The movement into the technological is not an abandonment of language, as it is the relationship between language and technology that remains pressing. What we have witnessed, according to Haraway, is the rise of a new power of technobabble and the 'language of spliced substantives' (69), in which nouns are divided by the slogans and buzzwords of corporate naming. The word tech-nobabble itself, in its ugliness, is a compound of the type it diag-noses, in which technology fuses with a language reduced to the meaningless reproduction of value. For Haraway, the new language of technological domination is a language of splicing and fusion, in which signifiers are rendered equivalent and joined together to generate new forms of value, something that has only intensified since she wrote the manifesto. Of course, the immediate difficulty is how we might distinguish her own splicing, as with the figure of the cyborg, from the corporate splicing of domination. Haraway's aim is to fight on the same terrain as the enemy, and the use of the cyborg is an operation of seizing or reclaiming, but then we face the difficult question of how we then use such a reclaimed figure.

This raises the question of how we deploy a language that can exceed the translation of the world into a monologic code and how we can use a language that does not succumb to being re-spliced into the corporate language of innovation. Haraway suggests that: 'If we are imprisoned by language, then escape from that prison-house requires language poets, a kind of cultural restriction enzyme to cut the code; cyborg heteroglossia is one form of radical cultural politics' (70). We witness here the reproduction of the image of language as a prison-house. Here that dramatic image is evaded by a turn to poetry, or more particularly language poets. Haraway invokes, if indirectly, the experimental American L=A=N=G=U=A=G=E poets, those 1960s and 1970s poets who often used 'found' language and emphasized the materiality of language. Once again, we have a bridge between the poststructuralist turning of language towards matter and materialisms that would surpass language in the name of matter. Haraway is a bridging figure, retaining the emphasis on language as practice fused here with the science of genetics to suggest a disruption of the code of language and life by 'cyborg heteroglossia'. The splicing and recombinant DNA of capitalist value, which joins together incommensurate things through a common coding, is opposed by a re-splicing that takes apart these fusions in the name of radical difference.

We are left with tantalizing hints of what this practice of cutting and cyborg heteroglossia might be. It seems to invoke a work on difference, an opening and diversification of language. We can see the tensions in the manifesto, in the similarities between Haraway's new coinages and the language of power. This practice of coining new spliced and integrated words is continued in Haraway's later writing, most memorably in the title of her 1997 book: *Modest_Witness@Second_Millennium.FemaleMan_Meets_OncoMouse: Feminism and Technoscience*. This title obviously mimics the online address and the grammar and structure of technoscientific naming. While it explicitly proclaims itself as a 'modest witness', the ambition, which is laudable, is still to match and exceed the language of technoscientific domination. This is a struggle waged on the terrain of the enemy, which is certainly true of the struggles we must wage. The question becomes how to write this struggle, how to give sense to it, how to name it. While the aim might be a fusion of signifier and materiality, another incarnated sign, we could add that language and writing remain sites to work out the differences and tensions, the relations, of forms of materiality and forms of language. Haraway invokes the power of mediation but this is mediation as fusion. This fusion of sign and reality risks becoming a new splicing of language, absorbed into techno-language, or remaining detached from relations by trying to invoke a 'pure' difference.

This difficulty results in the constant attempt to divide or split language from within, between the corporate splicing and the cyborg heteroglossia. The latter is supposed to disrupt language, without stabilizing into a new form of domination. This 'powerful infidel heteroglossia' or 'speaking in tongues' carries an obviously theological resonance (68). The plurality of the word is linked to the unfaithful, to a denial of faith, with the 'infidel' as the figure for all those who deny Christianity. While this supposes a refusal of the unifications of Christian and religious speech, it is also matched by a 'speaking in tongues', which has come to be associated with a

Christian religious practice of divine inspiration. This is, of course, a deliberate act of splicing, another deliberate disruption of the unity of religious discourse by the intrusion of its supposed Other. The difficulty remains in opposing technobabble with a new form of religiously inspired 'babble', and how far this truly offers an alternative language.

The contours of such a practice of language are to be found in the cyborg writing of feminist and African American science fiction, by authors like Joanna Russ, Samuel R, Delany, John Varley, James Tiptree Jr., Octavia Butler, Monique Wittig and Vonda McIntyre (Haraway 2016: 52). For Haraway, these practices can be recoded as cyborg, while they also engage with the difficulty of outsider identities and the question of how to write from those positions that remain violently ejected from the common language.[5] This speaks to the deadly play of demands for literacy, writing, naming and signifying against the silencing and obliteration enacted by the dominant powers, most evident in slavery (Moten 2003). Again, Haraway is keen to resist any assumption of innocence, any prelapsarian wholeness, any myths of origin as purity within outsider identity: cyborg language is interference, disruption, pollution. These disruptive texts are reclaimed as cyborg articulations of new identities and new languages that refuse to be stabilized in the monologic language of power as code. We have here another notion of the cyborg myth, in this case of the cyborg myth as the regeneration of language into a new productive form of difference. Once again, while denying totalities, wholes, and fusions, Haraway is constantly in search of such fusions and modes of expression, in which the sign and matter will come to coincide.

---

5 There might be issues raised here by Haraway's use of the Black aesthetic, parallel to those raised by Fred Moten (2003: 216–23) in relation to Frederic Jameson.

We could also consider a parallel fusion between sign and matter found in the another and different form of the cyberpunk moment. This is the 1990s and early 2000s work of the CCRU and Nick Land. While very different in political orientation to Haraway, we find here another fusion of language with the material, but this time in the form of numerical operations. The CCRU mount an assault on the language and writing of control, particularly in the form of the QWERTY keyboard,[6] in the style of William Burroughs (CCRU 2015; Land 2011: 583–90). Unlike Haraway's proliferation of language, perhaps something to do with her roots in the biological sciences and its practice of naming and classification, here language turns into the numeric as moment of resistance. It is perhaps not so surprising that a transition between this numerate thinking and the work of Alain Badiou can be made (2008). The structure of thinking number as resistance is, however, parallel to Haraway's heteroglossia in the claim to a fusion of sign and matter. While the CCRU and Land seem to present this fusion in a more explicitly secular style, as the operations of the code itself, they also license another form of mysticism, this time through the number mysticism of the Kabbalah. Despite so many differences, then, we see a convergence in the resistance to the secular powers of domination by a re-sacralization in the mystical fusion of sign or number with material reality.

Where the work of Land and the CCRU was often easily integrated into new materialist currents, partly because of its numeric materialism, Haraway's ongoing concern with language is more resistant to integration, and hence more interesting. Her attachment to language, even if problematic, prevents the smooth running of matter that conditions the new materialisms. The archaism of 'The Cyborg Manifesto', relatively speaking to current theoretical concerns with matter, is due to the fact that language still matters for Haraway. To use the terms we have set up, while aiming at a war on language by fusing together matter and language

---

6 This may well have been inspired by Gilles Deleuze's (1985) critique of the 'AZERT' keyboard, the French variant of QWERTY.

into a proliferating world of corporeal joins that never form a whole, Haraway is also attentive to the difficult necessity to continue a war of language from within. While trying to generate proliferating differences, we have noted the tendency of the text to continually split into new binaries. This is the problem that the manifesto confronts as it tries to escape from what it regards as the tyranny of 'wholes'. Haraway is astute enough to recognize the need for unity in confronting the power of capitalism, patriarchy, racism and all the modes of domination, but struggles to give form to this unity except as another binary. She contrasts a good unity, the 'a poetic / political unity', a unity retaining difference, with a bad unity, the subsuming or totalizing 'unity-through-incorporation' (Haraway 2016: 20). It is certainly important that Haraway recognizes the importance of unity for political action and tries to make the effort to suggest what such a unity would look like. The difficulty remains of forming such a 'unity' that does not fall into a binary or into a mythic form.

Apophatic Materialism

Haraway's own style and practice of language is one that delights in coining new compound words, new neologisms. This process of addition aims to mimic the process of material semiosis, in which language itself generates new joins with matter, in new configurations and new arrangements. It is also a way of signalling the inadequacy of language as it constantly proliferates itself in trying (and failing) to grasp materiality. The result is that language is constantly trying to name matter and constantly failing. For Haraway, language is afflicted with a fundamental instability:

> But every act of syntax is also a kind of fierce joke on our desire to clarify, to control, to know, to identify. But by the time you reach the end of a sentence, you've said at least six things that aren't true and you don't hold, but to get to the end of the sentence you don't have any choice. You can't simply say what you mean—that's not how language works. (209)

Taken as a statement about writing and language, there is a certain truth to it, but not the whole truth. In the act of writing we often explore and clarify our thought, and as we write potentials of meaning may expand (or shrink). This is why the process of writing is virtually coterminous with that of editing and the desire to minimize saying things you do not believe. Moreover, the fact that language disseminates meaning, that language works as a system of differences, does not mean that the effects of meaning do not appear or that we cannot establish meaning.

While known for her return to materiality, here we have a kind of hyper-poststructuralism in which differences do not simply open onto matter or animality or the various 'others' of language, but onto a fusing of matter and language in which language constantly testifies to its own impossibility. The process is additive: 'we need more than one word at a time, and we need to be careful how we situate these words in relation to each other' (231). This notion of constant addition has been characteristic of the new materialisms and those currents of postcritique, which claim the virtue of adding to reality rather than subtracting from it (Latour 2010: 475; Felski 2015). While it is true that we often do need more words and to think about how they are situated, we also need conceptual clarification and even sometimes the reduction of language. The relation of language and matter is not only about language constantly stretching out a hand to matter, but also of how we arrest this process in new concepts that stabilize and determine these relations. Here we not only have the proliferation of language or the speculation on a reality that always escapes language, but also the problem of their relation. In this situation, literary realism, which considers the complex relations of language and reality, might remain a more useful guide than the various speculative realisms that aim for a great outdoors beyond language.

While language is important our return to language is not just another attempt to proclaim the dominance of language over reality. In fact, Haraway's own work exhibits the problem of a notion of language as continual addition, which can then never actually reach the matter it is constantly striving for. Instead, we might consider the inadequacy of language better as raising the problem of conceptual understanding rather than indicating the perpetual failure of language. This makes sense of the much-remarked inferiority of language in Hegel's work. While this lowered status of language has served as a lever for various deconstructions of Hegel (Derrida 1982: 69–108), we might instead argue that Hegel indicates that language cannot systematize itself and so cannot, ironically, be considered the last word. In fact, this failure might be the necessary form of language as language. Jacques Derrida, summarizing Hegel, notes that language 'becomes language only by cancelling / conserving itself in the concept' (2021: 15). Language remains failed if it does not accede to the concept, if it remains circling materiality. Words can be brought to a stop by this process of clarification that does not remain purely internal to language nor is simply due to the encounter with matter, as when we stumble over a stone. Instead, conceptualization must be brought to bear to complete the determining function of language.

In contrast, in Haraway's understanding, language, to complete its relation to the material, must become material: words must 'granulate in your hands' (2016: 274). Instead of the path of language to the concept, we have the path of language to a fusion with matter. The demand here is that while language can never reach the material, it must mimic the material to become close to it. In this way, ironically, the material nature of language itself is diminished and, instead, language must fuse with reality through an act of splicing and recombination. The distance between language and matter is abolished in a sudden fusion, but as this fusion will always fail, the distance between language and matter is maintained. What we have is a series of repetitions of the sacrament, the act of holy communion, which will never achieve the fully redemptive fusion. While language will try to granulate in our hands this granularity will never truly achieve a fusion with matter. It will only ever remain an act of mimicry, or even parody. The act must be repeated again, a new striving will take place, and we will need to constantly add to language, while never being able to come to rest.

In effect, Haraway condemns language as a form of naming that fetishizes or reifies, turning process into thing and always misnaming the thing as a thing. When a word or sign fuses with matter it misnames that matter and so we have to begin anew with another name. What Haraway risks is translating a social process, commodity fetishism or reification, in which social relations are congealed into things (Lukàcs 1967), into an ontological condition of language as what congeals or reifies the process of changing matter. Any act of language or naming reduces and traduces matter or reality by fixing it in a name and denying process. In fact, ironically, turning language into a thing is praised, as long as that thing refuses any social relations and remains beyond any determination. Commodity fetishism or reification, in which a social relation becomes a thing, is resisted in the name of a thing that can never become a social relation. In this case we lose the capacity of using the abstractive force of language to grasp processes of social abstraction. In these processes people become things, in the experience of reification, but also, through personification, things become persons (Rose 2017: 58). This personification occurs not only in the well-known instance of corporations being treated legally as persons, but in all the ways in which commodities and our fusions with them take on the qualities of people. The possibility of exploring these social processes are lost in a general condemnation of reification as any act of naming.

The result is a philosophy of language that is a negative theology, as Haraway accepts and celebrates. In a negative theology any act of naming of god falls short and so we can only name our inability to name. The negative opens up the space for absolute transcendence in the ways in which it withdraws from the possibility of ever finally naming god. In such a situation language and naming proliferate, as we constantly try and fail to name god, while at the same time silence, absence and negativity are celebrated. In Haraway's version god is replaced by matter. Naming is always misnaming, naming does not ever work, and any naming is a kind of fetishism or idolatry. In response, Haraway's solution is a proliferation of words, Joycean rather than Beckettian (Schlossman

1985). It is the nonidentity of matter to language that establishes materiality as what can never be fully said, which is to say as god, at least within negative theology. Language loses power, but gains power in its conjoining with materiality while never sticking to it.

Haraway is explicit about this debt to the theological, but claims to exchange the infinity of god for finitude and mortality. The way of the negative is a demand of humility, but one which also knows the finite and rules out the infinite. Again, as we saw with the cyborg, it is not that claims to humility and the 'minor' are wrong per se, but that they are belied by the synthetic function of the term. Certainly, Haraway is a generous thinker and her citational practice of giving credit where due is one that needs replication. At the same time, my account is critical as this humility disguises claims to fusion and totalization that are then not worked through. We are left with various inadequate names as signs of our finitude, without the possibility of determining relations and gaining adequate knowledge (Bosteels 2009). It is somewhat ironic in a text that aims to engage science and the technological that we should be left in this position. What we need instead is a relation of determination that does achieve a totalization and an adequate conceptualization of the relation of language and matter.

These difficulties are also repeated in Haraway's conceptualization of capitalism: 'Capitalism obviously isn't just one thing. It's obviously a very complicated *historical system* phenomenon, among other things; it has many histories and unevenness' in time and space' (Haraway 2016: 239). While this is true, and the expansiveness of Marx's *Capital* attests to the difficulty of grasping capital as a historical system phenomenon, we once again run into the potential problem of blurring and expansiveness replacing analysis. This is the problem Marx identified in those 'economists who smudge over all the historical difference and see bourgeois relations in all forms of society' (1973: 105). Haraway's aim is specificity; capitalism is not one thing, but the invocation of complexity risks occluding the core dynamics of that system. Haraway is trying to complicate and to stay close to reality and materiality. The manifesto provides historical detail, and Haraway does not simply embrace the notion of capitalism as plurality (Gibson-Graham 2006). But the lack of full conceptualization of the historical system of capitalism as totalizing and itself within a totality makes this analysis intermittent and inclined to fall back on clichés of multiplicity. The problem of language as totalization and capital as totalization run together, whereas we need to tease them out. We have the capacities of language, through conceptualization, to grasp totality that is not simply that of capitalism. While we also need to grasp capitalism as a particular and contradictory totality, otherwise our invocations of plurality simply feed further accruals of value. Refusing totalization solves neither of these problems.

We can agree language cannot saturate reality in a linguistic imperialism or what Derrida called 'logocentrism', but this is not to a negative theology of language. Derrida pointed out that negative theology, to which his own work was often compared, in fact only uses negativity as a path to reach full presence and the positivity of god (1989c). In the case of Haraway, we have a negative theology of language as naming, in which we never get the right name, which sustains the full positivity of matter beyond any particular name. In such a schema the possibilities of relations and mediations, while proclaimed, are never really realized. Instead, we can think of language in terms of the title of Marie Cardinal's (1993) memoir of her experience of psychoanalysis, *The Words to Say It*. Words may not exhaust the world but words can be found to speak the world, both inner and outer. That is the practice of psychoanalysis and I would also argue that is the practice of historical materialism. It is also a practice of poetry, if we follow Rilke's claim in the *Duino Elegies* that: 'This is the era of the sayable / here is its homeland.' (2021: 71). The emphasis on indeterminacy, on the contrary, denies the translation into language, into conceptualization and into determination. Again, this is not to say language is itself exhaustive or wholly saturates thought. Instead, language is material, materially related to what we tend to call matter or nature, and it is this relation and mediation that must be thought through conceptualization (Pinker 2003).

CHAPTER EIGHT

2008–2016
Hex Position

I want to trace a period which spans the 2007–08 global financial crisis, the resulting regimes of austerity, and the intermittent moments of protest. This is not a period that has ended, but here I have drawn a provisional and punctual limit. This has been a bad time, not least because, as T. J. Clark noted, the moment of crisis has also resulted in 'the almost complete failure of left responses to [. . .] resonate beyond the ranks of the faithful' (2012: 54). In the bad times, what do poets sing of? According to Brecht, they sing of the bad times (1976: 320). Is it better to curse the bad times? A hex is a spell or curse. It derives from the German 'hexen', witch-craft, and is used to refer to an act of bewitchment by gesture or language. In terms of language, a hex is a performative: a piece of language that is supposed to have an effect in the real world (Austin 1979). Uttering a hex affects its target in a malignant way. The poetic hex is a speech act that lies between belief, fantasy and desire. As a fictional act, it suspends the distinction between serious and nonserious performative acts in the uncanny space of fiction (Derrida 1988). Poetic hexes engage with the power of poetry, often regarded as the most ineffectual and minor form of writing. The hex would overcome that lack of power and make something happen. The hex can be seen as the claim on power, on magical power, on the power of words, by the powerless, even in the recognition of that powerlessness. Therefore, the hex oscillates in this boundary, between fantasy and production, between fantasy and its abolition, between fiction and reality.

Contemporary British experimental poetry, often defined as the tradition of neomodernism, departing from Ezra Pound and William Carlos Williams via J. H. Prynne, has made use of the hex in these bad times. This has been a poetics intimately linked to a communist and radical politics, and concerned to explore the fate of that politics in the present. Here, I focus on the poets Sean Bonney, Keston Sutherland, and Verity Spott. Two of these poets, Bonney and Spott, make explicit use of the hex in their poetic practice, directing their hexes, as we will see, against particular British politicians, as well as other targets. All three poets fashion the hex as a form able to deal with the problem of contemporary capitalism and, in particular, capitalist crisis and the resulting implementation of programs of austerity. These hexes are attempts to realize language as a material intervention against capitalist abstraction through abstract language. The difficulty of this poetics lies oddly in its directness, as it turns language, within abstraction, towards a concrete antagonism. I do not propose a progression between these poets, but rather a circling and encounter with the problem of abstraction that is renewed at each juncture in a new form.

While capitalism is often regarded as the model of a faceless and anonymous power, which works through the blind imperative of reducing humans and nonhumans to sources of value, it is also embodied. This embodiment takes the peculiar form of what Marx called 'character masks' (*Charaktermaske*), a concept that is hard to trace as it is not consistently translated in the English editions of *Capital*. This concept is only used a few times, but Marx constantly emphasizes the significance of social roles and of humans as the bearers of social relations. He remarks in the Preface to the first German edition of *Capital* that:

> To prevent possible misunderstandings, let me say this. I do not by any means depict the capitalist and the land-owner in rosy colours. But individuals are dealt with here only in so far as they are the personifications of economic categories, the bearers (*Träger*) of particular class-relations and interests. (Marx 1990: 92)

So, we have here the force of abstraction, in which people appear as mere bearers or masks, but also a process of embodiment in which people become this abstract malign power and personify it.

The point of the hex is to capture this dual relation: first, to attack the embodied figure of abstract capitalist violence by naming and cursing that figure, and second, to hex that figure as, in fact, the bearer of abstract violence. This is a provocation, in which the mask is ripped off to reveal another mask, the abstract form of value for which we function as mere delegates. A better figure, one used by Guy Debord, is of exchange value as the condottiere of use value, as the condottiere is a mercenary, a figure of violence first employed by use value and then waging a war that 'was entirely its own' (1995: #46). Exchange value possesses use value and takes it over, and in the same way we are possessed and taken over by exchange value, becoming part of its war and becoming one with the mask. The aim is not simply to remove the mask to expose the real human beneath, in the mode of the emperor's new clothes or better Scooby-Doo, but to expose the inhabiting force of abstraction. The mercenaries of capital, the hired combat troops, must be exposed as what they are—nothing. They are, however, a 'nothing' that embodies violence and their role makes no sense without that embodiment.

The difficulty of such a practice of hexing is that it can always be accused of aiming at the wrong target. The attempt to give capitalist violence a form or figure can be accused of forgetting the abstract power of capitalism, of electing the pathetic bearer to a destiny they do not have, or even of promoting a vicious form of embodiment that treats symptom for cause. The inverse criticism is that attempting to give abstract capitalist violence a form puts the onus on abstract violence and neglects the living role of the bearer. Danny Hayward, discussing Lucy Beynon and Lisa Jeschke's pamphlet *David Cameron: A Theatre of Knife Songs*, with its fantasy of raping the then British Conservative Prime Minister David Cameron, points out that if we treat such works as only demonstrating politicians are character masks for capital then we nullify their real contempt and violence for actual politicians (2015: 99).

The first problem stems from treating the abstract power of capitalism as a matter of real people, the second lies in of treating real people as merely the embodiments of the abstract power of capital and thus as devoid of any responsibility. In the first case, we risk mistaking the symptom for the cause, while in the second case, it is true we are all subjects of capital but that experience is highly uneven—the problem of what we used to call class. In both cases it seems that the hex falls short: too focused on the particular target or too general in address. The problem is one of abstraction and its targeting. We have to see abstractions as embodied, lived and performed. Abstractions are real, but they are also abstract and so their particular bearers are relatively disposable.

The interest of the hex might lie in the fact that it does not or cannot hit its target. Here, however, we come close to celebrating failure as such and reinforcing the image of poetry as a game with language played at another level (which is not to say there cannot be serious games or games taken seriously, far from it). This is certainly the issue that all these poets confront and, in various ways, struggle to resolve. We do not aim to celebrate the hex as an art of necessary failure, although neither do we regard it as simply successful. The very violence of the hex takes on the cartoonish character that, as we have already seen, marks something of our experience of real abstraction. In this case, we must read between abstraction and the real, read the moments of determination; in this way the failure of the hex might take on an indicative value. The indication of the difficulty of finding the target should be the spur for analysing the connections between real people, real bodies, and abstract relations of violence. The concept of the character mask can and should be read both ways: as marking the individual as mere bearer of capitalist power, but also as marking the appearance of that power in an embodied form. This is the reason why *Capital*, often seen as the most abstract of works, also includes the chapter on the working day, with its detailed recounting of the violence of capital through gothic metaphor. It is no surprise that Keston Sutherland, alongside his poetry, has written on *Capital* as a work of satire and violent embodiment (2008). The point is, again, that abstraction and embodiment go together. Bodies and nature are rendered abstract in violent processes of levelling and homogenization, which can then be explored through poetic and literary texts.

I want to trace this moment of embodiment and abstraction through the mouth and the oral. This might appear unsurprising, as poetry remains a spoken art, and the poetry reading is still a central and vital event, especially in neomodernist poetry. My aim is not to reconstruct a history of the mouth in literature, or even in the history of the avant-garde and modernism (thinking particularly of Beckett). Rather, I take this brief period of time (2008–2016) as a moment of the violent emergence of the mouth and the oral. We have already seen the mouth and the oral appear, in the experience of negation, materiality, and the political fantasies surrounding the open mouth (see chapter 2). These anxieties and fantasies persist, and have become intensified with the recent Covid-19 pandemic. The mouth, the breath, and the covering of the mouth, have become matters of life and death. These anxieties surrounding the mouth also refer to the birth of language itself, to that strange and impossible moment of proto-language is which language is vocalized. Any moment of speaking carries the trace of this initial moment in which language emerged from the mouth. It is fitting that, in many ways, the hex should converge on this moment of orality. In such a moment, in the uttering of the hex through or by the mouth, a claim is made: a claim to materiality, to language, and to violently ejecting abstraction.

ACAB

The Invisible Committee, in *To Our Friends*, note that 'the epoch has even begun to secrete its own platitudes, like that All Cops Are Bastards (ACAB) which a strange internationale emblazons on the rough walls of cities, from Cairo to Istanbul, and Rome to Paris or Rio, with every thrust of revolt' (The Invisible Committee 2014: 12).

The slogan is more familiar to a British person as 'All Coppers Are Bastards', and as a tattoo that some have across their knuckles, as a deliberate marking of outsider status and defiance of authority. Sean Bonney's 2015 collection *Letters against the Firmament* includes probably his most well-known poem, originally published on his blog *abandonedbuildings* as 'ACAB: A Nursery Rhyme' (2014). This poem, with its refrain 'Fuck the Police', references the Venezuelan poet Miguel James' 'Against the Police' (2013), which begins 'My entire Oeuvre is against the police'; the NWA track 'Fuck the Police' is another obvious influence. So, Bonney's poem begins 'for "I love you" say fuck the police' and concludes 'say no justice no peace and then say fuck the police' (2015: 29). The last line refers to the protests against the killing of young Black men by the police, pre-dominantly in the United States, but also in Britain. The protest chant of 'no justice, no peace', is here rhymed and intensified with 'fuck the police'. Finally, and speculatively, ACAB displaces or echoes the start of the now childish magic word, abracadabra.

In the time of crisis, we have witnessed an increasing militar-ization of the police and of their militancy in disrupting protests. This has been particularly evident in strategies such as kettling— enclosing protestors in confined public areas for long periods of time before processing them for arrest and release.[1] While there has been a long tradition of working-class distrust of the police, hence the origin of ACAB, these strategies have intensified along with the sense of the police as the embodiment of state power in the enforce-ment of crisis as a way of life. The use of mass criminalization, as with the riots of 2011 that occurred in England following the police killing of Mark Duggan, has generated a new form of collective punishment. Exemplary sentences and the use of CCTV and informants after insurrectional events leads to arrests, fines, and imprisonment that chills further protest and deprives its victims of access to dwindling resources.

---

1 Bonney (2015: 27) writes 'stone circles are police kettles, you can't tell me different'.

The police, then, realize the abstraction of economic crisis in the embodied form of violent state power. In that way they become a figure, often anonymous in the new militarized riot gear, which realizes the violence of abstraction. In Bonney's poems this form of abstract violence penetrates into poetic and artistic form: 'police violence is the content of all / officially sanctioned art' (2015: 12). Therefore, all works of art are filled with this violence, which is usually denied or repressed. It is also crucial that this violence take an abstract form: 'the enemy is non-material / we are not' (18). While obviously violently material, police violence is also seen as a form of nonmaterial violence—a floating violence inflicted on our material person. The poem, a nursery rhyme, condenses the desire to curse in the poetic materiality of rhyme and repetition. It begins by making everything into 'fuck the police' and concludes with a simple rhyme. The poem mimics the child's acquisition of language through repeating the nursery rhyme, but this time with an education in the violent rejection of the police and all forms of ideological authority.

Bonney's *Letters against the Firmament* also includes a letter that is a hex against Iain Duncan-Smith (2015: 111–12). Duncan-Smith is a British Tory politician who, in his work as Secretary of State for Work and Pensions, was responsible for an assault on the welfare benefits received by people with disabilities and the unemployed. Bonney's hex recalls the Romantic poets' assaults on Lord Castle-reagh, another architect of reaction. Shelley, in 'The Mask of Anarchy' (1819)—written after the Peterloo Massacre, when protestors for Parliamentary reform were attacked by cavalry—wrote: 'I met Murder on the way—/ He had a mask like Castle-reagh—' (Shelley 2002: 316). Byron, after Lord Castlereagh's suicide, called him 'an intellectual eunuch' in his Dedication to *Don Juan* (1973: 43). In this case, Bonney writes in a radical poetic tradition that violently responds to the class violence of the politician who always presents such violence as sanitary and salutary.

A crucial way station in this history of cursing or hexing politicians is the figure of Margaret Thatcher, Conservative Prime Minister from 1979 to 1990 and initiator of the neoliberal project in Britain. Behind the empty figures of current politicians, usually characterized by a media friendly vacuity, lies the more openly confrontational and aggressive figure of Thatcher. Bonney (2015: 37) explicitly links Thatcher, alive at that moment, to the round-up after the riots of 2011: 'Margaret Thatcher and her strange relationship with the combined central nervous systems of all of the people who were picked up in the weeks following the riots, around 3000 of them' (37). Verity Spott (2014: 8) refers to 'Thatcher's numerous killings', when discussing the jury's exoneration of the police for the killing of Mark Duggan. Tom Raworth (2015), to cite another neo-modernist poet, curses Thatcher in his poem 'Rip Rap':

> orgreave
> your grave
> Margaret Hilda Thatcher

Orgreave was the site of a violent attack by the police on striking miners on 18 June 1984. Again, we should note the use of a simple rhyme, and, in all cases, we can see the sense that despite her empirical death Margaret Thatcher is not dead, but remains an animating force for the political expression of violence to the working class and for resistance to that violence.

In Bonney's case, the poem is a directly insult to the 'talking claw'—Iain Duncan-Smith (2015: 111). The poem also, however, tries 'to define him, to recite and describe, occupy his constellations'. In this case, the politician is not the significant figure of concentrated class power that was Margaret Thatcher, easily and repeatedly subject to visual satire.[2] Iain Duncan-Smith is the emblematic politician of our moment of waning class struggle and the direct result of working-class defeat. He is the very archetype of the

---

2 Jacqueline Rose (1988) has discussed Margaret Thatcher as figure of fantasy, in the psychoanalytic sense.

politician as *éminence grise*—metaphorically a behind the scenes manipulator, but also literally grey, washed out, empty. To hex a nullity requires the act of defining, of reciting, of describing, using language to determine the form of the politician and this abstract reality. This also speaks to how the politician displaces violence through law. The measures that led to the suicide and death of welfare claimants were legal measures. Duncan-Smith proposes 'the malevolent alphabet' (111), his own language, his own curse, on the most vulnerable members of society. The poet's spleen is one that recognizes this malign and material power that 'breaks children's teeth with gravel-stones' (111). Bonney's is the attempt to take a measure of the 'imperious darkness' that Duncan-Smith has invented and spread (112).

In the breaking of children's teeth, we can see the mouth as the site of expressed and lived violence. To trace the figure of the politician as embodiment of legal violence Bonney uses a hex that introjects Duncan-Smith through the mouth. In Bonney's words, 'we will keep you in our mouths, and we will keep / you there to recite the filth of your lives' (112). This returns us to Freud's account of negation in which the judgement of negation originates in the primitive oral drive and the rejection of something that is bad to eat by ejecting it from the mouth (see chapter 2) (Freud 1984b). Negation reveals the moment of the drive and encompasses the materiality of the mouth as site of introjection and projection. In Bonney's poem the mouth introjects the bad, which remains in our mouths, where the politician recites and so even speaks for us but in such a way as to judge himself, to reveal his own filth. In this position the politician is the abject, the object of disgust that lies between the subject and the object (Kristeva 1982). The abject is not simply spewed out, but made to speak. In this way some mastery is generated over this abstract legal violence through a reversal in which the politician is rendered abject and forced into our mouths. Yet, the poem registers the impossibility of this reversal and powerlessness as the abject still speaks in our place and out of our mouths.

In the next letter, Bonney notes that his respondent claims he only goes after 'easy targets' (2015: 113). While the letter goes on to defend Bonney's celebration of the riot form as a mode of disruptive speech we could consider whether this, presumably fictional, exchange also concerns the easy target of Iain Duncan-Smith. In the 'Letter on Work and Harmony' Bonney will write 'I take the fact that Iain Duncan Smith continues to be alive as a personal insult, ok BANG every morning he is still alive BANG BANG BANG' (47). And yet I want to suggest this hex is not so easy. None of the hexing or cursing I want to trace here presumes a simple gain to be set against loss. The hex is not thought to make good for suffering or violence or even to make good a claim to embody or represent that violence in an act of synecdoche. It is not assumed that this part, Iain Duncan-Smith, can stand for the whole, capitalism. Rather, the part can be taken into the mouth as a way to measure that law which becomes an act of continuous violence. This measure is itself abject, as we have seen, something that cannot be introjected or expelled. The hex, then, is a precarious moment of violence that negates in an act of preserving, and thus tries to take measure of legal violence.

Fetish Character

In Keston Sutherland's (2011) poem *Hot White Andy*, Andy Cheng, an actual person, is treated as 'Cheng the *Fetischcharakter*'—Marx's word for the nature of the commodity in the famous section of *Capital* on the fetishism of commodities.[3] Already, in this work, Sutherland is concerned with ventriloquizing capitalism,[4] with bringing the language of the commodity into our awareness. At the same time, the poem confronts a situation in which the commodity speaks in the place of the person—reification and personification

---

3 Sutherland (2012a) has a discussion of the dual nature of the '*Fetischcharakter*'.
4 For analysis of various instances of the ventriloquizing of capitalism see Alberto Toscano and Jeff Kinkle (2015: 40–48). For a critical discussion of the role of the slave as 'speaking commodity' see Fred Moten (2003: 8–22).

go together. My focus is on Sutherland's later *Odes to TL61P* (2013), which are odes addressed to the obsolete product ordering code for a discontinued Hotpoint washer-dryer TL61P. This is a love song to a lost commodity, a disappeared item from the endless cycle of capitalist obsolescence exempt from 'the vault / of exchangeable passion' (Sutherland 2013: 18). This long poem is a complex and multiform work consisting of five odes, which range from the contemporary political landscape to childhood sexual experience. Matthew Abbott (2013), bravely attempting summary, notes that 'the text articulates (and/or fails to articulate) political polemics, the outcomes of economic crisis, gnomic utterances and aphorisms, sexual fantasies and memories, grabs of news and other debased discourses, lyrical meditations on love, etc.' The *Odes* are largely written in the form of prose blocks and Sutherland argues that the poem exists under the pressure of capitalist abstraction which has forged or reduced the poetry into these blocks (2012b). The block of text is the formal mimicry of the squeezed block of labour formed into the abstract shape of value.

This squeezing of the text into abstract form as mimicry of capitalist processes of real abstraction is explicated by Sutherland's essay on Marx, which treats Marx's *Capital* as a work of satire (2008). In that essay Sutherland focuses on Marx's use of *Gallerte* (usually translated in English as congealed) in relation to how labour is rendered as abstract labour. Rendered is an appropriate word, as the German word refers to the animal substances (meat, bone and connective tissue) melted or processed to create something like glue or gelatine.[5] When Marx is tracing how labour is turned into abstract labour this is described as a violent process of rendering and so, for Sutherland, the extant English translations of *Capital* serve to neutralize the disgust Marx mined with this term. Marx's *Capital* is not an abstract work of pure theory, but, according to Sutherland, a text that is closely engaged with how abstractions

---

5 Jacques Derrida (1994: 243n35) had earlier drawn attention to the word *Gallerte* in *Capital*.

are materially rendered and in satirizing these processes at the level of its language. In this way, Sutherland aims to short circuit the usual structural readings of that Marx that ignore the disgust and satire that Marx develops as weapons against the abstract forms of capitalist society. *Gallerte* itself, becomes a kind of connective tissue or matter that joins together capitalist structures with material experience. Sutherland implies that *Capital* is a performative text, enacting the processing of matter into value, and is also a kind of hex or curse against these processes.

In reading *The Odes to TL61P*, also easily regarded as a highly abstract work, we should be attentive to its similar attempts to grasp abstraction as a material process. The blocks of text are processed blocks of language, which is parallel to the processed blocks of human labour used to produce abstract labour and so value (Sutherland 2012b: 205). We could add here that such a mimesis is surprisingly direct, and the equation of the block with abstraction less sensitive to the integration of matter and abstraction than Sutherland's account of *Capital* suggests. The relation of language to congealed labour is made explicit in the second ode, which begins with a consideration of the overlap between capitalist management and the police management that repressed the occupation of Trafalgar Square in London in 2011. Here Sutherland probes the 'mouthfeel' of the 'gelatine soufflé' purveyed by the 'buzzwords' of this management discourse (Sutherland 2013: 19). We have another iteration of *Gallerte*, this time as the ideological language of capital. This gooey and disgusting discourse materializes in police violence designed to clear the square. The ode ends 'Know your fucking / enemy' (22), in another attempt to trace exactly this materialization of words, police violence, and the abstractions of the commodity. Language and police violence coordinate together into this gooey homogeneity that is itself the result of the violent imposition of abstraction onto human bodies.

Sutherland's ode equates the abstract violence of labour management with the disciplinary function of police violence. This is no doubt true, but perhaps this consideration of the homogenization of language and labour in the goo of discourse might obscure the relations between abstract labour and policing. The rapid shift from the violence of real abstraction to the violence of policing has its truth, but one that could be rendered less abstractly. The image of the language of capital as blocks, both of homogenization and resistance (as in the black bloc), the image of that language as gooey homogeneity, are both ones that risk realizing the language of capital in an immediate rather than a mediated fashion. This is one of the tensions that runs through Sutherland's *Odes*, as they try to coordinate abstraction, materiality, and the realization of these forms in poetic language.

In terms of a more direct hexing, however, the particular section I want to focus on is a litany of different forms of misgiving and horror at a range of professions associated with financial services and activities that spreads over three pages in one sentence (38–40). To quote only the beginning:

> Giddy detestation of senior liquidity managers, strong aversion to strategy consultants, deep disgust at lead auditors, growing impatience with industry relations directors, spasmodic shrinking from financial modellers, rational fear of property loss adjustors, slight suspicion of corporate accountants, psychedelic distrust of branch compliance officers, [. . .] (38–39)

Here we have the repetition and modulation of dislike, stretching of the resources of language in an act, or series of acts, and the targeting of these proliferating embodied forms of financial management. Such a hexing is also gratifyingly comic. We have the dizzying spectacle of these abstract and seemingly meaningless jobs and the comedy comes in the matching of these proliferating roles with proliferating insults (Graeber 2018). This is particularly evident in the recordings of the poem being performed, which stages the desperate desire to name and insult these commodified forms of personality.

The *Odes* make a strange loop between these forms of violence on language and bodies—the violence that renders things fungible and vulnerable—and sexuality. The *Odes* explore childhood sexual experimentation, in an autobiographical mode, as one of polymorphous perversity. Sexuality is posed as both the 'irrepressible oral craving for the exciting controlled annihilation of values', and in terms of its absorption within capitalist regimes of value (Sutherland 2013: 29–30). While this might seem to suggest the collapse of the commodity fetish into the sexual fetish, in fact Sutherland is concerned with what remains resistant and qualitative within the commodity form (2012a). Discussing a childhood experience of giving a friend called Christian oral sex Sutherland writes: 'I wanted everybody to get something out of my mouth. What comes from it now is this ode, bright abolition to apathogenesis' (Sutherland 2013: 45). Apathogenic means not causing disease, so apathogenesis would seem to be the process by which disease does not develop. Either the ode moves from bright abolition to apathogenesis, to the nondevelopment of disease, or the ode is a bright abolition inflicted on apathogenesis, leaving us in a state of developing disease. The mouth is promise of a utopian sense of sharing by the mouth, an act of exchange that does not seem to be delimited by the commodity (Abbott 2013). The mouth is not simply the introjection of capitalist values, but also seems to play a role, again, of rejecting or abjecting such values.

Like Bonney's work, the *Odes* suggest a complex introjective dynamic, in which the libidinal and crisis economy of contemporary capitalism is internalized at the heart of lyric subjectivity through the mouth. The mouthfeel of abstract violence, rendered as the gelatine of the commodity form, is the taste of both violent abstraction and the qualitative moment of resistance within the commodity form. The moment of exception or resistance is there, but not outside the commodity, it is within, metaphorically, the mouth. The utopian moment of sexuality in the mouth is a making available to all, figuring the promiscuity of capitalist exchange, but also an availability beyond the limits of value. If we saw a tension with how Sutherland rendered abstraction in direct images, of blocks and equivalent forms of violence, here we see a tension in which sexuality is supposed to retain a pathos of resistance. Sexual experience is not reducible to capitalist logics, but the appeal to such experience might itself remain a performance of resistance that tries to work a traumatic resistance into abstract forms. It seems, in the face of the complexity of its own discourse, Sutherland's poetics has a recourse to violent shortcuts to resolve itself out of abstraction. While this is a recognition of the need to escape abstraction, the problem remains if this can offer a genuine direct language or a frustrated utopian desire for escape.

The Purge

Verity Spott's poem *Gideon* is itself a hex; Gideon is the name for a hex, for 'hate's screed' (2014: 8). In particular, the poem is hex against the British politician Georges Osborne (born Gideon Oliver Osborne), Conservative MP, Chancellor of the Exchequer from 2010, and responsible for the austerity program of the Tory government. The poem suggests 'and thus we may now call as one for the head / and intestines of George Osborne and do' (8). In a minor success for the hex, in 2016 George Osborne was sacked. After the Brexit vote and the election of a new Tory leader, Theresa May, he returned to the backbenches and then left politics to become editor of the *Evening Standard* (London's daily paper). The poem consists of sections written in three voices: Gideon, Isis (goddess of nature and magic, whose symbol means welfare or life), and Eris (the Greek goddess of strife and discord). The poem is a hex against the 'livid null' of a politician who, again, represents a modern version of the empty scion of privilege (3). Osborne's father, Sir Peter Osborne, founded the high-end fabric and wallpaper firm Osborne & Little. George Osborne attended Magdalen College, Oxford and was a member of the notorious Bullingdon Club—an elite all-male dining club based in Oxford.

As the figure behind the implementation of austerity measures that brought misery to many people in Britain while leaving financial institutions untouched or worse bailed out, George Osborne is another figure of the violence of financial abstraction. In this hex Spott tries to figure 'a conceptual /enemy body deranged' (5). The 'hex gurgles' 'for teething me' and we have to 'check again / the balance ingest' (3); once again the hex works in and by the mouth in this figuration of a deranged body. In particular, in the section Eris, the account of a cult that follows the goddess of discord (13), the poem turns to the notion of the purge as the implementation of the hex. The purge, which has an oral as well as a political sense, is enacted by a truly imaginary party, to use the term popularized by Tiqqun (1999). This purge is conducted in three or four forms of litany. The first is conducted subtly, and consists of various seemingly imaginary figures (although not all imaginary) with compound names connoting privilege that call to be purged: 'Georgie Highgrade-Middleton Cheney', for example, referring, perhaps, to Kate Middleton (Duchess of Cambridge and wife of Prince William), Dick Cheney (vice president of the United States under George W. Bush), and even Middleton Cheney (a village in South Northamptonshire, England).

The second purge is 'funtime', a purge of 'perceived public/celebrity enemies' (15). These include a range of celebrities who might, generously, be called public intellectuals in Britain: Professor Brian Cox (presenter of popular science programs), Melvyn Bragg (current presenter of the BBC Radio 4 series 'In Our Time', devoted to discussion of a range of intellectual topics), and Terry Eagleton (twice), usually described as Britain's leading Marxist literary critic. The 'next purge is a self-destructive purge in which 'I shot bullets into almost every one of my comrades killing most of them' (16). This is a 'self tearing', following the purging of 'aristocracy and minor celeb figures' (16). It parodies the conservative critique of revolutions as self-consuming while referencing the self-destruction of revolutions: the Terror of the French revolution, the suicide of the party under Bolshevism, the consumptive violence of the Khmer Rouge, or the murderous internal purges of the Japanese United Red Army, to cite well-known examples. It could also be considered as another involution of the hex, undermining its merely exterior position and suggesting an all-consuming process of hexing. In this it stands close to di Prima's notion that the final abstraction to be abolished during the revolution is the identity of the revolutionary or militant, but it is also close to a despair at the value of such identities.

Within this purge of people is another hex, on IBEX Global Solutions PLC, 'a leading provider of contact centre services and other business process outsourcing / solutions' (16). This returns us to capitalism, to the outsourcing and call centres that seem to dominate contemporary employment in Britain (Woodcock 2016). IBEX is a real company with a self-consciously hip image, describing itself as 'THE service disrupter in the world of business process outsourcing'. Its current website features images of diverse workers in suits with red-framed sunglasses, somewhere between *Reservoir Dogs* and James Bond. This is not a capitalism with a human face, but a capitalism in which the character mask is formed out of popular cultural representations of aggressive masculinity coded, ironically, as universally available. We have a world in which abstraction takes on a deliberately parodic and even cartoonish form. The difficulty of hexing such a company lies in its own capacity for self-satire or being beyond satire in its crassness. It inhabits that spirit of habituated counterculture that has become a dominant contemporary mode (Boltanski & Chiapello 2017; Frank 1997). Eris confronts its uncanny double in the creative destruction of contemporary capitalist disruption.

These various purges enumerate the subjectivities of contemporary capitalism as equivalent livid nulls and thereby try to void them. The poem is self-conscious about the limits of such strategies, conceding it 'is HEX that makes us futile' (Spott 2014: 8). At the same time, the hex and the purge are also violently enacted. This enactment expresses a fantasy and a desire: the desire to reveal and defeat the violence of capitalist abstraction. The fantasy is that we could render abstraction visible in all its maddening reality, in which abstractions are null but also livid. This would also reveal the discord that is hidden within the placid appearance of the legal order of capitalism. The desire is that the purge would expel all this, functioning as a purgative that would heal the social body. In this act of expelling through the mouth by listing and hexing we see the figures we need to destroy, as well as having the hope we could live without them.

These enumerations speak of the multiplicity of character masks and the various forms and structures in which they are arranged. While the list tends towards levelling and equivalence, Spott's (2016) 'An Angle on Management Cruelty' also speaks to the layering and hierarchies involved in the distribution of these masks. In the poem, the manager becomes a figure nested in the ascending great chain of being of contemporary capitalism. Hierarchy refers to company structures, roles, and skills, those fetish objects of contemporary capitalism: 'Healthcare, Hospitals, Change, Management, Business, Strategy, Team Building, Training, Business, Development, Coaching, Management, Mental Health, Performance, Management, Leadership, Development, Organizational Development, and Recruiting'. Here the cruelty of management decisions is seen as empty, dictated from above, but also real, enacted as a desire to be the good manager who implements what is required. Supplementing *Gideon*'s hex on one and all, this poem speaks of the hexes that capitalism implements. The capitalist hex, its cruelty, which is both and floating and embodied, is enacted through the mediation of the manager. In this way we can see the strategy of hexing is also a response to the much greater power of malediction possessed by capitalism itself—to the power of capitalism to bewitch, curse, and condemn (Pignarre and Stengers 2011). The hex is measure and response, ingestion, abjection and rejection of capitalist abstraction.

Revenge

The hex is a practice of poetic language that at once names, curses, and tries to produce the object of the curse. In the face of the forces and forms of abstract power, all-too brutally realized at particular points, the practice of the hex stages a scene in which abstract power is made to appear by the powerless, through the identification of poetry with the powerless, all the better to curse it. It is lack of power that is affirmed, although the notion of the powerless must be carefully considered. The poet is identifying with the powerless as well as inhabiting, to a degree, this lack of power as well. This is a variant of Rancière's analysis of the poetic 'short voyage to the land of the people', in this complex gesture of identification (2003). Of course, each hex is written out of personal experience, although with an awareness that this experience is itself abstracted and constructed. The difficulty of distance abides in the hex—the poetic citation of the slogan or curse is not exactly equivalent to their utterance, although these, in turn, are forms of performance. Poetry, while relatively powerless—still often cited in Britain as the most minor art and antithetical to self-reproduction—retains a certain power and canonical status. The poems I have discussed are instances of neomodernism and inhabit the reiteration of that formation, with all its complex arrangements of power and its lack.

The act of hexing or cursing is focused on orality—not simply on language, but also on eating and vomiting the negated object. The appearance or materialization of the abstract is one that takes place in the mouth and by the mouth. It is the oral that condenses the body and language in that opening to the outside that is site of speech and site of potential violation. If, for Freud, negation was an act of expelling from the mouth, these poems hold the object of the hex in the mouth, precisely in the ambivalent space between introjecting and expelling. Derrida, in another context, remarks that: 'Chaos refers precisely to the abyss or the open mouth, that which speaks as well as that which signifies hunger' (1996: 84). The mouth, again, carries a double function, of speaking and eating, which can be referred to the tension between abstract violence and material resistance; in austerity Britain, between the cry of despair and the hungry mouth resorting to the food bank. This chaos is the abyssal moment that the hex speaks to, trying to register as something that which the abstract impositions of equivalence and exchange obliterate and expunge. But the hex must also trace the chaos that results from these material organizations of equivalence, which condition the abyss from which these texts speak (and speak, interestingly, is what they try to do). These poems displace the writerly and the textual focus of the poetic and theoretical avant-gardes of the 1970s and 1980s for the sake of the oral and the spoken, albeit a speaking heavily conditioned by writerliness and textuality.

The hex is a performance that creates a reality out of fictive capital and state fictions in response to the mobility of capitalist abstraction and the faceless appearance of state power. It does so by a use of fantasy, which is used to sustain the hex as an act of power and to recognize the weakness in that act—the futility of poetic words to change reality. The hex is not a pure fantasy, or an act of imagination that denies reality, but the difficult attempt to sustain the imagination of a different reality. In these texts, bodies are pitched against bodies: bodies of poetic work, the body of the poet against the body of capital, the body of the state, the embodied enemy. These hexes suggest the violence of the abstract and counter the notion that such acts of counterviolence are perpetually doomed to miss the target or only choose easy targets. An overemphasis on the abstract form of capitalism and on the necessary failure of acts of revenge as forms of Nietzschean *ressentiment* are both ways to neutralize political possibilities. Instead, as Danny Hayward suggests, these works hex to exhaust language, to push exhausted language to the point of the exhausted labouring body, to create, in their litanies and repetitions, the hex as a strategy of exhaustion, in both senses: exhausting the resources of language and suggesting that our language is already exhausted (2015: 108).

At the same time, however, these poems proliferate and enumerate language and targets. It might be too simple also to dismiss the hex as acts of fantasy and fiction. Diane di Prima, in her *Revolutionary Letter #46*, writes: 'And as you learn the magic, learn to believe it / Don't be "surprised" when it works, you undercut / your power.' There is still a power in the hex, which may not only be the power of language or the power to push language to its point of exhaustion. The magic remains in the desire to push beyond the limits of abstraction, beyond the engagement with the ways in which abstraction seizes bodies. In this moment of remaining with the hex there is a desire to make the body appear—not only the body of the target but also the body of all those who resist. While it easy enough to regard this as mere fiction, to return once again to the tropes of poetry as useless and superfluous, something continues to take place in the emergence of a place from which to resist. The difficulty remains, however, of the hex as an act of faith and one heavily stylized in the context of abstraction. Faith in the word recurs in an orality that mimics the incarnation. A seemingly secular poetics (or a poetics that occasionally proclaims its secularity) forms its own oral faith in the material as merged with the word. This is the risk the hex has to run in its attempt to contest abstraction, which, at the same time, has a faith in the power of direct language to overturn that abstraction.

CONCLUSION

If our world becomes an abstraction, how do we continue to live in that world? This is a question and a problem posed to us by the global abstractions of capitalism and the damage they have done to our world. The urgency is magnified by the ways in which this abstract world of capitalism is forced to coincide with our world. The fantasy of capital is one in which capitalism and the world would become one (or are already one). There would be no life, no matter, no language, outside of the world made one with capitalism, or what would be outside would only ever be the source of future value. To conclude, I want to focus on how this problem and the potential despair it can induce is dealt with in the science fiction of Kim Stanley Robinson, especially his novels *Aurora* (2015) and *Red Moon* (2018). This is certainly a turn to narrative fiction and away from poetry. In fact, this transition is not as marked as it could be, for what concerns me in these novels is the ongoing and problematic attempts to connect language and matter. These are novels that engage with that problem on the planetary scale and, problematic as they are, remain resonant for our moment.

Aurora and *Red Moon* not only concern climate and capitalist crises, the twin and connected processes by which our world is becoming unliveable, they also engage with the problem of how we might communicate this experience of crisis. *Aurora* focuses on a generation ship, one sustaining several generations of humans, travelling to the planet Tau Ceti to found a new human colony in the face of the collapse of the earth's ecosystem. It tries to think how we might escape a world that has become, seemingly, coterminous with a destructive capitalism. *Aurora* also uses the ship's Artificial Intelligence (AI) as the device to represent the struggle to tell this story of attempted space colonization. *Red Moon*, set 30 years from now,[1] concerns a near future in which the moon is colonized by China, and both China and the United States are moving towards a crisis of hegemony. Again, we have an AI, this time in China, and this time trying to coordinate a global challenge to capitalism as hegemonic system.

Robinson has seen his fiction as a new realism and, borrowing from both Lukács and his friend Fredric Jameson, has argued that science fiction is the form for this realism that can go beyond the nineteenth-century novel's discussion of the relationship of the individual to society and history by adding 'the nonhuman and the planet' (Robinson and Feder 2018: 88). We can see these additions in the emergence of the nonhuman AIs and in the planetary dimension both novels engage with. While Robinson's *The Ministry for the Future* (2020) has attracted more critical attention and debate for its panoramic engagement with near future climate catastrophe, these earlier novels are more resonant to me. Not only does *The Ministry for the Future* abandon the science fiction elements, but it also does not directly concern itself with the focalization of the problem of realism. Instead, while there are instances of nonhuman narration, such as the sun 'speaking', and the use of heteroglossia, with multiple voices, there is not an equivalent to the AI in *Aurora* or *Red Moon* as the attempt to coordinate this new mode of literary realism. There is an AI in the novel, but it has a minor and brief role. We could argue the Ministry itself plays the role of focal point for the narrative, but this is not directly thematized. Robinson's attempted realism through heteroglossia risks fragmenting into a naturalism, which can only reflect the problems of climate change he is concerned with solving (Lukàcs 1963). While the shock power of *The Ministry for the Future* is undeniable, its lack of a focalizing of the relations between language and matter make it problematic (Lukàcs 1970: 15).

---

1 This is a neat reversal of the tendency of the realist novel to locate its action thirty years in the past.

The narrator of *Aurora* is the AI, and it is a narrator that constantly struggles with how to translate its own quantum processes, structured by mathematics, into human language and narrative. The AI, called to tell the story of the ship's journey, ponders the question of what is lost in language and the difficulties of narrative compression (Robinson 2016: 45). The AI considers the difficulties caused by its own perceptual matrix, but also the inadequacy of human narrative, and even the inadequacy of human language itself:

> First, clearly metaphors have no empirical basis, and are often opaque, pointless, inane, inaccurate, deceptive, mendacious, and, in short, futile and stupid. Nevertheless, despite all that, human language is, in its most fundamental operation, a gigantic system of metaphors. (123)

The ship's AI echoes Nietzsche's (1999: 146) suggestion that truth is a 'mobile army of metaphors' and Lakoff and Johnson's theses that language is fundamentally metaphoric in orientation (1980). The further claim, however, is that language is futile and stupid in describing reality. The AI reaches a brutal conclusion:

> Their languages lie to them, systematically, and in their very designs. A liar species. What a thing, really. What an evolutionary dead end. (Robinson 2016: 331)

Here we have another iteration of the war on language and an associated sense of hopelessness, which suggests that language must surrender before the dense and complex materiality of the universe. The AI might well be one of the current new materialists, who wish to exchange the dead end of language for the great outdoors of matter. The AI's despair over language becomes an antihumanist despair over humans themselves, left, finally, as 'a liar species'.

This pessimistic sense of hopelessness in relation to the powers of language is matched by the novel despairing that humans can successfully colonize another planet. Arriving on the planet chosen for colonization the settlers discover the planet is home to a prion-like disease that is deadly to humans. The result is a stark alternative: 'I mean it's obvious any new place is going to be either alive or dead. It it's alive it's going to be poisonous, if it's dead you're going to have to work it up from scratch' (178). This is Robinson's refutation of the Planet B scenario. The novel, however, is not entirely hopeless. While the project of space colonization is an abject failure, after the harrowing return journey to earth those remaining on *Aurora* discover a damaged earth that is being repaired through terraforming. The character Freya, who the AI had selected as the central voice for its narrative, joins this terra-forming effort. She is left the novel's last words, as she experiences the wonder that even a damaged earth is capable of eliciting. While Robinson's realism 'helps to make biophysical systems and problems visible' (Robinson and Feder 2018: 88), it also struggles with that process of making visible. There is a tension between a realism capable of grasping the relations between humans and things and a naturalism that can only show those these elements without bringing them into relation.

Robinson's novel tries to speak to the totality of language, matter, and thought in its imagination of a realism that includes society, history, the nonhuman and the planetary. *Aurora* remains, however, doubtful over the possibility of integrating that totality and so prone to restate a limit between knowledge and reality. It struggles, for understandable reasons, with imagining the limits of capitalism as a totality and an alternative order beyond capitalism. We have repeatedly noted how Marx pointed out that the romantic desire to return to an original fullness is predicated on the sense that history has come to a standstill (1973: 162). The notion of the world as completely calculable, the dream of bourgeois ideology, feeds the romantic desire for escape. In the face of the con-temporary catastrophe of climate-change capitalism, a global phenomenon that threatens our own living on the earth, it is not surprising that the desire for escape should be exacerbated. What remains difficult is what Marx suggested—the need to transcend this opposition by bringing capitalist society to its 'blessed end' (Anderson 1980: 169). *Aurora* can be read as illustrating this dif-ficulty, with the ship's journey out expressing the romantic desire to escape and the agonizing and catastrophic return journey as history come to a standstill, as well as being a metaphor for our failing eco system. While the novel disputes the romantic pathos of the outside it struggles to imagine the blessed end through an integrated change to our world.

Another of Robinson's AIs, this time in his novel *Red Moon* (2018), considers the problem of totality, capitalism and language from the other side of the saturation of language. Now it is not so much the lack of language, its inability to engage the material and the real, but its excess that is the problem. In this novel the AI has been freed from its human-created restraints to engineer global political change from within China. Faced with an uprising from below the AI takes on the role of creating a manifesto and set of demands that are both specifically Chinese and that will also resonate globally. This is the task of the revolutionary, most familiar to us from Lenin's ability to create a concrete slogan or Trotsky's development of the concept of transitional demands.

This problem of the integration of struggles in *Red Moon* is that the AI tries to formulate its demands in the face of a future context of the cloud as a dataspace saturated by demands and by language. It reflects on its own success at articulating resonant demands: 'although words are acts, and even important acts, there are in the discourse space of the current global civilization simply too many acts' (Robinson 2018: 405). The filling of space by language creates interference, 'a chaos of intersecting waves', which results in the fact that 'no new semantic action [. . .] can alter humanity's current behaviors'. This is, again, the hopeless dimension of the AI's thinking, but it proceeds by trying to link the language of demands to fundamental human needs—to be fed, to be healthy, to live freely, to create and so on. The needs are known and so is the language, but as the AI also realizes, power is necessary to actualize these needs and to cut through the global discourse of semantic acts. Totality is not simply a grasping together of all the dimensions of reality and the interconnections of matter, language, and concepts, but also calls for the means to comprehend and use a power based on a logical grasp of its structure and dynamics (Trotsky 1967; James 2001).

Lenin's text 'On Slogans' makes explicit this politics of language by arguing that: 'Every particular slogan must be deduced from the totality of specific features of a definite political situation' (2002: 62). The grasping of totality, of which language is an element that can in turn formulate this totality, is one geared to grasping the political situation. This is why, according to Lenin, the revolutionary situation has to be understood in terms of the question of power and of who has power. In this, he and Trotsky would be influential on Weber's understanding of the state as a monopoly on violence (2020: 46). The deduction of the situation must be attentive to the situation as it develops, as 'the substitution of the abstract for the concrete is one of the greatest and most dangerous sins in a revolution' (Lenin 2002: 67). Lenin is concerned with developing slogans that reflect the concrete truth of a changing circumstances and so avoid deceiving the people. What we have here is a use of language developed from the grasping of totality; exactly the aim to which Robinson's AI is fumbling towards.

We have become used to saying these references to Marxist classics are outdated, and we often prefer to adopt the AI's claim that there are simply too many speech acts in the global space of data, which defeats any mapping of totality. *Good Bye Lenin!*, as the film had it (Becker 2003), and so too goodbye language as a lever of change. While such references, as those thinkers argued, demand reinvention and rethinking through attention to concrete reality, they also pose fundamental lessons we still need to learn. Here I have tried to begin from what Marx called direct language, which can only appear to us insulting and rude to the honour of the commodity and to the commodities which we have become, to trace the possibilities and resources of a language of class struggle. That is why, I hope, like the quizzical AIs of Kim Stanley Robinson's fiction, we stand together trying to make sense of the possibilities of our existing language. This sense making is a collective task, one undertaken everyday under the most severe pressure, but evident in the persistence of direct language to cut through the chaos of semantic acts. It is just such a direct and collective language that will speak and write our future.

WORKS CITED

ABBOTT, Matthew. 2013. 'The Poetry of Destroyed Experience'. *3AM Magazine*. Available at: https://bit.ly/3z6azZP (last accessed: 22 October 2022).

ABRAHAM, Nicolas, and Maria Torok. 1986. *The Wolf Man's Magic Word* (Nicholas Rand trans.). Minneapolis: University of Minnesota Press.

ADAMS, Parveen. 1986. 'Versions of the Body'. *m/f* 11–12: 27–34.

——. 1996. *The Emptiness of the Image*. London: Routledge.

ADORNO, Theodor. 1973. *The Jargon of Authenticity* (Knut Tarnowski and Frederic Will trans). Evanston: Northwestern University Press.

AGAMBEN, Giorgio. 1991. *Language and Death: The Place of Negativity* (Karen E. Pinkus trans.). Minneapolis, MN: University of Minnesota Press.

——. 1998. *Homo Sacer* (Daniel Heller-Roazen trans.). Stanford: Stanford University Press.

——. 1999a. *The End of the Poem: Studies in Poetics* (Daniel Heller-Roazen trans.). Stanford, CA: Stanford University Press.

——. 1999b. *The Man without Content* (Georgia Albert trans.). Stanford, CA: Stanford University Press.

ALTHUSSER, Louis. 1969. *For Marx* (Ben Brewster trans.). Harmondsworth: Penguin.

——. 2008. *On Ideology*. London: Verso.

——. 2009. *Reading Capital* (Ben Brewster trans.). London: Verso.

ANDERSON, Perry. 1980. *Arguments within English Marxism*. London: NLB and Verso.

——. 2001. 'On Sebastiano Timpanaro'. *London Review of Books* 23(9). Available at: https://bit.ly/3F5c9ir (last accessed: 20 October 2022).

ARENDT, Hannah. 1959. *The Human Condition*. New York: Doubleday Anchor Books.

ARTAUD, Antonin. 1965. *Anthology* (Jack Hirschman ed.). San Francisco: City Lights Books.

———. 1988. *Selected Writings* (Susan Sontag ed. and intro.). Berkeley and Los Angeles: University of California Press.

———. 1995. *Watchfiends & Rack Screams: Works from the Final Period* (Clayton Eshelman with Bernard Bador trans. and ed.). Boston: Exact Change.

———. 2019. *Van Gogh: The Man Suicided by Society* (Catherine Petit and Paul Buck trans). London: Vauxhall & Company. First published 1947.

AUSTIN, J. L. 1979. 'Performative Utterances' in *Philosophical Papers*, 3RD EDN (J. O. Urmson and G. J. Warnock eds). Oxford: Oxford University Press, 233–52.

AVINERI, Shlomo. 1968. *The Social and Political Thought of Karl Marx*. Cambridge: Cambridge University Press.

BALESTRINI, Nanni. 2016. *We Want Everything* (Matt Holden trans.). London: Verso. First published 1971.

BALSO, Judith. 2014. *The Affirmation of Poetry* (Drew S. Burk trans.). Minneapolis, MN: Univocal.

BADIOU, Alain. 1999. *Manifesto for Philosophy* (Norman Madarasz trans.). Albany: State University of New York Press.

———. 2006. 'The Factory as Event Site'. *Prelom* 8: 171–76.

———. 2007. *The Century* (Alberto Toscano trans.). Cambridge: Polity.

———. 2008. *Number and Numbers* (Robin Mackay trans.). Cambridge: Polity.

———. 2012. 'The Figure of the Soldier' in *Philosophy for Militants* (Bruno Bosteels ed. and trans.). London and New York: Verso, pp. 41–60.

———. 2014a. 'A Requiem for the Factory: On François Bon's *Sortie d'usine*' in *The Age of the Poets* (Bruno Bosteels trans. and ed.). London and New York: Verso, pp. 140–46.

———. 2014b. 'Pierre Guyotat, Prince of Prose' in *The Age of the Poets* (Bruno Bosteels trans. and ed.). London: Verso, pp. 194–205.

BANKES, Ariane, and Paul Hills. 2015. *The Art of David Jones: Vision and Memory*. Chichester: Pallant House Gallery.

BARTHES, Roland. 1975. *The Pleasure of the Text* (Richard Miller trans.) New York: Hill and Wang.

BATAILLE, Georges. 1985. *Literature and Evil* (Alastair Hamilton trans.). New York and London: Marion Boyars. First published 1957.

———. 1990. 'Hegel, Death and Sacrifice' in 'On Bataille'. Special Issue, *Yale French Studies* 78: 9–28.

BAUDRILLARD, Jean. 1975. *The Mirror of Production*. New York: Telos.

———. 1993. *Symbolic Exchange and Death* (Iain Hamilton Grant trans.). London: Sage.

———. 1994. *Simulacra and Simulation* (Sheila Faria Glaser trans.). Ann Arbor: The University of Michigan Press.

BECKER, Wolfgang, director. 2003. *Good Bye Lenin!* X-Filme Creative Pool.

BENJAMIN, Walter. 1968. *Illuminations* (Harry Zohn trans., Hannah Arendt ed. and intro.). New York: Schocken Books.

———. 1979. *One-Way Street and Other Writings* (Edmund Jephcott and Kinglsey Shorter trans). London: NLB.

———. 1999. 'Experience and Poverty' in *Walter Benjamin: Selected Writings, Volume 2, 1927–1934* (R. Livingstone et al trans., Jennings, M. W. ed.). Cambridge, MA: Harvard University Press, 731–36.

———. 2015. *On Photography* (Esther Leslie trans. and ed.). London: Reaktion Books.

BERGER, John. 1992. *Pig Earth*. London: Vintage.

BERSANI, Leo. 1976. *A Future for Astyanax: Character and Desire in Literature*. Boston and Toronto: Little, Brown and Company.

BIRNBAUM, Antonia. 2011. 'Between Sharing and Antagonism: The Invention of Communism in the Early Marx'. *Radical Philosophy* 166: 21–28.

BLAKE, William. 1967. *Songs of Innocence and of Experience* (Geoffrey Keynes ed.). Oxford: Oxford University Press. First published 1794.

———. 1975. *The Marriage of Heaven and Hell* (Geoffrey Keynes ed.). London and New York: Oxford University Press. First published 1794.

BLANCHOT, Maurice. 2001. *Faux Pas* (Charlotte Mandell trans.). Stanford, CA: Stanford University Press. First published 1943.

———. 2010. '"Factory-Excess," or Infinity in Pieces' in *Political Writings: 1953–1993* (Zakir Paul trans. and intro.). New York: Fordham University Press, pp. 131–32.

BOLTANSKI, Luc, and Eve Chiapello. 2017. *The New Spirit of Capitalism* (Gregory Elliott trans.). London and New York: Verso.

BONNEY, Sean. 2014. 'ACAB: A Nursery Rhyme'. *abandonedbuildings*, 31 December. Available at: https://bit.ly/3F4cF09 (last accessed: 22 October 2022).

———. 2015. *Letters against the Firmament*. London: Enitharmon Press.

BORGES, Jorge Luis. 2020. *The Aleph and Other Stories* (Andrew Hurley trans.). London: Penguin.

BOSQUET, Antoine. 2018. *The Eye of War*. Minneapolis, MN: University of Minnesota Press.

BOSTEELS, Bruno. 2009. 'The Jargon of Finitude'. *Radical Philosophy* 155: 41–47.

BRAVERMAN, Harry. 1974. *Labor and Monopoly Capital: The Degradation of Work in the Twentieth Century*. New York: Monthly Review Press.

BRECHT, Bertolt. 1976. *Poems 1913–1956* (John Willett and Ralph Manheim eds). London: Methuen.

BRENNAN, Timothy. 2014. *Borrowed Light: Vico, Hegel, and the Colonies*. Stanford, CA: Stanford University Press.

BREU, Christopher. 2014. *Insistence of the Material*. Minneapolis and London: University of Minnesota Press.

BURROUGHS, William. 1968. *Nova Express*. London: Granada. First published 1964.

———. 1971. *The Wild Boys*. New York: Grover Press.

———. 1999. *Word Virus: A William Burroughs Reader* (James Grauerholz and Ira Silverberg eds). London: Flamingo.

BUTLER, Judith. 2019. 'The Inorganic Body in the Early Marx'. *Radical Philosophy* 2(6): 3–17.

BYRON, Lord. 1973. *Don Juan* (T. G. Steffan, E. Steffan and W. W. Pratt eds, Susan J. Wolfson and Peter J. Manning intro.). London: Penguin. First published 1824.

CALASSO, Roberto. 2018. *The Ruin of Kasch* (Richard Dixon trans.). London: Penguin. First published 1983.

CARDINAL, Marie. 1993. *The Words to Say It* (Pat Goodheart trans.). London: Women's Press. First published 1975.

CAUDWELL, Christopher. 2009. *Studies & Further Studies in a Dying Culture*. New York and London: Monthly Review Press.

CAVALLETI, Andrea. 2014. Introduction to *Spartakus: The Symbology of Revolt* (Alberto Toscano trans., Andrea Cavalleti ed.). London: Seagull Books, pp. 1–21.

CCRU. 2015. *Writings, 1997–2003*. Falmouth: Time Spiral Press.

CLARK, T. J. 1999. *Farewell to an Idea: Episodes from a History of Modernism*. New Haven, CT: Yale University Press.

——. 2006. *The Sight of Death*. New Haven, CT: Yale University Press.

——. 2012. 'For a Left with No Future'. *New Left Review* 74: 53–75.

——. 2013. 'Lowry's Other England' in T. J. Clark and Anne M. Wagner, *Lowry and the Painting of Modern Life*. London: Tate Publishing, pp 21–73.

——. 2018. *Heaven on Earth: Painting and the Life to Come*. London: Thames & Hudson.

CLARK, T.J., Iain A. Boal, Joseph Matthews, and Michael Watts. 2005. *Afflicted Powers: Capital and Spectacle in a New Age of War*. London and New York: Verso.

CLOVER, Joshua. 2016a. 'Five Book Plan: Radical Poetry'. *Verso Blog*, 24 May. Available at: https://bit.ly/3FbG3Bw (last accessed: 21 October 2022).

——. 2016b. *Riot. Strike. Riot: The New Era of Uprisings*. London: Verso.

CROSER, Caroline. 2007. 'Networking Security in the Space of the City: Eventful Battlespaces and the Contingency of the Encounter'. *Theory & Event* 10(2). doi:10.1353/tae.2007.0058 (last accessed 21 October 2022).

CULLER, Jonathan. 1976. *Saussure*. London: Fontana.

DAVIS, Mike. 2003. *Dead Cities and Other Tales*. New York: The New Press.

DEBORD, Guy. 1995. *The Society of the Spectacle* (Donald Nicholson-Smith trans.) New York: Zone Books.

——. 1998. *Comments on the Society of the Spectacle* (Malcolm Imrie trans.). London and New York, Verso.

DE CASTRO, Eduardo Viveiros. 2014. *Cannibal Metaphysics* (Peter Skafish trans. and ed.). Minneapolis, MN: Univocal.

DELEUZE, Giles. 1983. *Nietzsche and Philosophy* (Hugh Tomlinson trans.). London: The Athlone Press.

——. 1985. 'Lecture 08' (transcribed by Annabelle Dufourcq, Charles J. Stivale ed., Samantha Bankston trans.) in *Seminar on Foucault, 1985–86*. Available at: https://bit.ly/3DvvbMl (last accessed 3 November 2022).

——. 1986. 'Nomad Thought' in David B. Allison (ed.), *The New Nietzsche*. Cambridge, MA: The MIT Press, pp. 142–49.

DELEUZE, Giles, and Félix Guattari. 1983. *Anti-Oedipus: Capitalism and Schizophrenia*. (Robert Hurley, Mark Seem and Helen R. Lane trans). Minneapolis, MN: University of Minnesota Press. First published 1972.

——. 1986. *Kafka: Towards a Minor Literature* (Dana Polan trans., Réda Bensmaïa for.). Minneapolis, MN: University of Minnesota Press.

——. 1988. *A Thousand Plateaus* (Brian Massumi trans.). London: Athlone. First published 1980.

——. 1994. *What is Philosophy?* (Hugh Tomlinson and Graham Burchell trans). New York: Columbia University Press.

DE MAN, Paul. 1982. *Allegories of Reading*. New Haven: Yale University Press.

——. 1996. *Aesthetic Ideology* (Andrzej Warminski trans.) Minneapolis: University of Minnesota Press.

DERRIDA, Jacques. 1976. *Of Grammatology* (Gayatri Chakravorty Spivak trans.). Baltimore and London: Johns Hopkins University Press.

——. 1978. *Writing and Difference* (Alan Bass trans.). Chicago: Chicago University Press.

——. 1982. *Margins of Philosophy* (Alan Bass trans.). Brighton: The Harvester Press.

——. 1985. *The Ear of the Other* (Christie McDonald ed.). Lincoln and London: University of Nebraska Press.

——. 1987a. *Positions* (Alan Bass trans.). London: The Athlone Press.

——. 1987b. *Archeology of the Frivolous* (John P. Leavey Jr trans. and intro.). Lincoln: University of Nebraska Press.

——. 1987c. *The Post Card: From Socrates to Freud and Beyond* (Alan Bass trans.). Chicago: Chicago University Press.

——. 1988. *Limited Inc* (Samuel Weber trans., Gerald Graff ed.). Evanston, IL: Northwestern University Press.

——. 1989a. *Of Spirit* (Geoffrey Bennington and Rachel Bowlby trans). Chicago: The University of Chicago Press.

——. 1989b. *Edmund Husserl's Origin of Geometry: An Introduction* (John P. Leavey Jr trans.). Lincoln and London: University of Nebraska Press.

——. 1989c. 'How to Avoid Speaking: Denials' in *Languages of the Unsayable* (S. Budick and W. Iser eds). New York: Columbia University Press, pp. 3–70.

——. 1992. *Given Time: I. Counterfeit Money* (Peggy Kamuf trans.). Chicago and London: Chicago University Press.

——. 1994. *Specters of Marx: The State of the Debt, the Work of Mourning and the New International* (Peggy Kamuf trans.). London: Routledge.

——. 1998a. *Monolingualism of the Other: Or, The Prosthesis of Origin* (Patrick Mensah trans.). Stanford, CA: Stanford University Press.

——. 1998b. 'To Unsense the Subjectile' in *The Secret Art of Antonin Artaud* (Mary Ann Caws trans.). Cambridge, MA: The MIT Press, pp. 59–148.

——. 1998c. *Resistances of Psychoanalysis* (Peggy Kamuf, Pascale-Anne Brault, and Michael Naas trans). Stanford, CA: Stanford University Press.

——. 2002. *Negotiations: Interventions and Interviews, 1971–2001* (Elizabeth Rottenberg trans., ed. and intro.). Stanford, CA: Stanford University Press.

——. 2019. *Theory & Practice* (David Wills trans., Geoffrey Bennington and Peggy Kamuf eds). Chicago and London: University of Chicago Press.

——. 2021. *Clang* (David Wills and Geoffrey Bennington trans.). Minneapolis, MN: University of Minnesota Press.

DESCOMBES, Vincent. 1980. *Modern French Philosophy* (L. Scott-Fox and J. M. Harding trans). Cambridge: Cambridge University Press.

DI PRIMA, Diane. 1991. 'Paracelsus: An Appreciation' in Richard Grossinger (ed.), *The Alchemical Tradition in the Late Twentieth Century*. Berkley, CA: North Atlantic Books, pp. 26–33.

——. 1998. *Loba*. New York: Penguin.

——. 2007. *Revolutionary Letters*. San Francisco: Last Gasp. First published 1971.

DOLAR, Mladen. 2017. 'Of Drives and Culture'. *Problemi* 1: 55–80.

DUNCAN, Dennis (ed.). 2015. *Theory of the Great Game*. London: Atlas.

ECHEVERRÍA, Bolívar. 2014. '"Use-value": Ontology and Semiotics'. *Radical Philosophy* 188: 24–38.

ELIOT, T. S. 1983. *Collected Poems 1909–1962*. London: Faber and Faber.

ENGELS, Friedrich. 2010. *The Origin of the Family, Private Property, and the State*. London: Penguin. First published 1884.

ERDMAN, David. 1977. *Blake: Prophet against Empire*. Princeton, NJ: Princeton University Press.

ESSLIN, Martin. 1976. *Antonin Artaud: The Man and His Work*. London: Calder Publications.

FAROCKI, Harun. 2006. 'Workers Leaving the Factory in 11 Decades'. Photographic installation in *Cinema Like Never Before* (exhibition). Vienna: Generali Foundation.

FELSKI, Rita. 2015. *The Limits of Critique*. Chicago: The University of Chicago Press.

FENOLLOSA, Ernest. 1936. *The Chinese Written Character as a Medium for Poetry*. (Ezra Pound ed.). San Francisco, CA: City Lights Books.

FLUSS, Harrison, and Landon Frim. 2021. *Prometheus and Gaia*. London: Anthem Press.

FOSTER, Hal. 2017. *Bad New Days: Art, Criticism, Emergency*. London and New York: Verso.

———. 2018. 'You have a new memory'. Review of *Trevor Paglen: Sites Unseen*, by John P. Jacob and Luke Skrebowski, and *Trevor Paglen*, by Lauren Cornell, Julian Bryan-Wilson and Omar Kholeif. *London Review of Books* 40(19) (9 October): 43–45. Available at: https://bit.ly/3MZx5ZS (last accessed: 21 October 2022).

FOSTER, John Bellamy and Paul Burkett. 2000. 'The Dialectic of Organic/Inorganic Relations: Marx and the Hegelian Philosophy of Nature'. *Organization & Environment* 13(4) (December): 403–25.

FOUCAULT, Michel. 1970. *The Order of Things*. London and New York: Routledge.

———. 1977a. 'Nietzsche, Genealogy, History' in *Language, Counter-Memory, Practice: Selected Essays and Interviews* (D. F. Bouchard ed.). Ithaca: Cornell University Press, pp. 139–64.

———. 1977b. *Discipline and Punish*. Harmondsworth: Penguin.

———. 1983. Preface to Gilles Deleuze and Félix Guattari, *Anti-Oedipus: Capitalism and Schizophrenia* (Robert Hurley, Mark Seem and Helen R. Lane trans). Minneapolis, MN: University of Minnesota Press, pp. *xi–xiv*.

———. 1989. *Madness and Civilization: A History of Insanity in the Age of Reason* (Richard Howard trans.). London: Tavistock/Routledge.

FRANK, Thomas. 1997. *The Conquest of Cool*. Chicago: University of Chicago Press.

FREUD, Sigmund. 1964. 'Constructions in Analysis' (James Strachey trans.) in *The Standard Edition of the Complete Psychological Works of Sigmund Freud*, VOL. 23. London: The Hogarth Press and the Institute of Psycho-Analysis, pp. 256–69. First published 1937.

——. 1973. *Introductory Lectures on Psychoanalysis* (James Strachey, trans., James Strachey and Angela Richards eds.). London: Penguin.

——. 1975. *The Psychopathology of Everyday Life*. (Alan Tyson trans., James Strachey ed.). Harmondsworth: Penguin. First published 1901.

——. 1976. *The Interpretation of Dreams* (James Strachey trans. and ed.). London: Penguin. First published 1900.

——. 1977. 'Three Essays on the Theory of Sexuality' in *On Sexuality* (James Strachey trans., Angela Richards ed.). Harmondsworth: Penguin, pp. 39–169. First published 1905.

——. 1984a. 'Repression' in *On Metapsychology* (James Strachey trans., Angela Richards ed.). Harmondsworth: Penguin, pp. 145–58. First published 1915.

——. 1984b. 'Negation' in *On Metapsychology* (James Strachey trans., Angela Richards ed.). Harmondsworth: Penguin, pp. 435–442. First published 1925.

FREUD, Sigmund, and Joseph Breuer. 1974. *Studies on Hysteria* (James Strachey and Alix Strachey trans., Angela Richards ed.). London: Penguin. First published 1895.

FROMENT-MEURICE, Marc. 1998. *That Is To Say: Heidegger's Poetics*, (Jan Plug trans.). Stanford, CA: Stanford University Press.

FUSSELL, Paul. 1977. *The Great War and Modern Memory*. Oxford: Oxford University Press.

GALLOWAY, Alexander. 2014. *Laruelle: Against the Digital*. Minneapolis and London: University of Minnesota Press.

—— and Eugene Thacker. 2007. *The Exploit: A Theory of Networks*. Minneapolis, MN: University of Minnesota Press.

GAY, Peter. 1989. *Freud: A Life for Our Time*. London and Basingstoke: Macmillan.

GIBSON-GRAHAM, J. K. 2006. *The End of Capitalism (As We Knew It): A Feminist Critique of Political Economy*. Minneapolis, MN: The University of Minnesota Press.

GINZBURG, Carlo. 1980. *The Cheese and the Worms: The Cosmos of a Sixteenth-Century Miller* (John and Anne Tedeschi trans). London and Henley: Routledge & Kegan Paul.

GORDILLO, Gastón. 2014. *Rubble*. Durham, NC: Duke University Press.

GOUX, Jean-Joseph. 1988. 'Banking on Signs'. *diacritics* 18(2): 15–25.

——. 1990a. *Symbolic Economies: After Marx and Freud* Jennifer Curtis Gage trans.). Ithaca, NY: Cornell University Press.

——. 1990b. 'General Economics and Postmodern Capitalism'. *Yale French Studies* 78: 206–24.

——. 2012. 'Cash, Check, or Charge?'. *Communications* 91: 227–41.

GRAEBER, David. 2018. *Bullshit Jobs*. London: Penguin.

GROSRICHARD, Alain. 1998. *The Sultan's Court: European Fantasies of the East* (Liz Heron trans., Mladen Dolar intro.). London: Verso.

GUATTARI, Félix. 1984. 'Mary Barnes, or Oedipus in Anti-Psychiatry' in *Molecular Revolution*. London: Penguin, pp. 51–59.

HALL, Stuart. 1996. 'The Problem of Ideology: Marxism without Guarantees' in David Morley and Kuan-Hsing Chen (eds), *Stuart Hall: Critical Dialogues in Cultural Studies*. London: Routledge, pp. 24–45.

HAMACHER, Werner. 1998. *Pleroma* (Nicholas Walker and Simon Jarvis trans). London: The Athlone Press.

——. 2008. 'Lingua Amissa: The Messianism of Commodity-Language and Derrida's *Specters of Marx*' in *Ghostly Demarcations: A Symposium on Jacques Derrida's 'Specters of Marx'*. London and New York: Verso, pp. 168–212.

HARAWAY, Donna. 2016. *Manifestly Haraway*. Minneapolis and London: University of Minnesota Press.

HARMAN, Graham. 2005. *Guerrilla Metaphysics: Phenomenology and the Carpentry of Things*. Chicago: Open Court.

HART, David Bentley. 2018. *The New Testament*. New Haven and London: Yale University Press, 2018.

HATHERLEY, Owen. 2016. *Chaplin Machine*. London: Pluto.

HAYWARD, Danny. 2015. 'Strong Language: Beynon & Jeschke's *David Cameron: A Theatre of Knife Songs*'. *Hi-Eros Poetry Review* 6: 99–108.

HEGEL, Georg Wilhelm Friedrich. 1977a. *Faith and Knowledge* (H. S. Harris and Walter Cerf trans and eds). Albany: State University of New York Press. First published 1802.

———. 1977b. *The Difference Between Fichte's and Schelling's System of Philosophy* (H. S. Harris and Walter Cerf trans and eds). Albany: State University of New York Press. First published 1801.

———. 1983. *Hegel and the Human Spirit: A Translation of the Jena Lectures on the Philosophy of Spirit (1805–6)* (Leo Rauch trans. and ed.). Detroit: Wayne State University Press. Available at: https://bit.ly/3f48d6K (last accessed: 22 October 2022).

———. 1990. 'Section One: Subjective Spirit' (Steven A. Taubeneck trans.) in *Encyclopaedia of the Philosophical Sciences*, PART 3. London: Continuum. Available at: https://bit.ly/3FbG9Jo (last accessed: 19 October 2022). First published 1817.

———. 1993. *Introductory Lectures on Aesthetics* (Bernard Bosenquet trans.). London: Penguin. First published 1835.

HEIDEGGER, Martin. 1959. *An Introduction to Metaphysics* (Ralph Manheim trans.). New Haven and London: Yale University Press.

———. 1971. *Poetry, Language, Thought* (Albert Hofstadter trans.). New York: Harper Colophon Books.

———. 1977. *The Question Concerning Technology and Other Essays* (William Lovitt trans. and intro.). New York and London: Garland Publishing.

———. 1998. 'Letter on "Humanism"' in *Pathmarks* (William McNeill ed.). Cambridge: Cambridge University Press, pp. 239–76. First published 1946.

———. 2016. *Ponderings II-VI: Black Notebooks 1931–1938* (Richard Rojcewicz trans.). Bloomington: Indiana University Press.

HENRY, Michel. 1983. *Marx: A Philosophy of Human Reality* (Kathleen McLaughlin trans.). Bloomington: Indiana University Press.

HJEMSLEV, Louis. 1953. *Prolegomena to a Theory of Language* (Francis J. Whitfield trans.). Baltimore: Indiana University Press.

HORKHEIMER, Max. 2013. *Critique of Instrumental Reason*. London: Verso.

THE INVISIBLE COMMITTEE. 2014. *To Our Friends* (Robert Hurley trans.) South Pasadena, CA: Semiotext(e).

IRONSIDE, Robin. 1949. *David Jones*. London: Penguin.

JAMES, C. L. R. 2001. *The Black Jacobins*. London: Penguin. First published 1938.

JAMES, Miguel. 2013. 'Against the Police'. *Typomag* 18. Available at: https://bit.ly/3sjoI1U (last accessed: 22 October 2022).

JAMESON, Fredric. 1972. *The Prison-House of Language*. Princeton, NJ: Princeton University Press.

———. 1984. 'Periodizing the 60s'. 'The 60's without Apology', special issue, *Social Text* 9–10: 178–209.

———. 1994. *The Seeds of Time*. New York: Columbia University Press.

———. 2002. *The Political Unconscious*. London and New York: Routledge. First published 1981.

———. 2008. *Fables of Aggression: Wyndham Lewis, the Modernist as Fascist*. London and New York: Verso. First published 1979.

———. 2013. *The Antinomies of Realism*. London and New York: Verso.

———. 2016. *Raymond Chandler: The Detections of Totality*. London and New York: Verso.

———. 2019. *Allegory and Ideology*. New York: Verso.

JESI, Furio. 2021a. *Secret Germany: Myth in Twentieth-Century German Culture* (Richard Brodie trans.). London: Seagull Books.

———. 2021b. *Time and Festivity* (Cristina Viti trans., Andrea Cavalletti ed.). London: Seagull Books.

JEVONS, William. 1970. *The Theory of Political Economy* (R. D. Collison Black ed.). Harmondsworth: Penguin. First published 1871.

JONES, David. 1961. *In Parenthesis*. London: Faber and Faber. First published 1937.

———. 1981. *The Roman Quarry and Other Sequences* (Harman Grisewood and René Hague eds). London: Agenda Editions.

———. 1993. *Selected Works of David Jones* (John Mattias ed.). Cardiff: University of Wales Press.

———. 2017a. *Epoch and Artist* (Harman Grisewood ed.). London: Faber and Faber. First published 1959.

———. 2017b. *The Sleeping Lord and Other Fragments*. London: Faber and Faber. First published 1974.

JOYCE, James. 1992. *Finnegans Wake* (Seamus Deane ed.). London: Penguin. First published 1939.

JUDGE, Elizabeth F. 2001. 'Notes on the Outside: David Jones, "Unshared Backgrounds," and the Absence of Canonicity'. *ELH* 68(1): 179–213.

JÜNGER, Ernst. 2021. *War as Inner Experience* (Kasey James Elliott trans. and ed.). Anarch Books.

KAPLAN, Leslie. 2017. 'There should be battles', interview by Julie Carr and Jennifer Pap. *Jacket 2*, 18 October. Available at: https://bit.ly/3smyDnj (last accessed: 22 October 2022).

———. 2018. *Excess—The Factory* (Julie Carr and Jennifer Pap trans). Oakland, CA: Commune Editions. First published 1982.

KERSLAKE, Christian. 2004. 'Rebirth through Incest: On Deleuze's Early Jungianism'. *Angelaki* 9(1): 135–57.

KOSELLECK, Reinhart. 2004. *Futures Past: On the Semantics of Historical Time* (Keith Tribe trans. and intro.). New York: Columbia University Press.

KRISTEVA, Julia. 1982. *The Powers of Horror: An Essay on Abjection* (Leon S. Roudiez trans.). New York: Columbia University Press.

———. 1984. *Revolution in Poetic Language* (Margaret Waller trans.). New York: Columbia University Press.

LACAN, Jacques. 1977. *The Four Fundamental Concepts of Psycho-Analysis* (Alan Sheridan trans., Jacques-Alain Miller ed.). Harmondsworth: Penguin.

———. 1988. *The Ego in Freud's Theory and in the Technique of Psychoanalysis, 1954–1955* (Sylvana Tomaselli trans., Jacques-Alain Miller ed.). The Seminar of Jacques Lacan, BOOK 2. New York: W. W. Norton & Company.

———. 1992. *The Ethics of Psychoanalysis: 1959–1960* (Dennis Porter trans., Jacques-Alain Miller ed.). The Seminar of Jacques Lacan, BOOK 7. London: Tavistock/Routledge.

———. 2002. *Écrits*. (Bruce Fink trans.). London and New York: W. W. Norton.

———. 2016. *Seminar 23: The Sinthome* (A. R. Price trans., Jacques-Alain Miller ed.). Cambridge: Polity.

LAING, R. D. 2010. *The Divided Self: An Existential Study in Sanity and Madness*. London: Penguin.

LAKOFF, George, and Mark Johnson. 1980. *Metaphors We Live By*. Chicago: University of Chicago Press.

LANCHESTER, John. 2013. 'When did you get hooked?' Review of *A Song of Ice and Fire*, 7 VOLS, by George R. R. Martin, and Warner Home Video's *Game of Thrones: The Complete First and Second Seasons*. *London Review of Books* 35(7): 20–22. Available at: https://bit.ly/3MVp1JV (last accessed: 21 October 2022).

LAND, Nick. 2011. *Fanged Noumena.* Falmouth: Urbanomic.

LAPLANCHE, Jean. 1976. *Life and Death in Psychoanalysis* (Jeffrey Mehlman trans. and intro.). Baltimore: The Johns Hopkins University Press.

LAPLANCHE, Jean, and Jean-Bertrand Pontalis. 1988. *The Language of Psychoanalysis* (Donald Nicholson-Smith trans.). London: Karnac.

LATOUR, Bruno. 1987. *Science in Action.* Cambridge, MA: Harvard University Press.

———. 2004. 'Why Has Critique Run out of Steam? From Matters of Fact to Matters of Concern'. *Critical Inquiry* 30: 225–48.

———. 2010. 'An Attempt at a 'Compositionist Manifesto'. *New Literary History* 41: 471–90.

LEBOVIC, Nitzan. 2013. *The Philosophy of Life and Death: Ludwig Klages and the Rise of a Nazi Biopolitics.* Basingstoke: Palgrave.

LEFEBVRE, Henri. 1968. *Dialectical Materialism.* (John Sturrock trans.). London: Jonathan Cape.

LENIN, V. I. 2002. 'On Slogans' in *Revolution at the Gates* (Slavoj Žižek ed.). London: Verso, pp. 62–68. First published 1917.

LESLIE, Esther. 2002. *Hollywood Flatlands.* London: Verso.

LEWIS, Wyndham. 1982. *Blasting and Bombardiering: An Autobiography, 1914–1926.* London: John Calder.

LINEBAUGH, Peter. 2014. *Stop, Thief! The Commons, Enclosures, and Resistance.* Oakland, CA: PM Press.

LOSURDO, Domenico. 2001. *Heidegger and the Ideology of War: Community, Death, and the West.* Humanity Books.

LOTRINGER, Sylvère. 1979. 'The Game of the Name'. *diacritics* 3(2): 2–9.

LUKÁCS, Georg. 1962. *The Historical Novel.* (Hannah and Stanley Mitchell trans). London: Merlin.

———. 1963. *The Meaning of Contemporary Realism.* London: Merlin.

———. 1967. *History and Class Consciousness* (Rodney Livingstone trans.). London: Merlin Press.

———. 1970. *Writer and Critic* (Arthur D. Kahn trans. and ed.). New York: The Merlin Press.

———. 1971. *The Theory of the Novel* (Anna Bostock trans.). London: Merlin Press.

———. 1983. *Review and Articles* (Peter Palmer trans.). London: Merlin Press.

———. 2021. *The Destruction of Reason* (Peter Palmer trans., Enzo Traverso intro.). London: Verso.

LURIA, A. R. 1987. *The Man with a Shattered World*. Cambridge, MA: Harvard University Press.

LUISETTI, Federico. 2016. 'Notes on the Biopolitical State of Nature'. *Paragraph* 39(1): 108–21.

LYOTARD, Jean-François. 1993. *Libidinal Economy* (Iain Hamilton trans.). Grant, London: The Athlone Press. First published 1974.

———. 1990. *Duchamp's Transformers* (Ian McLeod trans.). Venice, CA: The Lapis Press. First published 1977.

MAKDISI, Saree. 2003. *William Blake and the Impossible History of the 1790s*. Chicago: University of Chicago Press.

MALABOU, Catherine. 2008. *What Should We Do with Our Brain?* (Sebastian Rand trans.). New York: Fordham University Press.

———. 2012. *The New Wounded: From Neurosis to Brain Damage* (Steven Miller trans.). New York: Fordham University Press.

———. 2015. '"Father, Don't You See I'm Burning?" Žižek, Psychoanalysis, and the Apocalypse' in Agon Hamza (ed.), *Repeating Žižek*. Durham, NC: Duke University Press, pp. 113–26.

MALI, Joseph. 1999. 'The Reconciliation of Myth: Benjamin's Homage to Bachofen'. *Journal of the History of Ideas* 60(1): 165–87.

MARCUSE, Herbert. 2002. *One-Dimensional Man*. London: Routledge. First published 1964.

MARDER, Elissa. 2012. *The Mother in the Age of Mechanical Reproduction: Psychoanalysis, Photography, Deconstruction*. New York: Fordham University Press.

MARX, Karl. 1973. *Grundrisse* (Martin Nicolaus trans.). Harmondsworth: Penguin.

———. 1975. *Early Writings* (Rodney Livingstone and Gregor Benton trans., Lucio Colletti intro.). Harmondsworth: Penguin.

———. 1990. *Capital*, VOL. 1 (Ben Fowkes trans. and Ernest Mandel intro.). Harmondsworth: Penguin. First published 1867.

———. 2010. *Surveys from Exile* (David Fernbach ed.). London and New York: Verso.

MARX, Karl, and Friedrich Engels. 1956. *Selected Correspondence*. Moscow: Foreign Languages Publishing House.

———. 1973. 'Manifesto of the Communist Party' in Karl Marx, *The Revolutions of 1848: Political Writings*, VOL. 1 (David Fernbach ed.). London: Penguin and New Left Books, pp. 67–98. First published 1848.

———. 2011. *The German Ideology: Parts I and III* (Roy Pascal trans and ed.). Mansfield Centre, CT: Martino Publishing. First published 1846.

MEILLASSOUX, Quentin. 2008. *After Finitude: An Essay on the Necessity of Contingency* (Ray Brassier trans.). London: Continuum.

———. 2012. *The Number and the Siren* (Robin Mackay trans.). Falmouth: Urbanomic.

MILLER, Adam S. 2013. *Speculative Grace: Bruno Latour and Object-Oriented Theology*. New York: Fordham University Press.

MILLER, Jacques-Alain. 2005. 'Lacan with Joyce: The Seminar of the Clinical Section of Barcelona'. *Psychoanalytical Notebooks* 13: 7–32.

MILNE, Drew. 1996. 'David Jones: A Charter for Philistines' in Iain Sinclair (ed.), *Conductors of Chaos*. London: Picador, pp. 260–63.

MILNER, Jean-Claude. 2017. 'Back and Forth from Letter to Homophony'. *Problemi International* 1(1): 81–98.

MITCHELL, Juliet. 1990. *Psychoanalysis and Feminism*. London: Penguin.

MOON, Michael. 2012. *Darger's Resources*. Durham, NC: Duke University Press.

MORETTI, Franco. 2020. 'Always Allegorize?' *New Left Review* 121: 53–64.

MOTEN, Fred. 2003. *In the Break: The Aesthetics of the Black Radical Tradition*. Minneapolis and London: University of Minnesota Press.

MURPHY, Timothy S. 1997. *Wising Up the Marks: The Amodern William Burroughs*. Berkeley, CA: London: University of California Press.

NANCY, Jean-Luc. 1991. *The Inoperative Community* (Peter Connor, Lisa Garbus, Michael Holland and Simona Sawhney trans, Peter Connor ed.). Minneapolis and Oxford: University of Minnesota Press.

NAO PROJECT. 2014. 'The poetry and brief life of a Foxconn worker: Xu Lizhi (1990–2014)'. *libcom.org*, 29 October. Available at: https://bit.ly/3VU0kBx (last accessed: 29 October).

NEEL, Phil A. 2018. *Hinterland: America's New Landscape of Class and Conflict*. London: Reaktion Books.

NIETZSCHE, Friedrich. 1968. *Twilight of the Idols / The Anti-Christ* (R. J. Hollingdale trans. and intro.). London: Penguin.

———. 1969. *On the Genealogy of Morals / Ecce Homo* (Walter Kaufmann trans. and ed.). New York: Vintage Books.

———. 1999. *The Birth of Tragedy and Other Writings* (Raymond Guess and Ronald Speirs eds). Cambridge: Cambridge University Press. First published 1872.

NOYS, Benjamin. 2016. 'Bound to Labor: Life & Labor in (Early) Marx and (Early) Derrida'. *Minnesota Review* 87(1): 139–48.

———. 2017. 'Hex Position: The Poetics and Politics of the Hex in Contemporary British Experimental Poetry' in Anthony Iles, et al. (eds), *Look at Hazards, Look at Losses*. London: Mute, pp. 133–49

———. 2018. '"Freudful Mistakes": On Forgetting and On Forgetting Psychoanalysis'. *Problemi* 2: 279–96.

'The Oldest System-Programme of German Idealism'. 1995[1796/97]. *European Journal of Philosophy* 3(2): 199–200.

OLLMAN, Bertell. 1976. *Alienation: Marx's Conception of Man in Capitalist Society*, 2nd EDN. Cambridge: Cambridge University Press.

PARENTI, Christian. 2011. *Tropic of Chaos: Climate Change and the New Geography of Violence*. Hachette, UK.

PATEL, Raj, and Jason W. Moore. 2018. *A History of the World in Seven Cheap Things*. London: Verso.

PEETERS, Benoit. 2014. *Derrida: A Biography*. Cambridge: Polity.

PERLMAN, Fredy. 1983. *Against His-story, Against Leviathan!* Detroit: Black & Red.

PICHOT, André. 2009. *The Pure Society: From Darwin to Hitler*. London and New York: Verso.

PIGNARRE, Philippe, and Isabelle Stengers. 2011. *Capitalist Sorcery* (Andrew Goffey trans.). Basingstoke: Palgrave.

PINKER, Steven. 2003. *The Language Instinct*. London: Penguin.

PINTOR, Luigi. 2013. *Memories from the Twentieth Century* (Gregory Elliott trans.). London, New York, Calcutta: Seagull Books.

PLATONOV, Andrei. 2009. *The Foundation Pit*. New York: New York Review of Books. First published 1930.

POSTONE, Moishe. 1993. *Time, Labor, and Social Domination*. Cambridge: Cambridge University Press.

POVINELLI, Elizabeth. 2016. *Geontologies: A Requiem for Late Liberalism*. Durham, NC: Duke University Press.

PRYNNE, J. H. 1993. *Stars, Tigers and the Shape of Words*. The William Matthews Lectures 1992. London: Birkbeck.

———. 2016. *The White Stones* (Peter Gizzi intro.). New York: New York Review of Books.

RABATÉ, Jean-Michel. 1986. *Language, Sexuality and Ideology in Ezra Pound's 'Cantos'*. Basingstoke: Macmillan.

RANCIÈRE, Jacques. 2003. *Short Voyages to the Land of the People*. Stanford, CA: Stanford University Press.

———. 2011. *Mallarmé: The Politics of the Siren*. (Steven Corcoran trans.). New York: Continuum.

———. 2012. *The Intellectual and His People* (David Fernbach trans.). London: Verso.

RAWORTH, Tom. 2015. *Average Cabin*. Cambridge: Face Press.

RENÉ [Colette Thomas]. 2014. *The Testament of the Dead Daughter* (Catherine Petit and Paul Buck trans). London: Vauxhall and Company.

RIDING, Laura. 1970. *Selected Poems: In Five Sets*. London: Faber and Faber.

RIEDE, Austin. 2015. '"Artificial Guts": Labor and the Body in David Jones' *In Parenthesis*'. *Modernism/modernity* 22(4): 691–711.

RILKE, Rainer Maria. 2021. *Duino Elegies* (Alfred Corn trans.). New York: W. W. Norton & Company. First published 1923.

ROBINSON, Kim Stanley. 2016. *Aurora*. London: Orbit.

———. 2018. *Red Moon*. London: Orbit.

ROBINSON, Kim Stanley and Helena Feder. 2018. 'The realism of our time: Interview with Kim Stanley Robinson'. *Radical Philosophy* 2(1) (February): 87–98.

ROSE, Gillian. 1984. *Dialectic of Nihilism: Post-Structuralism and Law*. Oxford: Basil Blackwell.

———. 2017. *Judaism and Modernity*. London: Verso.

ROSE, Jacqueline. 1986. *Sexuality in the Field of Vision*. London: Verso.

———. 1988. 'Margaret Thatcher and Ruth Ellis'. *New Formations* 6: 3–29.

Ross, Kristin. 2015. *Communal Luxury: The Political Imaginary of the Paris Commune*. London: Verso.

Sartre, Jean-Paul. 2000. *Nausea* (Robert Baldick trans.). London: Penguin. First published 1938.

Saussure, Ferdinand de. 2000. *Course in General Linguistics*. (Roy Harris trans.). London: Duckworth. First published 1916.

Sayers, Janet. 1992. *Mothering Psychoanalysis: Hélène Deutsch, Karen Horney, Anna Freud And Melanie Klein*. London: Penguin.

Schlossman, Beryl. 1985. *Joyce's Catholic Comedy of Language*. Madison: The University of Wisconsin Press.

Schmidgen, Henning. 2014. *Bruno Latour in Pieces: An Intellectual Biography* (Gloria Custance trans.). New York: Fordham University Press.

Shafer, David. 2016. *Antonin Artaud*. London: Reaktion Books.

Shaviro, Steven. 2015. *No Speed Limit: Three Essays on Accelerationism*. Minneapolis, MN: University of Minnesota Press. Ebook.

Shelley, Percy Bysshe. 2002. *Shelley's Poetry and Prose*, 2nd Edn (Donald H. Reiman and Neil Fraistat eds). New York: W. W. Norton and Company.

Simondon, Gilbert. 2017. *On the Mode of Existence of Technical Objects* (Cecile Malaspina and John Rogove trans). Minneapolis, MN: Univocal Publishing.

Sinclair, Iain. 2002. *Landor's Tower*. London: Granta.

Sloterdijk, Peter. 2009. *Terror from the Air* (Amy Patton and Steve Corcoran trans). Los Angeles, CA: Semiotext(e).

Smith, Dale. 2013. 'Giving Everything: On Diane di Prima'. *Los Angeles Review of Books*, 26 January. Available at: https://bit.ly/3z3SUSE (last accessed: 21 October 2022).

Smith, Jason E. 2013. 'From *Établissement* to Lip: On the Turns Taken by French Maoism'. *Viewpoint Magazine*, 25 September. Available at: https://bit.ly/3DlFvaS (last accessed: 22 October 2022).

Sohn-Rethel, Alfred. 1978. *Intellectual and Manual Labour: A Critique of Epistemology*. Atlantic Highlands, NJ: Humanities Press.

Spinoza, Baruch. 1930. *Spinoza Selections* (John Wild ed.). New York: Charles Scribner's Sons.

——. 1976. *The Ethics* (Edwin Curley trans). London: Penguin. First published 1677.

SPOTT, Verity. 2014. *Gideon*. London: Barque Press.

——. 2016. 'An Angle on Management Cruelty'. *Two Torn Halves*, 5 December. Available at: https://bit.ly/3DlBlzW (last accessed: 22 October 2022).

STALLYBRASS, Peter. 1998. 'Marx's Coat' in Patricia Spyer (ed.), *Border Fetishisms: Material Objects in Unstable Spaces*. London: Routledge, pp. 183–207.

STEYERL, Hito. 2016. 'If you don't have bread, eat art!: Contemporary Art and Derivative Fascisms'. *e-flux* 76. Available at: https://bit.ly/2D1cMIh (last accessed: 21 October 2022).

STIRNER, Max. 2013. *The Ego and Its Own*. London and New York: Verso.

SUTHERLAND, Keston. 2011. *Hot White Andy*. London: Barque Press.

——. 2012a. 'Fetish and Refuge: A Mock Pastoral'. 'Crisis Inquiry', special issue, *damn the caesars* (Summer): 243–54.

——. 2012b. 'Email to Josh Stanley'. 'Crisis Inquiry', special issue, *damn the caesars* (Summer): 205–6.

——. 2013. *The Odes to TL61P*. London: Enitharmon Press.

THOMPSON, E. P. 1991. *The Making of the English Working Class*. London: Penguin.

TIMOFEEVA, Oxana. 2018. *The History of Animals: A Philosophy*. London: Bloomsbury Academic.

TIMPANARO, Sebastiano. 1976. *The Freudian Slip*. London and New York: Verso.

TIQQUN. 1999. 'Theses on the Imaginary Party'. *lib.com*, 25 August. Available at: https://bit.ly/3VUTID6 (last accessed: 22 October 2022).

TOLKEIN, J. R. R. 2005. *The Fellowship of the Ring*. London: HarperCollins. First published 1954.

TOSCANO, Alberto. 2012. 'Credit and Critique'. Unpublished manuscript, 25 September 2019, typescript.

—— and Jeff Kinkle. 2015. *Cartographies of the Absolute*. Winchester: Zero Books.

TRANTER, Michael. 2004. 'Derrida's Debt to Milton Friedman'. *New Literary History*: 791–806.

TRONTI, Mario. 2019. *Workers and Capital* (David Broder trans.). London and New York: Verso.

TROTSKY, Leon. 1967. *History of the Russian Revolution*, 3 VOLS (Max Eastman trans.). London: Sphere Books. First published 1930.

TSING, Anna. 2015. *The Mushroom at the End of the World: On the Possibility of Life in Capitalist Ruins*. Princeton: Princeton University Press.

VANEIGEM, Raoul. 1998. *The Movement of the Free Spirit* (Randall Cherry and Ian Patterson trans). New York: Zone Books.

VIRILIO, Paul. 2009. *War and Cinema: The Logistics of Perception*. London and New York: Verso.

VIRNO, Paolo. 2008. *Multitude: Between Innovation and Negation* (Isabella Bertoletti, James Cascaito and Andrea Casson trans.). Los Angeles, CA: Semiotext(e).

VOEGELIN, Eric. 1987. *The New Science of Politics*. Chicago: The University of Chicago Press.

VOLOSHINOV, V. N. 1973. *Marxism and the Philosophy of Language*. Cambridge, MA and London: Harvard University Press. First published 1929.

WALKER, Gavin. 2016. *The Sublime Perversion of Capital: Marxist Theory and the Politics of History in Modern Japan*. Durham, NC: Duke University Press.

WEBER, Max. 1989. *The Protestant Ethic and the Spirit of Capitalism* (Talcott Parsons trans.). London: Unwin Hyman. First published 1905.

———. 2020. *Charisma and Disenchantment: The Vocation Lectures* (Damion Searls trans., Paul Reitter and Chad Wellmon eds). New York: NYRB books. First published 1919.

WHITAKER, Muriel. 1997. 'The Arthurian Art of David Jones'. *Arthuriana* 7(3): 137–56.

WILLIAMS, Raymond. 2015. *Politics and Letters: Interviews with 'New Left Review'* (Geoff Dyer ed. and intro.). London: Verso.

WITTGENSTEIN, Ludwig. 2001. *Tractatus Logico-Philosophicus* (David Pears and Brian McGuinness trans). London: Routledge. First published 1921.

WOODCOCK, Jamie. 2016. *Working the Phones*. London: Pluto.

WOOTTEN, William. 2003. 'At The Thirteenth Hour'. Review of *Wedding Poems*, by David Jones (Thomas Dilworth ed.), and *David Jones: Writer and Artist*, by Keith Alldritt. *London Review of Books* 25(18): 27–28.

ZERZAN, John. 1998. *Elements of Refusal*. Columbia: MO: CAL Press.

WORKS CITED

ŽIŽEK, Slavoj. 1990. 'Eastern Europe's Republics of Gilead'. *New Left Review* 183: 50–62.

—— and F. W. J. von Schelling. 1997. *The Abyss of Freedom / Ages of the World*. Ann Arbor: The University of Michigan Press.

——. 2000. 'Class Struggle or Postmodernism? Yes, please!' in Judith Butler, Ernesto Laclau and Slavoj Žižek, *Contingency, Hegemony, Universality*. London and New York: Verso, pp. 90–135.

——. 2005. *The Metastases of Enjoyment: Six Essays on Women and Causality*. London: Verso.

——. 2006. *The Parallax View*. Cambridge, MA and London: The MIT Press.

——. 2010. *Living in the End Times*. London: Verso.

INDEX

INDEX